Bob Kimball, PhD
Jerold "Buck" Hall

Selling in the New World
of Business

Pre-publication
REVIEWS,
COMMENTARIES,
EVALUATIONS . . .

"This is a unique book compared to other books targeted at the sales industry. So ma to focus on 'R may provide two. The auth lined a definiti allow a salesp ful sales caree impressive be evaluate how the past. Many the presentation as a pitch or long dialogue in which they can talk and talk while the potential customer will merely listen. The authors ask us to look at the process from a different and unique angel. The sales presentation becomes a sales interview, and instead of merely pitching the product, the salesperson works with the customer to help uncover any unmet needs or dissatisfactions with current vendors. With our business environment becoming more competitive day by day, it is refreshing to receive new outside perspectives.

This book inspired me to reevaluate how we approach potential customers. It redefines the 'old school' sales processes and will prepare our sales force for the challenges in the ever-changing professional selling arena. I would recommend that anyone looking to enhance their selling success or revitalize their ead this book as

"You can't make tomorrow's sales with yesterday's skills! *Selling in the New World of Business* gives you a step-by-step process to make the transition from salesperson to strategic partner with your key customers. It's a must read for everyone who wants to develop business-building ideas and add value for their company and clients."

Fred J. Lewis
Author, *Selecting Stars:*
The Handbook for Hiring Success

More pre-publication
REVIEWS, COMMENTARIES, EVALUATIONS . . .

"**B**ob Kimball and Buck Hall have written a book that reveals the art of professional selling versus the old methods of the unethical, stereotypical 'snake oil' salesman. This book is easy to read, well organized, and packed with ideas and recommendations that will help anyone increase his or her sales effectiveness and develop a rich portfolio of repeat customers and referrals. Just as our world has changed, the world of buying has also changed. This book focuses on how we as salespeople need to change to be successful and take advantage of the new environment we live in. I highly recommend this book for anyone who wants to improve his or her success in business, and I only hope my competition never finds it."

Charles "Chuck" Howard, MBA
Executive District Sales Manager,
AstraZeneca Pharmaceuticals

"**W**hether you are leading a sales force or are part of one, this book provides food for thought as well as tangible and actionable instructions on how to succeed in today's world. Readers willing to do the work will improve their success rate and avoid becoming today's Willy Loman. This book is written in a very friendly but pointed conversational style that gives readers plenty of opportunity to practice their listening skills. The examples will strike home to nearly everyone—buyer or seller. This book provides an easy-to-read summary of what most people know but fail to remember as they pursue success without planning on how to achieve it."

Robert G. Dawson
President and CEO, Southern LINC

BEST BUSINESS BOOKS

Best Business Books®
An Imprint of The Haworth Press, Inc.
New York • London • Oxford

Selling in the New World
of Business

BEST BUSINESS BOOKS
Robert E. Stevens, PhD
David L. Loudon, PhD
Editors in Chief

Selling in the New World of Business

Bob Kimball, PhD
Jerold "Buck" Hall

Best Business Books®
An Imprint of The Haworth Press, Inc.
New York • London • Oxford

Published by

Best Business Books®, an imprint of The Haworth Press, Inc., 10 Alice Street, Binghamton, NY 13904-1580.

PUBLISHER'S NOTE
Due to the ever-changing nature of the Internet, Web site names and addresses, though verified to the best of the publisher's ability, should not be accepted as accurate without independent verification.

Cover design by Marylouise E. Doyle.

Library of Congress Cataloging-in-Publication Data

Kimball, Bob.
    Selling in the new world of business / Bob Kimball, Jerold "Buck" Hall.
       p. cm.
Includes index.
    ISBN 0-7890-2271-0 (case : alk. paper)—ISBN 0-7890-2272-9 (soft : alk. paper)
    1. Selling. I. Hall, Jerold. II. Title.

HF5438.25.K547 2004
658.85—dc21
                                                  2003014675

CONTENTS

ABOUT THE AUTHORS

Bob Kimball, PhD, is Professor of Marketing at the University of West Florida in Pensacola, where he teaches Marketing Fundamentals, Professional Selling, and Sales Management. He is the author of the *AMA Handbook for Successful Selling,* and is the author, executive producer, and narrator of "Secrets of Professional Selling," a video sales training program. Dr. Kimball worked for thirteen years in sales and marketing with Coca-Cola USA and for seven years managed The Kimball Organization, specializing in developing and conducting sales and management training programs for a wide variety of firms in the southeastern United States.

Jerold "Buck" Hall is Business Development Manager with Amstaff Human Resources. He has worked for IBM, Mainline Information Systems, and Southern Company in the areas of technology and complex sales cycles, specializing in sales training, direct sales, channel sales, and sales management. Mr. Hall is also a contributing columnist to the *Pensacola News Journal.*

Preface

Businesspeople today will likely tell you things are very, very different than they were just a few years ago. Breakthroughs in technology have affected every organization in every industry. Competition is more intense, with the number of rivals increasing daily. The pace of business has accelerated dramatically, and information can be transmitted almost instantaneously. With that information in hand, attendant decisions must be made quickly, lest opportunities be lost. Business professionals must get much more done in much less time, just to keep up. Making a profit is a luxury afforded only to those who work hard for it every step of the way. On those rare occasions when a businessperson tells you that things are about the same as they were ten years ago, well, those people may not be in business anymore, and if they are, may not be for long. Doing things the same old ways is no longer an option.

Still, many ostensibly professional salespeople may believe that the essence of selling really hasn't changed. Sure, they use e-mail more than snail mail and submit reports electronically instead of filling out paper forms. They've found some really helpful Web sites that offer everything from selling tips to stock market tips. Perhaps they've mastered the fundamentals of PowerPoint or have read a book on 1,001 ways to prosper online. But still, they'll tell you the basics of selling are the same as they've always been. Get the appointments, demonstrate to prospects how your product's features translate to benefits for them, and negotiate the most favorable terms and conditions. The more things change the more they stay the same. Selling is still selling. Unfortunately for salespeople who believe that, such an attitude is a recipe for disaster in the new world of business.

Think about it: Using that same line of reasoning, we could argue that the essence of business hasn't changed either. A company must still develop products or services that prospects want and need, communicate information about the products or services, and establish a distribution channel or system to deliver them. Business is still business. Yes, but the *process* of running a business has fundamentally changed.

This is a key point, and it leads us to the reason this book is important for every professional salesperson. Every aspect of selling has been affected by the revolution in technology, and in the chapters that follow, we'll describe what the professional salesperson must do to prosper in the new world of business. You'll see how business relationships have changed and how you need to approach them differently. We will discuss managing your time and communication more effectively; modifying your approaches to prospecting; enhancing the professionalism of your presentation; and dealing with objections, closing the sale, and negotiating the *relationship* instead of just haggling over terms and conditions.

Chapter 1

Building Your Foundation

If you want to put up a building, you have to start with a foundation. It's the same for becoming a sales professional in the new world of business. Before you can start operating, it's essential to understand the new business relationships and things that must be done to be a viable player on the new business playing field. In this chapter, we'll look at the five key concepts for building your foundation, those things that will differentiate you as someone embracing the revolution in technology and flourishing instead of being someone struggling just to get by.

CONCEPT 1: THE NEW AGE WILLY LOMAN

One of the most significant changes in the new world of business is the nature of business relationships. A professional salesperson must become a strategic partner, not merely a supplier of products and services. Part of this is knowing where to go to get the information that will make you an expert, consultant, and helper. You must also have confidence in yourself, your company, and your personal network of professional colleagues.

Many professional salespersons are familiar with Willy Loman, the tragic figure in Arthur Miller's *Death of a Salesman.* Willy is the consummate negative role model, the epitome of what we are *not.* Just as sales pros cringe at the thought of being associated with the likes of a stereotypical used-car salesperson, we insist with confidence that we will never become a Willy Loman. Perhaps not, but a Willy Loman clone is emerging: the New Age Willy Loman.

So, who is this New Age Willy Loman? If you've ever seen *Death of a Salesman,* you know one thing for sure: Willy Loman is *old.* To Buck, "old" is anyone over fifty. For Bob, "old" starts sometime be-

1

tween 105 and 110. And few readers in their early to mid-thirties think of themselves as old. How old, then, is "old"? Thirty-five? Fifty? 115? Answer: none of these. Experts on aging tell us there is no specific chronological age at which we become old. You can be young at seventy-five or old at thirty. What makes the difference is mostly how we live, how we think, and how we act. If you're looking forward to new challenges, are open to new ideas, and seek ways to do things better and differently, you're probably young. By contrast, if you're doing the same things the same way with the same people and feel a bit resentful that no one seems to appreciate you or the good old days, you're probably old. It took Willy Loman until his late fifties or early sixties to become old, but that's because when Arthur Miller wrote the play, the world was changing at a much slower pace than today. We now experience as much change in one year as would have occurred in five years of Willy's life. To a twenty-four-year-old sales professional, a thirty- or thirty-two-year-old, who was a rising star in his or her mid-twenties but who is still doing the same old things the same old way, is, well, old. And very shortly, if not already, that twenty-four-year-old will leave his or her aged counterpart in the dust.

If you remember Willy, you'll recall that in his yearning for the good old days he talked a lot about relationships, the old friends he called on in his territory. Those old friends had retired or moved on, and the replacement buyers were giving business to Willy's competitors, who were undercutting him on price. Willy thought it reprehensible that someone would disregard friendship in the name of the almighty dollar, but therein lies the fallacy in his thinking. For Willy to believe that a buyer should pay more for something that could be purchased elsewhere for less is to imply that business friendships must be subsidized: *If I'm your friend, you, in effect, owe me a living.* That line of logic didn't fly in Willy's day and will literally get you laughed out the door in today's business environment. But that's precisely the attitude of the New Age Willy Loman, who whines that he or she can't make a decent living against online competitors undercutting his or her prices at reverse auctions sponsored by customers inviting him or her to submit a bid to the virtual purchasing agent at their Web site.

What the traditional and New Age Willy Lomans have lost sight of is the basic concept of price versus value. Price is what they pay;

value is the benefits they receive in return. Basically, if value exceeds price, it makes sense for the customer to buy. That customer, then, will buy from the company and salesperson who provides the greatest value for the price.

Professional salespeople often mistakenly believe that buyers make decisions based on price. Buyers *want* you to believe that, and it's their job to *make* you believe that. Their objective is to purchase the very finest product with the best features and reputation, at the price of the lousiest product with minimal features and a terrible reputation. They will tell you that your competition has the same thing for less, and will prove it by pulling up the competitor's Web site. You, in turn, either cut your price to the point you're barely covering expenses or you lose the sale entirely. *And I thought we were friends.* Sorry, Willy.

Over an eighteen-month period, we interviewed over 300 customers and asked them, on a scale from one to ten, how important was price in a buying decision. Over 90 percent of the time, they gave it a ten. Then, we asked them to list their most important considerations in selecting a vendor with whom they would establish a long-term relationship. Price was among the top five reasons less than 10 percent of the time.

It's simple. Competing on price is the road to nowhere. And professional salespeople don't just cut the price, they sell value. Today's sales pros know something Willy Loman didn't: buyers *talk* price, but they *buy* value, the most important component of which is the expertise and professionalism brought to the table. Buyers will gladly pay more to do business with you if you can provide business-building ideas and other professional resources that add up to value. Ask yourself, "What value do I generate above and beyond that of the online competitor?" If you can't satisfactorily answer that question, why should anyone buy from you? Customers have changed the way they buy, investigate, and treat suppliers. Ask yourself, "Am I merely reacting to those changes, or am I taking a proactive role in teaching and training my customers, directly involved in helping them achieve their objectives?" Are you a consultant and partner, or just another salesman, Willy?

Another thing implicit about Willy Loman was that he talked about all his accounts, calling on them and servicing them year after year, but never once mentioning going out and prospecting for new customers. The New Age Willy Loman is busy servicing his or her established customer base but fails to identify evolving accounts that may offer the best opportunities for long-term consultative relationships. That's a prescription for certain disaster in today's business environment, where start-ups and small businesses account for the majority of economic growth. New Age Willy not only doesn't call on them, he or she doesn't even know where they are. In the old, old days, salespeople would prospect by "smokestacking," driving around looking for smokestacks. *See a new one, gee, I guess they make something there. I'll just drop in and see if they want to buy something today.* In the new world of business, of course, there may not be smokestacks, and, in fact, a very significant prospect might have an 800-square-foot office on the back end of a strip mall. The old ways of prospecting for these nuggets just won't get you where you want to go. (We'll cover this further in Chapter 4.)

One thing you can say for Willy: He didn't have to worry about keeping up with the latest developments in technology, except for knowing how to type and remembering which side of the carbon paper went where. New Age Willy knows that technology is important and here to stay but lives under the illusion that he or she is technologically competent because he or she can use e-mail, surf the Net to buy plane tickets, and write a memo with Word instead of a Selectric. He or she doesn't realize it, but that twenty-four-year-old he or she calls a kid could do all that by the third grade and has been on an exponential learning curve ever since. What takes New Age Willy half a day shuffling through paper at home and the library, the kid does in fifteen minutes, with ten times the useful output. Every December, Willy dutifully visits the office supply store to buy next year's planning calendar, sits down every evening to write out the next day's schedule, and relies on the office staff to call and remind him or her of an important meeting or deadline he or she might have overlooked. Meanwhile, the kid is modifying his or her schedule on the go as events and opportunities unfold, and his or her electronic calendar beeps at the exact moment he or she needs to wake up or call a prospect.

It's not news that technology has become an essential tool for today's professional salesperson. But technology is more than that. It has fundamentally altered the way people do business, and it has altered the profession of selling. Sure, New Age Willy uses technology, but he or she has not *embraced* technology. The original Willy Loman was a tragic figure because he lived in the past and could not adapt to the future. Once his old friends were gone, he was finished. *Why did all my old friends have to go away? Everything was so great then. Things worked so well. Why? Why? Why?*

Our ideas and our habits are our friends, too. They provide us comfort and stability, a foundation of certainty. When something or someone begins to undermine and overturn them, we become defensive. That's New Age Willy. All the ways of doing things six or eight years ago worked so well, he or she figures that all he or she must do is keep doing them, and keep doing more of them, and everything will be all right. *But why am I beating my head against the wall day after day and getting nowhere? And that hotshot kid, who's getting all those lucky breaks, why does he look at me that way? I'm barely thirty, and he looks at me as though . . . as though I'm old.*

That's because you are, Willy.

CONCEPT 2: EVERYTHING IS THE SAME, ONLY DIFFERENT

We've noted that technology has fundamentally altered the profession of selling. That does not mean, however, that there has been a sort of radical paradigm shift in which all the assumptions of the past have been overthrown. Yes, things are being done differently, but the same things are being done. Don't throw out the baby with the bathwater.

Until very recently, numerous "experts" were predicting that the Internet would replace salespeople in business-to-business (B2B) transactions. Some of the same experts also told us that virtual retailers would run brick-and-mortar companies out of business in a very few years. We hope those experts didn't invest all their retirement savings in e-tailer stocks.

The parking lots are still full at the mall because of a simple characteristic of human nature: people generally like to be around, and do business with, other people. We want and need technology to facilitate and enhance the buying process, to free us from unnecessary manual tasks, but ultimately we live to share experiences with others. I don't need human interaction to buy a plane ticket, but ultimately it's people and personal service that determine my satisfaction, or lack thereof. I'll use an airline Web site to book my flight, but if the plane is late, the gate agent incompetent, and the flight attendants insult my mother, I probably won't fly them again, even to save a few bucks. You may know exactly what you want and can easily place the order from your home computer, but if you need help you'll want a human being, in person or through an 800 number, to resolve the problem. To get the best price, you might buy a product online, but if it's defective and then you have a hassle getting it fixed, you likely won't buy from that company again. And you might just post a note on an online message board to share your experience with a few thousand of your "closest friends."

Today's businessperson must utilize technology to communicate information and make it easier to buy. But what is a computer, anyhow? Nothing but a very dumb, albeit fast, adding machine that does what a human being tells it to do. Computers relieve us from rote, mundane tasks that take time and energy but do not require intelligent thinking, which is why the professional salesperson has become *more* important, not less. To buy a commodity, with no unique selling proposition or differential advantage except price, use a computer. If you're a salesperson selling a commodity with no added value, well, you're probably now out of sales and working elsewhere.

The reason that professional salespeople have assumed an even more important role in the new world of business is because only *people* can think, come up with business-building ideas, or imagine what the future might be and work cooperatively together to turn those dreams into realities. These are the things professional salespeople do; it's part of the added value they bring to the table. It's one of the reasons why customers buy from them instead of the faceless competitor quoting a cheaper price online. A salesperson can be relied on to make sure that what's supposed to happen does happen, when it's supposed to. That's value. When there's a special need and customers call, a salesperson is there. That's value, and it's well worth paying for.

Professional salespeople work continuously to generate value for their prospects and customers. In fact, they are often as important and contribute as much as their customers' best employees. The critical difference is those customers don't have to pay the professional salesperson a salary and have no expenses for benefits or other ancillaries. Think of it this way. If you, as their partner, bring them unique business-building ideas that help them earn an extra $200,000 in profits this year, you've done the job of a good $100,000-a-year employee. So, it's just not in their best interest to go online to find a supplier who says he or she has the exact same thing for $50,000 less. As a professional salesperson, you've created more than that in value, and, in essence, you and your customer split the profits.

This perspective is absolutely essential in the new world of business. A professional salesperson must go beyond looking at the specifications and price of his or her product or service compared to the competition. You might have been able to get away with that a decade ago, but if that's what you're doing now, you're doomed. In effect, you're going head to head on price against the online competitor, and you can no longer make much of a living doing that.

How many times in the past month have you heard someone say, "You have to sell yourself"? That's probably the most trite platitude of all time. It's also the most true. It makes no difference whether you sell land or Land Rovers, computer chips, chocolate chips, or cow chips. Not only do you have to sell yourself, but *all* you have to sell is yourself and the business-building ideas you create. Put the focus on your customers and prospects and ask yourself, "What can I do to help build their business, increase their profits, and help make life easier and better for them?" As long as you're doing that, you are creating value, and if you're creating value, you are going to make money. Create a lot of value and make a whole pile of money, but always focus on how you can create value for your customers and prospects, not on how much money you can make. Put the focus on others and what you can do for them, and the money will be there. Of course, even more money will be there once you master the skills of professional selling and negotiation in the new world of business, with both you and your customers dealing with each other in a relationship of trust, respect, and enlightened self-interest.

This brings up another key point about the art of selling in the new world of business. Selling is a skill and a process, not a natural-born trait and technique. This has always been the case, but until recently the illusion of the just-born-that-way sales wonder still persisted. Usually, this salesperson stereotype was good-looking, gregarious, and always the center of attention, and his or her people skills were perceived as excellent because everyone was so drawn to him or her. Well, of course, people are drawn toward good-looking people, which makes them, by definition, the center of attention. And it's natural, if you're the center of attention, to be gregarious. So different for us mere mortals with our imperfections who must stand in the corner eating hors d'oeuvres. But the characteristics that bring success at the evening social simply do not translate to success in professional selling, where success is measured in business-building ideas and value. Success in selling comes from mastering skills and working hard. Period.

It's very important to make this point early on, because some people still tend to make an analogy between success in selling and success in sports. In sports, or in other fields as diverse as art and music, it is often proposed that people are either born with or not born with a predisposition for success. Sure, it takes a lot of hard work to get to the top, but if you have that predisposition you can get there. The flip side is no predisposition, no way.

This is *not* the way it is in sales. It is *all* hard work and skill, and *anyone* can do it if he or she wants to and is willing to pay the price. We don't have illusions of you accepting this at this early point, but we're confident you'll agree with us by the time you finish this book.

And while we're talking about paying the price, there's something we want from all of you. We want you to fail. You got that right: *we want you to fail.* You won't hear that said in most of those rah-rah "motivational" books cluttering up the shelves, but it's a fact. To succeed in sales, you must be willing to fail, because that's the only way to learn anything. As Mary Kay put it, fail forward toward success.

Think about it. If you never fail, you just aren't trying hard enough. Failure, although it's not fun at the time, provides the opportunity to critique yourself to ascertain how you can do things differently and better the next time. Thomas Edison, one of history's most renowned inventors, put it most succinctly when asked about 2,000 consecutive experiments that had failed, saying that he hadn't failed 2,000 times but had discovered 2,000 approaches that would not work. Have that perspective in the front of your mind as you read through this book and execute its strategies and approaches. Face it, the first time you try something new and different, you may fail. No problem. Just critique and do better next time. Above all, don't quit and revert to the old way of doing things. In the new world of business, the old ways are not an option.

Throughout this book, you're going to discover our emphasis on selling as a process and not as an application of techniques. There are a number of books out there on techniques to get more appointments, to close sales, and to negotiate, and they have some, albeit limited, value. And we will note a number of techniques, some of which have been around since Eve bought the apple. They can be useful but when applied in isolation can come across as manipulative. No doubt you've been exposed to them by telemarketers and used-car salespeople whose pushiness made you feel uncomfortable. That's not what this book is about.

What this book *is* about is the mastery of the process of identifying potential colleagues with whom you could develop a mutually beneficial business relationship. The advances in technology that we'll cite will facilitate the "doing" part of that job. But ultimately, success will be determined by your ability to form strategic alliances and partnerships with other competent professionals who feel comfortable having you actively participate in their business. Of course, this is not just going to happen by random chance. You will have a plan through which you actively manage the process to make it happen by helping your customers and prospects make decisions that help them achieve their objectives as you achieve yours. Yes, it's a subtle difference between managing a process and applying techniques, but it's nonetheless an important difference. Essentially, it comes down to this: Never lose sight of the fact that in everything you do, your focus is to help customers and prospects make decisions that are in *their* best interest, not just yours. If you always operate with that in mind, people will like doing business with you and they will tell their friends about you. Repeat business and referrals are the keys to success in selling.

Professional selling is high-paid but hard work. In the new world of business, it's more important than ever to not only work hard but to work smart. As in the past, the professional salesperson must be organized and set priorities. He or she must know everything there is to know about everything, be able to communicate effectively, and negotiate the terms and conditions of the business relationship. But today, it's essential to do those things *efficiently* and in a manner appropriate to the new environment. We'll get into all these considerations, covering the aspects of the selling process, later in this and subsequent chapters.

We've pointed out the importance of the professional salesperson being a source of knowledge and expertise. Today, that too is the same, only different. In the past, vendors to the retail trade found it easy to get appointments with headquarters buyers because they had category market share data the buyers were interested in. Along came scanners, though, and those buyers had all the data they wanted at their fingertips instantaneously, so the vendors had to come up with another type of "carrot" to get them in the door. This example is now applicable for salespeople calling on all kinds of business, even the very small. The Internet provides access to all sorts of information, so don't try to impress anyone with goodies gleaned off a Web site your prospect may have already looked at two weeks ago. More important, the Internet has given your prospects extensive and detailed information about you and how you compare with the competition, thus fundamentally changing the buyer-seller relationship. Technology has given the small business owner the power of a professional purchasing agent.

Traditional purchasing agents (PAs) were university and company trained buying professionals salespeople had to deal with in the larger companies. Often, they specialized in narrowly defined product lines, and 90 percent of the time were better informed and better trained than most of the better salespeople. You knew you were in for a rough time of it when you called on one of these people. They let you know right up front that their objective was to buy the best products at the absolute best price, in direct opposition to your objective of selling them your products at the highest possible profit margin. They'd casually mention a meeting with Competitor A the day before, and refer to an appointment with Competitor B later that afternoon. Immediately, your expectation level was reduced to the point where you were calculating how much you needed to clear to fill the car up with gas and check into the budget motel at the next stop down the road.

If you thought it was tough before, the new world of business makes you yearn for the good old days. Today's PAs have access to an ever-expanding information pool, with hundreds of Web sites catering to every industry. They no longer need a fifteen-minute appointment to check out your competition. Now they can do it all in sixty seconds with a couple of clicks. If anything, they're *better* trained than ever, thanks to courses and articles from sources such as the American Purchasing Society <www.american-purchasing.com> and the National Institute of Governmental Purchasing, Inc., <www.nipg. org>. PAs know about everything that's going on, thanks to message boards and chat rooms where they share experiences and post helpful hints about pricing, tactics, procedures, and vendors. In some places, it used to be that there was enough anonymity to permit an unreliable salesperson to slide for months or years before the PAs could share experiences with their colleagues. In the old days, if you messed up, buyers would tell five or ten colleagues over the next week or two. Today, they tell 10,000 people instantly. There's simply no place left to hide for less-than-professional salespeople who don't follow through with their commitments.

Salespeople used to get a break when dealing with small businesses. Sure, they were a bit more discriminating with money because, after all, it was *their* money, but at least you didn't have to worry about them playing you against the competition like the big guys did. No longer. Today's small business has access to all the information and tools previously available only to the big guys, and they'll utilize online vendors and search engines to compare and contrast you with the competition. They can readily check out your company's credit rating to verify that you're stable and reliable. They'll log on to the Better Business Bureau to confirm that you're a member and don't have a history of customer complaints. Yes, everything's the same; you still have to meet with customers and prospects face to face. But everything's different, too. Everyone you deal with is better informed and is a tougher sale. It never made sense to sell the same product as your competitor or to compete on price. Today it's impossible. You're right if you believe some of those online competitors can't sell at their prices and make a profit. That's demonstrated by their steady stream of operating losses. But by the time they go belly up, you'll be flipping burgers at the local fast-food emporium unless you generate and sell the value of yourself as a professional and consultant.

Before moving on to the next segment, review the following Web sites that are devoted to selling to or buying from individuals, businesses, or the government. Check them out in detail, and then seek out other sites dealing specifically with your industry, your customer's industry, or your customer's customers industries.

    Institute for Supply Managment (formerly known as the
      National Association of Purchasing Management)
      <www.napm.org>

American Purchasing Society
  <www.american-purchasing.com>
mySimon (price comparisons from around the Web)
  <www.mysimon.com>
National Institute of Governmental Purchasing, Inc.,
  <www.nigp.org>
Purchasing for Purchasing and Supply Chain Managers
  in Manufacturing
  <www.Purchasing.com>

CONCEPT 3: BEING A SUPPLIER, OR BEING A PARTNER

At this point, it should be abundantly clear that the only way to prosper, or even survive, as a professional salesperson in the new world of business is by creating value and having a differential advantage in yourself personally. In sum, this comes down to forming a strategic alliance with your customers—becoming a partner—instead of merely being a vendor efficiently providing them with products and services.

The concept of partnership has been around for years. In consumer products: We're not just another company that sells its stuff off your shelves; we want to help you manage the category to optimize shelf space and maximize your profits. As a producer of industrial components: We don't just sell you widgets; we'll coordinate deliveries to match your production schedule, ensure you have what you need when you need it, and help you reduce costs of warehousing and tying up funds carrying excess inventory. As a personnel service: We aren't just sending over temporary help; we can enhance the efficiency of your entire operation and help your business grow.

If anything, it's even *more* important than ever to form strategic alliances and partnerships with customers, but as with every other aspect of selling in the new world of business, it's different.

Back in Selling Skills 101, we learned about the "sales triangle," consisting of the product, the customer, and you, the sales rep. The untrained salesperson, we were told, focuses only on the facts and features of the product: specifications, prices, terms, and other items about the company, service, systems, etc. But the professional salesperson talks benefits, what the features mean in value to the customer and his or her company. Then, about twenty minutes into the first day, we learned the first rule of selling: Every time you mention a feature, translate it to a corresponding benefit, and personalize the benefit. This tie is made of silk. That means it won't wrinkle and will always look good. Your boss will be so impressed, he or she will promote you to vice president. Fundamental stuff that's as true as it ever was. In the new world of business, however, we must go beyond the sales triangle, features-benefits, and the traditional view of partnership.

The sales triangle is adequate for describing a sale to an individual, whether it's a new car or a dishwasher, since there's no implied partnership. The sales rep wants to help prospects buy the product that best meets their needs, follows up to ensure satisfaction, and stays in touch to encourage repeat business and referrals. The follow-up and relationship add value to the customer experience, value that they and the friends they refer may be willing to pay a little more for in a future buying situation.

Traditionally, the sales triangle and repeat business/referral scenario described B2B sales. Show them the benefit, provide service and follow-up, and just wait for the repeat business and referrals to come rolling in. But as we've noted, those days are no more, and any sales rep hoping for their return is living in the past.

In the new world of business, the sales triangle is inadequate for describing B2B selling and in dealing with small businesses because it only has three components: product, customer, and sales rep. It does not include the critical fourth component, the key to developing a strategic alliance and partnership today: the *customer's* customers.

After the first coffee break in Selling Skills 101, we returned to our seats to learn the importance of knowledge: Know everything there is to know about your product, company, industry, competition, customer, and the customer's customers. The value you create as a sales professional, as an expert, consultant, and helper, lies in *directly* assisting your customers to enhance and serve their customer base, to identify opportunities, and then to *directly* help them exploit those opportunities. You create a joint-venture partnership relationship in which the two of you together utilize suppliers to obtain the absolute lowest price on the products and services you need to attain your mutual objectives.

Forming strategic alliances is the essence of business relationships in the new world of business, and throughout the book we'll describe how this fundamental change has affected every aspect of the selling profession.

CONCEPT 4: KNOW WHAT YOU NEED TO KNOW AND WHERE TO GET IT

Not much has changed for salespeople. They still have to be experts about everything. But in the new world of business, there's a lot more they need to know, and to be effective, different approaches to obtaining what they need. For example, consider your products and your company. In the old days, you had to know everything there was to know about your products: specifications, features-benefits, pricing, terms, delivery, etc. You also had to know everything there was to know about your company: who everyone was, what they did, and how they could be a resource to you. You still need to know these things, but now you must also be an expert on your company's Web site to be able to educate your customers and help them utilize it to get information and generally enhance their experience with you and your company. In Concept 5 of this chapter, we'll discuss thoroughly evaluating your company and its user-friendliness, online and off. At this point, let's just say that you must know everything about your company's Web site and every aspect of technology you have in place to serve and communicate with your customers and prospects.

Along the same lines, you must be thoroughly familiar with every aspect of your customer's Web site. You may think you know your customer, but an in-depth tour through his or her site is bound to reveal many things about the customer you never knew. Take that tour with two different sets of eyes. First, as a partner in a strategic alliance. Look for new opportunities and ways you might serve the customer better. Then, tour as a customer and prospect, and critique your experience to generate ideas for changing and improving that site. Now, when you call on *your* customer, you'll bring in business-building ideas to help the customer do business with *his or her* customers. This is just one of the ways to become, as described in the previous section, a partner instead of a supplier.

If you do not know your customer's Web site address, you can always ask what it is, but you can probably find it on your own pretty easily. The first step would be to check the customer's letterhead or business card for an e-mail address. Nothing on the cards or letterhead? Try a search engine such as Ask Jeeves <www.ask.com>. Inquire, "Where can I find (blank) company?" and hit the "Ask" icon.

If you're at the Web site of a publicly held company, the first thing to look for is a copy of its annual report, from which you can learn what its markets are, the channels of distribution it employs, information on any acquisitions or other organizational actions, and management's outlook for the direction of the company, its respective strategic business units, and various product lines. Often, the annual report is available at the site in links such as "Investor Information" or sections such as "About Us" or "Company Information." If you can't find the annual report on the company's Web site, check out such sites as <www.finance.yahoo.com>, <www.edgar-online.com>, or <www.wilink.com>, from whom you can also procure hard copies. While you're there, also check out the company's 10-K financial report. Most important to you is Item 7: Management's Discussion and Analysis of Financial Condition and Results of Operations. This segment expands upon their financial condition, including relative performance of the company's respective strategic business units and plans for future periods. Since few employees read these documents, you may come to the table knowing more about the company than the employees do.

Whenever you're at a prospect's Web site, it's important to study every page, no matter how mundane, since you never know where a critical piece of information may be buried. Recently, Buck was researching a large privately held company, finding little of use at its Web site when he noticed an obscure button off to the left corner, called "Customer Value." Goldmine! It was a link to the internal site to which the company sent its customers for research and problem solving, replete with information about its products and detailed bios on all its executives. This wealth of information was crucial in helping Buck get an appointment on the first contact.

Be sure to check out all "Press Releases" and "News" pages. You'll find much of the information you might have previously obtained through search engines, such as newspaper articles about companies and individuals, but also purely internal items such as who won employee of the year and whose kid was awarded a scholarship at the local university. Mention those when you meet in person. Everyone likes to feel important, and everyone appreciates recognition.

Also check out the "Employment Opportunities" page, not to look for a job but to see what positions the company is trying to fill. If the company is looking for salespeople, it could signal a move into new territories or an expanded product line. If the company is seeking warehouse or office staff, demand for its products may be on the upswing. In any case, who the company is hiring, or the fact that it is not hiring, may give you some valuable insights.

In the new world of business, it is absolutely essential that professional salespeople be thoroughly familiar with the Web sites of their company and their customers. If you're not, don't look behind you because, as Satchel Paige warned us, someone might be gaining on you. That person gaining on you, of course, is your competition. Everything you know about your company and its products, you must also know about competing companies and their products: their strengths, their weaknesses, and their vulnerabilities. No one ever won a football game or a war contemplating his or her strategies and tactics to the exclusion of planning how to deal with those of the opposition. Know your competitor's Web site cold. What you need to know to prevail against him or her might be only a mouse click away. In any case, you can feel confident that your prospect is familiar with the competitor's Web site and will use it as leverage against you. It is best to be prepared with a response.

Selling Skills 101 also taught you to learn everything there was to know about an industry: key trends, issues, legislation, competition at home and globally, product innovations, etc. Pursuant to the last section, now you must go one step beyond. You must also know the industries of your customers and prospects. Let's make that *two* steps beyond: You must know everything about the industries of your customers and prospects, who *their* customers and prospects are, and then everything about the industries of *their* customers and prospects. Wow! That sounds like *three* steps beyond. But it's the expertise you need to bring value to your business relationships. You're already familiar with the trade publications for your industry and their Web sites, aren't you? Now develop the same level of expertise for those other industries. Be it for diapers or microchips, a plethora of Web sites and magazines is dedicated to promoting the industry. Next time you're waiting for an appointment in the lobby of a prospect's office, look over some of the trade publications that are invariably there. Glance at the subscription cards contained within, and you'll be pleasantly surprised at how many of them offer free subscriptions or at the least a free copy. They'll also note an industry Web site for you to check out. Now you'll not only be receiving the same publications as your customers and prospects, you'll also get on the same mailing lists and be aware of all the information and competitive solicitations being sent to them. Becoming an expert in your customer's industry can also help you prospect, identifying important players and businesses. If you, your products, and your services can benefit one company in an industry, it's very possible they could also benefit other companies in that industry. But before calling for an appointment, go to their Web sites and learn all you can about them and their business.

All this leads us to one of the most important things we need to know: where to find qualified prospects to seek out new professional relationships. We'll discuss the process of networking and prospecting in Chapter 4. Here, we'll limit the discussion to identifying who and where those prospects are.

You probably already know who the large companies are in your territory. They're often mentioned in trade publications or the business sections of local newspapers, most of which are available online as well as in hard copy. If the company is publically traded, you can research it through sites such as <www.moneycentral.msn.com>, which will usually feature a link to the company's Web site. Generally, large businesses will have beautifully designed Web sites detailing the company, its history, and its products, perhaps along with details on how to contact the company about product information or employment. However, Web sites tend to have limited information about decision makers in particular specialties, and you may need to revert to more traditional approaches to identify targets for appointments. Often, larger companies have limited local buying authority and multistep buying procedures that will try anyone's patience. Also, since they're so visible, other sales reps are already calling on the company. Everyone in Orlando, Florida, wants to do business with Disney. Everyone in Atlanta, Georgia, wants a shot at Coca-Cola.

As previously mentioned, most of the growth and emerging opportunities are with smaller businesses. Many sales reps don't even know who these businesses are, let alone researched them or approached them for an appointment. In the new world of business, these companies are easy to find, and once you uncover them it's a whole lot easier to identify the decision maker, get in the door, and get a commitment.

The most effective method for finding these small businesses is a search by Standard Industrial Classification (SIC code) or North American Industry Classification System (NAICS code). These codes classify businesses according to their predominant business activity, though firms may, and often do, engage in other business activities. A SIC or NAICS code is similar to the zip code we use on letters sent through the post office. The smaller the number of digits, the more general the classification; the larger the number of digits, the more specific. Thus, a zip code beginning with 3 denotes the Southeast, 32 is Florida, and 32514 the north side of Pensacola. Similarly, the NAICS code of 51 denotes the general category of information, 513 denotes broadcasting and telecommunications, and 51332 denotes wireless telecommunications carriers (except satellite). NAICS replaced the SIC code in the United States with the advent of the North American Free Trade Agreement (NAFTA) in 1994 and includes new classifications to accommodate new technologies and diverse services not envisioned when SIC was established in the 1930s. NAICS is a superior classification system and will ultimately replace SIC entirely. We make note of SIC, however, because it may remain in use in some places for some time.

Until recently, comprehensive lists of prospects by SIC or NAICS codes were products only affordable by large companies who contracted with printing houses and companies specializing in mailing lists. No longer! Today, any salesperson can purchase CD-ROM programs such as ProCD and Selectphone, which sort businesses by NAICS code by state, county, city, zip code, and street. You can even identify their latitude and longitude. You may have known about prospects in a certain industry who were in the major office parks or downtown high-rises. Now you have them all!

Obviously, you want to spend your time prospecting qualified and reputable companies, so you might want to check them out with the Better Business Bureau <www.bbbonline.com> or Dun & Bradstreet <www.dnb.com/us/>. The address <www.businesscreditusa.com> will give you a basic credit report on businesses for no charge, and a detailed report for a modest fee, a worthwhile consideration if you don't only wish to sell to them but also want to get paid by them.

In Chapter 3, we'll go into detail about customer relationships and helping customers buy the way they like to buy. At this stage, though, let's stick with finding out who they are and being sure to locate information about them on the Web.

If you still haven't been able to identify the appropriate decision maker, call the company and ask the receptionist. Remember that at this point, you're not yet ready to talk to the decision maker or ask for an appointment. You haven't done all your homework yet. So, a good approach might be to introduce yourself to the receptionist, identify your company, and say that you need to send some information to the person in charge. Ask who that would be, how does he or she spell his or her name, and what is his or her title? Remember, of course, that when you ultimately talk to the decision maker, you will never just put something in the mail in lieu of a face-to-face appointment. You might drop a quick note as a prelude to a call, and by all means send a follow-up thank-you for the appointment.

Initially, you will want to uncover everything that's out there about the decision maker and his or her company. You can search newspapers and news groups online for articles, or obtain software such as Copernic, which will enable you to search multiple sites at once. Check it out at <www.copernic.com>. All the news items about the person and his or her company will pop up at once, providing invaluable information about what he or she is doing and what's being said about this individual. Think about how competent and well informed you'll appear when you meet with him or her and mention, "I noticed in the business section of the *Saint Pete Times* that your company was expecting to become a market leader in xxx within the next five years," or "I was looking at the write-up in the *Wall Street Journal* which described your plans for expanding distribution to the Midwest." Imagine the opportunities for finding common ground with the decision maker by uncovering the fact that he or she has particular community involvements and affiliations. On the other side of the coin, think of the pitfalls you might avoid by discovering that a person was under indictment for fraud or a company was being sued by its vendors for nonpayment.

Whether you're a salesperson making a call or on a job interview, know what information you need to know and where to get it. It distinguishes you as someone who is competent and knowledgeable, the kind of person a company would like to do business with in a partnership relationship.

CONCEPT 5: EVALUATE YOUR COMPANY AND THE COMPANY YOU KEEP

Recently, Buck was having a heart-to-heart discussion with a colleague in a slump. His friend is in all ways a professional salesperson who had his priorities right and felt he was doing all the right things. Still, performance was sluggish and he was becoming increasingly frustrated and discouraged. After exploring all the day-to-day activities and routines, Buck happened to ask him some questions about his company, its products, and its services. His friend looked down, shrugged his shoulders, and said hesitatingly, "Well, we've got some problems." They sure did: a product line clearly inferior to competitive offerings, a totally unreliable service arm, and a management culture dedicated to assessing blame rather than coaching employees to succeed. Buck asked, "Is there anything you can do to improve your products and services, and to influence the company environment?" No. Buck's advice was to go to work for the competition. The friend did, and it was a happy ending.

Before ever going to work for anyone, you need to investigate the company, its products, it services, and its culture, just as you would investigate a customer or prospect. Even more so, you have an even deeper partnership relationship with your company, and though you regularly may be off on your own enjoying free time, you're connected to it twenty-four hours a day, seven days a week. It is a good idea to regularly evaluate your company and do everything you can do to make that relationship work. If it's not working and nothing can be done to make it work, move on.

Every business must start with its special reason for being, its niche. It must then serve its markets by being in some way better, its differential advantage or unique selling proposition. If you can't describe what makes your company different or better, it has no reason to be in business and probably won't be for long. The differential advantage is what the salesperson sells: Why should a customer or prospect do business with you instead of the competition? The differential advantage is what a graduate sells in a job interview: Why should you hire me instead of that other person, who is better looking and has a higher grade point average? There is simply no way anyone is going to form a strategic alliance with you unless you can demonstrate a benefit to him or her for doing so.

Everything can and must be differentiated, or you are forced to compete by selling a commodity at the lowest price online. As we've seen, there is no future to that. There are extremely limited opportunities selling an inferior product or service at a lower price. There are many more opportunities and you can make a lot more money selling a superior product or service at a higher price, assuming that the attendant benefits add more in value than you charge as a price premium. Your company must put this in your portfolio when it sends you out the door, or you will fail.

Often, the key differential advantage comes down to intangibles, especially when physical products are fairly similar. One of our favorite authors is Harvey "Swim with the Sharks" Mackay, whose company manufactures the consummate commodity product, envelopes. As everyone knows, "Envelopes is envelopes." Well, at least the physical product specifications are the same. Harvey differentiates his envelopes through superior product quality and impeccable customer service. Evaluate Mackay Envelope Company and you'll see something else. Every employee is considered to be a salesperson. In the military, every person on staff has one directive: serve the soldier on the ground. At Mackay Envelope, every employee is dedicated to helping the sales force serve the customer better. Take a good look at your company, or a company you're considering working for. Is everyone there to help you satisfy the customer, or are managers and employees more concerned about their own personal agendas and power plays? We've already described one of the most important intangibles you offer customers and prospects: the value you add as a professional sales consultant. But you can't deliver that value unless your company is dedicated to customer service. Your word is your bond in selling, and you must have confidence that your company will follow through on promises made to customers. There's no future in going back to customers and telling them you couldn't help it.

Every company will tell you it values its employees, and that it invests in those employees to train them to do their jobs. And every company will tell you it's committed to customer service. But look behind the words to be sure they walk the talk at any company you represent. A few years ago, Bob was talking to the manager of a small business who was concerned about sales-force turnover. After describing the company's superior product and customer service, the manager went on to say that he told his people to ignore follow-up and service promises and to concentrate on cold-calling for new accounts. "I don't care if yesterday's customer is about to throw it out the window," he said. "My bonus is based on sales." Bob told the manager why he thought salespeople might be leaving, but that was not what the manager wanted to hear.

The topics discussed so far have always been true and remain so. They are the foundation upon which a company is built, absolutely essential. But in the new world of business, there's more. Put simply, if a company continues to run its business the same way it did as little as five or six years ago, it may no longer be competitive. Just as the professional salesperson must embrace technology, so must the company.

Put yourself in the shoes of your customers and prospects and evaluate how easy you are to do business with as compared to your competition. Can customers and prospects get the information they need? Can they identify and get in touch with your people? Can they track the status of their order? Is your billing timely and convenient, and does it provide them the information they need? Does your system automatically e-mail them notifications that facilitate their operations and planning? How user-friendly is your Web site, and does it feature links that would be of interest?

Bob is 100 percent loyal to a particular brand and style of jeans, but they're not available in the east, so he looked up the manufacturer's Web site. The company didn't offer product sales online, but listed its 800 number, which Bob called. The company then gave him the name of a retailer and another 800 number to call to place an order, which Bob did. That retailer, it turns out, also sells everything through *its* Web site. Which begs the question: Why didn't the manufacturer's Web site have a direct link to the appropriate page on the retailer's Web site? There aren't that many customers out there as brand-loyal as Bob who will endure two 800 calls to buy from you when one mouse click should have done the job. This is a very important intangible in the new world of business. If you make it easier and more convenient for people to do business with your company at every stage of the process, you will be providing a valuable benefit to your customers.

Just as it's important to evaluate your company, it's equally important to take a look at yourself and the company you keep. As an old and famous football coach once said, "I don't coach football, I coach people." Good sales managers also coach people, and the professional salesperson is a self-coached entrepreneur constantly seeking to excel in all three areas of life: mental, physical, and personal. Already, we've given you plenty of things to do on the mental side, but when you set priorities and do your weekly and daily plans (see Chapter 2), be sure to make time for enough physical activity to keep fit and relieve the stress that is an inherent by-product of the new world of business.

The mental and physical areas are things you make time for and *do.* The personal area is what you *are,* and it comes down to one simple thing: unimpeachable integrity. Remember that you are not a supplier conducting a transaction but a partner in a strategic relationship. Though that does not obviate the need for written understandings of specific expectations, the relationship is predicated on one basic tenet: trust. This implies reliability, of course. You can be depended upon to do what you said you'd do, when you said you'd do it, no excuses. It's why it's so important that you, in turn, have confidence your company will make good on the promises you make to your customers.

But trust goes far beyond reliability. In a joint-venture partnership, you and your customers share objectives and risks. You share dreams and, to a large extent, you share your lives. There will be good times and bad. But just as in any relationship, the venture will succeed only to the extent to which there is implicit trust among the parties. Rather than reduce the importance of relationships, the new world of business has actually created the opportunity to develop a few close personal professional relationships based on integrity and trust, while relieving us of impersonal transactions that can be replaced by a mouse click. As we'll see in succeeding chapters, this has fundamentally changed how professional salespeople do business, prospect, network, and negotiate.

In this chapter, we've challenged the sales professional to take a look at how he or she is doing things, suggesting that what worked a few years ago might be inadequate today. The same will be true for many of the affiliations, organizations, and individuals that are part of your life—the company you keep.

In the new world of business, the people at the top will be achievement-oriented individuals in achievement-oriented environments. They will do business together, send business to each other, share leadership roles in their profession, and take active roles in their community. They will uphold standards of integrity and insist on the same from others for the simple pragmatic reason that anything less can be messaged to a million people overnight and greeted by lawyers and the media the next day. They will be in all ways competent and will not tolerate incompetence. They will not suffer fools gladly. They are the winners. Those not among them are not winners, but losers.

In the old days, this might have described a good-old-boy network, the exclusive province of a few, inaccessible to us mere mortals. But no more. The revolution in technology has totally leveled the playing field, making all forms of information available to anyone who will go out and get it. As sales pros know, knowledge and information equate to power in selling and negotiation. Each individual makes choices about his or her character and integrity. Each individual decides whether to do what it takes to be among the winners.

Tough as it will be to move beyond individuals you've known as friends, it will be even more difficult to bid farewell to friends and colleagues at your company if you determine a change must be made. Many of those folks are fine people who care about what they do and are trying to do the best they can. You'll miss them and may believe you're letting them down. But if you don't have faith in the company and can't see it turning around any time soon, it's time to go.

As you can see just from this first chapter, you have a lot of work ahead of you. There are a lot of challenges to getting up and running with the leaders in the new world of business. Nothing's changed. Success has its price. What is different, though, is that the new level playing field affords opportunity to anyone who knows what to do and is willing to pay the price to get it done. And as you move in this exciting new direction, you're going to notice a significant change in the personal areas of your life. You're going to become more confident and motivated.

We've all heard sales managers talk about how they want to motivate their sales force and give them confidence. Often, they'll send reps to luncheon speeches or all-day programs with sales and marketing gurus in an attempt to do so. You've probably been to this sort of thing yourself. They don't work. They are, essentially, entertainment and stand-up comedy. Sure, you may pick up a few acronyms and tid-bits of wisdom, but you can get that from reading an article on a trade publication Web site. The motivational gurus basically give you a good laugh, show you a good time, and give you a nice warm-and-fuzzy feeling about yourself, until the first time you go back into the field and reality smacks you square in the face.

Although this is not a motivational book, it identifies many specific things you can do to get more of the right things done. Those will make you a better professional salesperson, and provide you with skills that can enhance your income. If you're better, you'll be more confident. And when you're better and more confident, you'll be more successful. Then, when you're better, more confident, and more successful, you'll be motivated to do even more. Motivation is a result of success, not a prelude to it, but only if sales is your passion and not your prison. If you're going to be motivated and successful at what-ever you do, you've got to feel you're doing exactly what you'd want to be doing even if you weren't being paid for it.

CONCLUSION

In this chapter, we've challenged you to take a look at yourself and how you're managing yourself as a professional salesperson. All those things which led to success a few years ago are still essential, but they're not enough. It's absolutely critical to be getting better every day or you'll soon find yourself falling behind.

If you've made the commitment to excellence, and you've affiliated yourself with the right people and the right organizations, you're ready to get started. In the next chapter, we'll address how to be more efficient, more effective, and more focused.

Chapter 2

Yesterday's Good Habits Are Today's Time Wasters: Time and Territory Management

Most sales professionals believe that success comes to those who do all the right things and do them consistently. It's a matter of developing good work habits and doing the things that need to be done, day in and day out. Selling is a numbers game. You may not be successful on any one single sales call, but if you keep throwing that spaghetti up against the wall, some of it is going to stick. Unfortunately, many of yesterday's good habits are today's time wasters. Doing the right things isn't enough. *How* you do those right things is equally important.

In this chapter, we'll explore the five key concepts of time and territory management in the new world of business. First, similar to points made in Chapter 1, we'll see that some things never change. There are many essentials from the past that are still important today. Then, in Concept 2, we'll challenge you to carefully assess what you're doing now and how you're doing it; figure out where you are now before deciding where you want to be. In Concept 3, we'll discuss how technology can help you plan and operate more efficiently and more effectively. Then, in Concept 4, we explain how to get twice as much done in half the time. And finally, Concept 5 focuses on new perspectives on old traditions such as the business lunch, wining and dining, and other business socializing.

CONCEPT 1: SOME THINGS NEVER CHANGE

Recently, we were talking to a woman who had been in sales for about a year. She was on the job market, seeking *anything* but another job in sales. Here's what she told us:

I get up every morning at five. By the time the kids have break-fast and get out the door, it's seven. I stuff and address envelopes till eight. Then I spend the day fighting traffic, going by the of-fice to get things, running them out to customers, sitting in wait-ing rooms because prospects had something come up and can't see me for another hour, only to make my presentation and have them tell me they'll think it over. I'm beating my head against the wall an average of eighty hours a week, and after expenses I'm lucky to clear six bucks an hour. I have never worked so hard in my life. If I'm working this hard, I ought to be making more money.

Unfortunately, the company doesn't pay you for working hard; it pays you for results. It's not how hard you work; it's what you get done.

Something that will never change is that salespeople get paid for one thing: sales. This truism has become the norm in business. Not all that long ago, loyal employees had moved up in the ranks, worked hard all their lives, but couldn't directly demonstrate how what they did contributed to the bottom-line profitability of their company. They were called *middle management.* They are no more, replaced by technology and a flatter, leaner, and meaner organizational structure. Whether you're an employee or the owner of a small business, work-ing hard is a given. But it's even more important to work smart and to be effective. Do the right job. Don't merely do the job right.

To be successful in sales, you must set goals and have a plan for achieving them. When the U.S. military landed at Normandy, they did not merely round up whoever was available, send them toward the beach, and wait to see what happened. When the University of West Florida sends its football team down to Gainesville to play the Gators, they do not lull themselves into complacency by thinking, *These guys will be a pushover. We can win by six, seven touchdowns easy. All we have to do is show up.* When Procter & Gamble or Microsoft launch a new product, they do not simply throw it over the fence, run for cover, and hope it will sell.

For you, it's absolutely essential to start by setting a goal of how much you want to make in the next year. It should be realistic but challenging, perhaps a little more than you think you can do but po-tentially attainable. Let's say your goal is $100,000. Now you have a number in front of you, something to shoot for. But don't stop there.

Next, determine how many sales you'll need to achieve the goal. In all likelihood, you have many different types of customers and prospects, each with different product/service needs and different sales potential, each requiring different amounts of effort, and each having a different probability of success. To keep things simple, let's consider only one type.

You want to make $100,000. If you make $2,000 per sale, you need fifty sales a year. Now figure out how many face-to-face contacts you need to get those fifty sales. If you close one out of three prospects you see in person, you'll need to meet with 150 prospects in the next year, fifty of whom will buy and 100 of whom will not. Next, calculate how much time that will take including travel to and from appointments and all types of communication between meetings. If the fifty who ultimately buy each take ten hours of your time, that's a total of 500 hours. If the 100 who ultimately do not buy each take six hours of your time, that's a total of 600 hours. So, you will need 1,100 hours to meet with prospects.

Next, determine how much time you will need to prepare for those appointments. If each of the 150 prospects requires two hours for preparation, that's another 300 hours a year.

Finally, calculate how many solicitations it will take to get 150 prospects to see you in person. If one in twelve agrees to meet with you, that's 1,800 solicitations you must make every year. How much time will that take? For example, if it takes eight minutes for the 150 who agree to meet with you, that's 1,200 minutes or twenty hours. And if it takes four minutes for the 1,650 who will not meet with you, that's 6,600 minutes or 110 hours. So, you will need 130 hours to solicit appointments.

Now, add it all up: 1,100 hours meeting with prospects + 300 hours preparing + 130 hours soliciting = 1,530 hours a year, or nearly thirty hours a week in direct selling activities to meet your goal of earning $100,000. Remember that none of this includes time for networking, business-related socializing, or commitments and obligations to your manager, your company, or your profession. Ask yourself. "Is this doable?" If not, your goal of $100,000 may not be realistic and should be revised downward. On the other hand, if it's doable in just eight months, it might be reasonable to revise it upward.

Throughout this book, we address advanced selling skills and applications of technology to enhance your effectiveness so that you can close a higher proportion of sales, have a higher proportion of solicitations result in appointments, and enable you to get a lot more done in a lot less time. When you complete Action Plan Assignment #1 one year from now, compare it with the numbers you calculate today. Hopefully, you'll be pleasantly surprised to find you need fewer hours to generate more money. Going through Action Plan Assignment #1 should make one thing abundantly clear: To achieve your income goal, you're going to need to get organized, have a plan for every week and every day, and make the commitment to do those things which have to get done.

In our example, we calculated that it would take thirty hours a week of direct selling activities to earn $100,000 a year. Sounds pretty good, right? Most anyone would gladly put in a thirty-hour week to make that kind of money. It's not quite that easy, though, as any sales professional will tell you. That's because, in addition to direct selling activities, there are other must-do activities. For starters, how many hours a week do you need for reports, meetings, paperwork, etc. for your company? We talked about the time required for soliciting appointments, but before you can make a call you have to figure out *who* you're going to call. How much time will it take to network and research for potential qualified prospects? We'll go into these issues in detail later in this and succeeding chapters, but as a guideline, figure on needing about one hour of other must-do activities for every hour of direct selling activities. In our example, to have thirty hours a week in direct selling activities translates to a sixty-hour week. What you may well discover, however, is that the way you're doing things now is taking *two* hours of other must-do activities for every hour of direct selling activities, which means you must work ninety hours a week to get the needed thirty hours of direct selling activities. Since it's unlikely you can put in ninety-hour weeks for long before losing both your marriage and your sanity, it's more than likely you're working sixty hours a week but netting only twenty hours for direct selling activities. That means you're only going to make $67,000 instead of $100,000, and that costs!

Let's take another look at Action Plan Assignment #1 to see one of the most important numbers it calculates for you. Remember, you make your money in direct-selling activities. Everything else just supports those activities. Take the income goal for the year and divide it by the number of hours necessary to achieve that goal to determine

Action Plan Assignment #1: Annual Activity Commitment

Complete this exercise for every type of current customer and potential prospect. Be sure the sum of income goals for all customer/prospect types adds up to your total income goal. Here, we've included the numbers from our example.

Current customer: _____
Potential prospect: _____
Customer/prospect type: _____

1. Income goal: $100,000
2. Average income per sale: $2,000
3. Sales goal (#1 ÷ #2): 50
4. Average number of customers/prospects to meet with to get one sale: 3
5. Goal number of customers/prospects to meet with (#3 × #4): 150
6. Appointment and follow-up time required for each customer/prospect who buys: 10 hours
7. *Total* appointment and follow-up time required for *all* customers/prospects who buy (#3 × #6): 500 hours
8. Number of customers/prospects met with who do *not* buy (#5 − #3): 100
9. Appointment and follow-up time required for *each* customer/prospect who does *not* buy: 6 hours
10. *Total* appointment and follow-up time required for *all* customers/prospects who do *not* buy (#8 × #9): 600 hours
11. Grand total appointment and follow-up time (#7 + #10): 1,100 hours
12. Preparation time for each customer/prospect meeting: 2 hours
13. Grand total preparation time (#5 × #12): 300 hours
14. Number of solicitations required to get one in-person appointment: 12
15. Total number of solicitations necessary (#5 × #14): 1,800
16. Time required for each successful solicitation: 8 minutes
17. Total time required for successful solicitations (#5 × #16): 1,200 minutes or (#17 ÷ 60): 20 hours
18. Total number of unsuccessful solicitation (#15 − #5): 1,650
19. Time required for each unsuccessful solicitation: 4 minutes
20. Total time required for unsuccessful solicitations (#18 × #19): 6,600 minutes or (#20 ÷ 60): 110 hours
21. Grand total solicitation time (#17 + #20): 130 hours
22. Total time in direct selling activities (#11 + #13 + #21): 1,530 hours or (#22 ÷ 52): 30 hours/week

what your time is worth. In our example, to make $100,000 took 1,530 hours, which means your time is worth sixty-five dollars an hour. Of course, your numbers may vary, but figure it out. Just how much is your time worth? You'll probably be surprised how high that number is. If your time is worth sixty-five dollars an hour, every hour you waste or every hour your company makes you lose costs you sixty-five dollars.

CONCEPT 2: CAREFULLY ASSESS WHAT YOU'RE DOING NOW AND HOW YOU'RE DOING IT

Once you have an idea of how much your time is worth, it's time for a detailed assessment of what you're doing now. If you've ever been in a time management program, you're probably familiar with time logs. They are detailed, minute-by-minute trackings of all your activities, every minute of the day, for one week. Essentially, that's what you need to do in Action Plan Assignment #2, but with an added dimension. Don't just note *what* you do, but also note *how* you do it because, as the title of this chapter suggests, yesterday's good habits are today's time wasters. Choose a day to start—a Saturday, Sunday, or Monday would be best—and make the commitment to do this.

Action Plan Assignment #2: Time Log

For seven days, keep a detailed record of all your activities, all day long, minute by minute, and note details of how you were conducting that activity. No details necessary for free time/family time.

We cannot overemphasize how important it is that you really *do* these action plans and not just read through them. Action Plan Assignment #1 helps you pinpoint what you need to do in direct-selling activities to achieve your goals, and Action Plan Assignment #2 gives you a detailed critique of where you are now. Doing these is an essential prelude to the process of effective planning, and without a plan you'll never get where you want to go. As the old adage says, plan your work and work your plan. It's tough to figure out where you want to go if you don't know where you're at. And as a well-known ballplayer also renowned for his eloquence put it: If you don't know where you're going, you might wind up somewhere else. Yes, those are all platitudes. Yes, they're trite. They're also true.

Traditionally, the next step in time management is to assess everything you're doing or would like to do and assign it an A, B, or C priority:

> **A priority:** Direct-selling activities, such as prospecting and networking, and obligations to your manager and company
>
> **B priority:** Items of secondary importance, which yield some limited benefits
>
> **C priority:** Activities that sap your time and contribute little or nothing

Effective time management and planning, then, consist of getting you to focus on the A's, reduce the B's, and eliminate the C's. We'd like to modify that just a tad to fit the new world of business.

First split the A's into two parts: true A's and what we call AX priorities (activities which get a top priority but which you should either not do yourself or do differently). For example, in your time log you might have activities such as spending two hours a week stuffing and addressing envelopes to send out to customers and prospects. Stop doing that. Get some kid in the neighborhood or in a youth group to do it. *But,* you say, *that'll cost me six bucks an hour!* No, that will free up two hours a week for direct-selling activities. As you discovered when you did Action Plan Assignment #1, direct-selling activities yield you sixty-five dollars an hour. That kid doesn't cost you six dollars an hour, he or she frees you up to make fifty-nine dollars an hour. Along the same lines, there are things you *should* do, but differently. In Chapter 1, we described software packages that enable you to identify potential prospects. You might look at such a package and balk at its price tag. But if that package does for you—and does it a whole lot better—in fifteen minutes what used to take you three and a half hours a week at the library, it's more than paid for itself in a week. Once you have an appreciation of what your direct-selling activities earn for you, it becomes very clear that investments in the tools available will pay off quickly.

We also suggest that you don't just reduce B's but eliminate them entirely. There really is no limit to the possibilities for finding A's, and you'll simply never get to the point of addressing items of secondary importance. On the other hand, there might be some B's or C's that you simply enjoy doing. Perhaps you joined a certain community organization awhile ago, believing it would be a good networking opportunity. When you assess that organization in the action plan assignment in Chapter 4, you may have to agree it's not helping you as a prospecting tool, but you really like the people there and enjoy being part of things. Fine. Just acknowledge, though, that the organization is a social activity you're engaged in for fun on your own free time, and eliminate any pretense that you're "working."

There are some time wasters that are so subtle you may not even have noted them in Action Plan Assignment #2. One of those is excessive socializing. Of course, some socializing is necessary and, as we'll see in Chapter 3, some types of prospects require more socializing and rapport building than others. But if you meet with twenty people a day and spend an extra three minutes socializing with each of them, that kills an hour a day or five hours a week. That five hours a week, at sixty-five dollars an hour, costs you $325 a week. We trust you are not one of those people who sits around the office socializing with colleagues and peers. The folks who do that, you will discover, are the marginal performers. The sales winners are out of the office doing A priorities. If you find you're spending a significant number of hours exchanging stories with co-workers, it's time to evaluate the company you keep.

Here's another subtle time waster you may have overlooked. How many hours a week do you spend in waiting rooms before seeing customers and prospects? In some fields, such as pharmaceutical sales, you may spend more time waiting than actually selling. Instead of just sitting there watching the second hand go around on the clock, put that time to use. We already suggested checking out trade publications that might be there. After that, use those minutes to catch up on paperwork, read, or to do your expense account. Many sales reps discover that using those few minutes several times a day, every day, enables them to get done what previously took them half a day on the weekend. *Their* weekend!

The same principle applies to time gaps between appointments. If you finish with one prospect at 10:45 a.m. and the next one is set for 1:00 p.m., what do you do? Kill two hours for lunch? Put that time to work! Take a look at the appointments themselves. Is it taking two or three meetings to cover an agenda that could have been handled in one session with proper up-front planning? Meetings often waste time, but the real killer can be the time it takes going to and from them.

Along those lines, don't delude yourself into believing that travel time is productive time. Yes, you can fire up the laptop on the plane and you can use your cell phone, hands free, of course, in the car, but neither environment is as productive as being by yourself working in a distraction-free environment, and even that is no substitute for direct-selling activities. So, if you're doing something in one end of your territory, plan ahead and get everything done that needs attention there. Traffic is awful *everywhere* now, and driving is an expensive way to spend your day, mostly because sitting in traffic is costing you sixty-five dollars an hour. Keep that in mind the next time you think about taking an hour to run something out to a customer instead of having a courier service do it for twenty bucks. Just as with stuffing envelopes—that courier services doesn't cost you twenty dollars, it saves you forty-five dollars.

Once you've carefully assessed what you're doing now and how you're doing it, you're ready to begin planning. You're going to notice that by the time you identify all the AX priorities and start implementing all the improvements in how you do things, your daily and weekly plans will look a lot different than they do today. No matter. Starting now and from now on, you must do a plan, without fail, every week and every day. In the next section, we'll introduce you to technologies that will make your planning and your doing easier and more effective. But no matter whether you're using a Palm Pilot and Meeting Maker or a paper calendar and index cards, planning starts now. This is nothing you keep floating around in your head, either. It is absolutely imperative that you write it down, or, as the case may be, key it in. Action Plan Assignment #3 lets you practice this planning method.

Action Plan Assignment #3: Daily Planning

At the same time every day, in fifteen-minute time blocks, do your daily plan for the next day. At the same time every week, do your weekly plan and seven tentative daily plans.

The best time to do a weekly plan is *before* the weekend. If you wait until Sunday night, you may discover there were things that needed to be done over the weekend to get ready for the week. Too late then. Far better to knock it out Friday night or Saturday morning and enjoy the weekend knowing you have all your ducks in a row. Each evening, then, before any free time or family time, do the next day's daily plan.

Weekly and daily plans will closely resemble the process you followed in Action Plan Assignment #1, where you started with a goal and broke it down to a series of activities and times required. Keeping that annual goal in mind, ask yourself, *What do I need to do this week? What do I need to do tomorrow to get me there?* What gets you there, of course, are A priorities and AX priorities you're going to modify into A priorities, and that's all you list on your weekly and daily plans.

Something you'll notice about daily and weekly plans is that they resemble battle plans. That is, they remain intact only until the first shot is fired. Depending on what happens between 8:00 and 10:00 a.m. Monday morning, the rest of the day may be very different from what you envisioned Sunday night. Let's say, for example, that starting at 8:00 a.m., you make twenty-four calls soliciting appointments. Based on the ratios in our example, you expect two of these to be successful. But you might confirm four appointments or none. And depending on what happens all day Monday, Tuesday will look quite different from the tentative plan. By the time you get to Friday, it may bear almost no resemblance whatever. Don't get frustrated. Effective planning requires flexibility. In sales, you can't plan the entire week ahead in fifteen-minute time blocks. For those who like structure and predictability, this can be frustrating, but it's also why sales is fun. What you *can* do is stay focused on A priorities at all times, and every time you get even a few minutes, ask yourself, *What can I be doing now?* To help you do that, designate one item as your A1 priority, *the* most important thing you need to get done. When it's completed, cross it off the list and designate something else as the A1. If you're always focused on those priorities as you execute your plan, you will be organized, will get things done, and will begin to make a lot more money.

CONCEPT 3: RUNNING WITH TECHNOLOGY
OR RUNNING IN PLACE

Remember the Rolodex? Used to be there was one on every desk. For those of you who aren't into collectibles, the Rolodex was an alphabetized card file on a roller that you turned around to look up names, addresses, and phone numbers. According to the <www. newelloffice.com> Web site, the Rolodex has been around for fifty years, and the average one is twenty years old. Doesn't sound like something entering the growth stage of the product life cycle. If you have a Rolodex, you won't come in one morning and find it lying on its back, feet in the air, bleeding cards. But believe us, the Rolodex is dead.

There was a time when a sales rep submitted paperwork that was actually on paper. Really, no kidding. Didn't you ever wonder why it was called "paperwork"?

Ever see a law firm commercial? Invariably, an attorney in an expensive dark suit is standing in a nice office with shelves of books in the background. Those are law books. At one time, when they were researching a case they'd get a whole staff of law clerks and first-year law students to go rummaging through all those books looking for statutes and precedent. Yes, it did take several weeks, they probably missed as much as they found, and the books were out of date the day they came out. But that's the way it was done; at the time there were no other choices

Along the same lines, doctors used to have to search through books, journals, and a hard copy of the *Physicians' Desk Reference* to make a diagnosis and determine treatment. No, we're not making this up.

The world of academia has never been renowned as trendsetting, but in the mid-1980s, when Bob started his doctoral program, his chairperson told him they had embraced technology and would allow him to do his dissertation on a word processor, despite objections from some of the senior faculty. Until then, dissertations had to be typed with no errors and no corrections. It had always been done that way. Why mess with a good thing?

In the Middle Ages, when you wanted to make a copy of something, someone had to sit down and write it out in longhand. They were called scribners, and made a pretty good living of it until high tech came along and gave us carbon paper.

We hope you see where we're going with this. Certainly, you're not living in the sixteenth century. Your office is stocked with carbon paper or you might even have a copy machine. You've probably even graduated beyond the 1970s. You utilize word processing instead of a typewriter. But it's entirely possible that you're still using card files and looking things up in hard copy. We'll also bet you may not even know about some of the technology innovations we're about to share with you. If you're not running with technology, you're running in place. And someone's gaining on you.

It's understandable that an individual or small business might be a bit behind the times, particularly if they have steady business with a few regular clients and aren't looking to expand between now and an imminent retirement. But it's hard to believe that a growth-oriented person or business in a highly competitive industry could continue to do things the same old way just because it's always been done that way. Yet many do.

Recently, Buck was called in to consult with top management of a multimillion-dollar retailing organization. His assignment was to assess their current operations and make recommendations for changes that might enhance their system. He and his staff interviewed inventory personnel and inside salespeople, and spent some time observing procedures. What they found was most interesting. A customer would phone in to place an order. The salesperson would leaf through a hard copy of the catalog to find it, often asking the customer, "You wouldn't happen to know what page that's on, would you?" The salesperson would then write out the order on an index card and place it in a shoe box. Periodically, a runner would come by to empty the shoe boxes and take them to the next step in the process. If a customer inquired as to whether the item was in stock, the sales rep would put the caller on hold and walk into the warehouse to physically check stock, returning to inform them, "Yup, we got it" or "Nope, we're out just now." If an item was out of stock and the customer asked when it might be available, the response went something along the lines of, "Well, we get a truck in every Wednesday. Might be in then." The really fun scenario was when a customer called in asking about the status of an order. Then, it was, "I'll call you right back on that," followed by a desk-to-desk hunt in search of the elusive index card and another walk back to the warehouse to confirm, "Nope, it ain't come in yet."

Bob had a similar experience. He has a few expired cars in his yard, and some of the neighbors in his country club and resort community were complaining a little, so he decided to plant some English Ivy to grow over them and cover them up until he could decide what to do with them. He went down to the lawn and garden center at one of the nation's largest retailers and bought up all the English Ivy they had, filling his 1979 Cutlass to capacity. Still, this was only about half of what he needed to complete the job, so a week later he went back to get some more. There were only four more baskets in stock, so he asked a clerk when more would be coming in. She told him that a truck came in every week, and every week they got four baskets of English Ivy. But what if someone had come in the week before and bought all twenty-four baskets they had in inventory? "It doesn't make any difference what we sell or what we've got in inventory," she said. "They send us the same amount of everything every week."

Certainly you'd expect the health care industry to be up to speed. But a recent experience Buck had with a leading medical placement firm has to call that into question. The firm has over 1,000 clients that it places in facilities all over the United States. They, too, were using those ubiquitous index cards to store information on their clients, and file folders to store account information on facilities where clients were placed. If a hospital called needing, for example, an anesthesiologist in Denver, the firm would then search through their card file for someone with the requisite qualifications and, in turn, further narrow the search to those persons who could make the trip on short notice. On average, it took the placement manager thirty minutes to conduct this manual search. This was obviously an incredible waste of time. Hospitals in need of personnel have no time to waste. They need to find someone immediately, not thirty minutes from now. As a result, by the time this firm was able to respond, in many cases the hospital had already located someone somewhere else. The sale was lost, as were possibilities for repeat business and long-term partnerships and strategic alliances.

If these stories hit home for you or your company, it's time to get up and running with technology. You should no longer be writing things down on paper or index cards. You should no longer be looking things up in books or hard copies of magazines, journals, or newspapers. And, you should no longer be glancing at a shelf to see if something's in stock or phoning a colleague to check on the status of an order.

Time and territory management are as important as they ever were in the new world of business. Many of the basics, as you've seen, are the same. But a lot is different. For one thing, territory management now includes far more than the geographical sales territory it used to connote. The revolution in technology has blurred the concept of physical distances and geographic territories so that today, as our examples have illustrated, territory management might address the process of taking customers orders, expediting and tracking goods, then doing billing and follow-up. Or it might be applied to retrieving information, and how you utilize that information to create and communicate valuable services which people will buy. Same thing on time management. Traditionally, time management was a task for individual self-management. Today it's something business owners and managers must consider for their employees. Your employees may be dealing with all the top priorities you want them to focus on, but if it's taking them thirty minutes to do something that could get done in thirty seconds, you're sure not getting optimum productivity. And you know what? That kind of working environment is murder on morale. Employees who really want to do a good job and be productive just won't stay around. Beyond that, it gets back to what we said about the individual sales rep stuffing envelopes. If you pay employees twenty dollars an hour, including benefits and direct expenses, a task that takes thirty minutes costs you ten. If it could have been done in thirty seconds, it would have cost you seventeen cents. You just burned $9.83, and you have less satisfied customers besides. Repeat that 200 times a day and see how long you stay in business. But take heart! The revolution in technology has made it possible for big companies, a small business, or even an individual to run with technology.

Buck helped the medical placement firm convert from index cards and paper files to a local area network (LAN) equipped with a vertical-market software package. An in-house data and information management system now stores all information about their candidates and clients, maintains all accounts payable and accounts receivable, and does in thirty seconds any of the tasks that previously took thirty minutes to do manually.

Vertical-market software packages are not cheap, and until a few years ago they were out of reach for small businesses. In the new world of business, though, all that has changed. Just as you can timeshare for a luxurious beach condo two weeks a year, so can companies or individuals share services and expenses of software packages once solely the province of the big guys. These services are made available by firms known as application solution providers (ASPs). With an ASP, smaller businesses can utilize a wide variety of software packages, all of which are the latest and the greatest. It's an attractive alternative to the significant investment of purchasing such software, much of which might be obsolete in a short time. The medical placement firm utilized an ASP to obtain customer relationship management (CRM) software. Individuals can benefit by utilizing ASPs for sales force automation (SFA) software, which we'll touch on briefly in the next section.

To get you started, the following are some ASP sites you might find of interest:

CRM Online <www.salesforce.com>
Oracle Online Services <www.oraclesalesonline.com>
Siebel Systems <www.sales.com>
Upshot <www.upshot.com>
Xsellsys <www.xsellsys.com>

If at first you don't find an ASP that has exactly what you need, keep looking. Someone out there has a package to address precisely whatever it is that will specifically fit your unique business situation.

How can companies still be doing things the way they were six or eight years ago? Hard to say. But people have a natural propensity to stay with what they know and to resist change. Many people have a fear of anyone or anything that's different. If it's always the way they did things and it works, leave it alone. If it ain't broke, don't fix it.

In the old days, you could get away with such an attitude because change occurred relatively slowly. American automobile companies were slow to accept that they were in the total personal transportation business, not the new car business, but they finally got it right and are now producing good products with the service people expect. We wonder how Smith Corona could have gone on year after year believing they were in the typewriter business and not the information-processing business. It never did dawn on them, and they're history.

Some people seem to believe that it's fine to let something go until it breaks, and then fix it. We wonder if they maintain their cars that way. They do no preventative maintenance until there's a road failure, and then they have it towed in. But today, in business or in sales, by the time you realize it's broke, it's already too late to fix it. So we implore you: If it ain't broke, break it. Get up running with technology, or you're running in place.

CONCEPT 4: THE DYNAMIC DAY— GETTING TWICE AS MUCH DONE IN HALF THE TIME

In the olden days, life ran at a snail's pace compared to today. The telephone had been invented, so people would talk to one another occasionally, but then, as now, verbal understandings were subject to misinterpretation, so you would always follow up with a letter, sent by the only means available, the post office. It was also a time of large corporations with layers of middle management, each of which had to note every activity every step of the way. When Bob was in the corporate sales department of a Fortune 500 company, the norm was that a memo from him to the appropriate person in a regional office took six weeks to disseminate, since it had to be noted and then expedited up through every layer in corporate headquarters and then noted and expedited down through every layer in the region office before getting to the person to whom it was directed. In the Fortune 500 today, those middle managers are all gone, since their only real contribution, disseminating information, has been replaced by technology.

But a more significant change in the economy has been a shift toward small business. We continue to hear of layoffs in the big companies, and yet the size of the workforce has continued to grow. The reason is simple. *All* the growth in our economy is in small- to medium-sized companies who operate with little or no middle management and whose employees, at the point of encounter, are expected to make decisions and take action on the spot. Plus, through the wonders of technology, these same employees manage all the dissemination of information once handled by middle management. Fortune 1000 companies who have not adopted the small-business style model are— well, they're no longer in the Fortune 1000.

This does not surprise anyone working in sales or managing a small business today. The pace is very fast, people work very long hours, and making a profit is getting tougher than ever. The casual business trip is a thing of the past. Gone are the days of leaving the office at noon to catch a midafternoon flight that would get you to your destination in time for a couple of shooters in the bar, a nice dinner on the company's money, a meeting around 10:00 the next morning, lunch, and a flight too late to drop by the office but just in time to beat the traffic home. Today, business trips are expensive. They also take a lot of time, which costs you sixty-five dollars an hour. Now, you make the business trip only if it's the only way to get the job done, and even then you may be out on the 6:30 a.m. flight, have a meeting at 9:00 a.m., and be back in the office by 2:00 p.m. If an e-mail, a phone call, or a teleconference will handle it, don't make the trip. But you know that, don't you?

When you *must* travel, you do work on the go. At the airport or in flight, instead of sipping on Johnnie Walker Black, you're grinding it out on your laptop. You get a hotel room with an Internet connection and get in a couple hours work after a quick dinner. Thanks to your cell phone and pager, people can contact you anytime, anywhere. But you're already doing that, aren't you?

You and your company no longer have index cards and paper files, and you're using e-mail in lieu of snail mail. Furthermore, you check your e-mail regularly. If people have your e-mail address and send you a message, they have the right to expect a prompt reply. Check your mailbox two or three times a day, not every fifteen minutes. That's a time waster. Similarly, if you have voice mail you should check it regularly. You do not answer the phone every time it rings if you're in the middle of an A priority. Instead, a couple of times a day, ideally just before lunch and just before evening rush hour—when everyone wants to get to the business at hand and not waste time—you reply to all your e-mails and return all your phone calls. But this describes your present routine, doesn't it?

We've just described changes in the typical business day, changes that reflect today's faster pace and enhanced productivity. They should describe you. If not, you're in trouble. These are the givens, but they're not enough. They don't describe a dynamic day.

Just as your company has chucked index cards and paper files, it's time for you to toss the leather-bound daily/weekly planner and organizer. Your local office supply store has off-the-shelf products such as Act! or GoldMine that offer basic database features such as appointment scheduling, personal phone book, simple records management, and plug-ins for proposal writing and forecasting. These products will run something in the neighborhood of $200, which means one will pay for itself in the first three hours of your time it saves, not to mention the savings in pencils and erasers.

Now just imagine having a supercomputer that stores all the information available on all your current customers and potential prospects: A complete purchase and payment history by product line by day/week/month/time of the quarter/phase of the moon, whatever. Further imagine that this supercomputer would automatically keep you apprised of any press releases or stock market information pertaining to those customers and prospects. In addition, imagine that you could gain secure access to all this information from practically anywhere in the world with your laptop, handheld device, or even cell phone. How much would you pay for a supercomputer such as this? A million dollars? Nope. Try about sixty dollars a month.

These SFA software packages geared at automating things such as contact management, forecasting, and reporting are available through ASPs. A few years ago, SFA packages such as these cost hundreds of thousands of dollars to purchase outright, so were affordable only to large companies. No longer. This is just one more example of how the availability of technology has expanded to make it not only affordable but also *essential* to small businesses or individuals.

You can log onto these packages through any Internet connection. Now, you and your colleagues, or you and all your employees, are always in touch with one another and have all the information in your company's decision support system (DSS) at their fingertips. Virtual offices all over the world can share real-time information, Web conference, and check on or change the status of orders, whether subscribers are at home, in the office, or in front of a customer who needs to know something right now. All this is delivered through a secure Internet connection with service level agreements (SLAs) that guarantee your information is private, secure, and always available. Costs can be as low as ten to thirty dollars per month per user. The following are a few ASPs you can look up to investigate SFA software:

OnContact <crm.oncontact.com>
Upshot <www.upshot.com>
Avantgo, Inc. <www.avantgo.com>
OpenAir <www.openair.com>
Xsellsys <www.xsellsys.com>

With SFA software customized to your needs, you and all your colleagues will have all their sales, marketing, and customer service information in one system. Everyone will always be up to date and in the loop, no matter where he or she is.

The software innovations we've described illustrate our point about AX priorities. Already, you've probably seen examples of how A priorities can be handled differently and more effectively, freeing up time for direct-selling activities. To really do it right, however, we're going to suggest one more step: graduate up and away from your laptop or notebook.

There's nothing wrong with what a laptop or notebook can do, which is as much as a room-sized mainframe could do in the dinosaur days. It's just that technology has made them too big and bulky for day-to-day applications.

Think about it. If you're an outside salesperson going from appointment to appointment all day, it can be impractical and cumbersome to lug a laptop around. And when you're in a meeting with customers and prospects, it's inconvenient to whip out the laptop and fire it up to take notes and schedule appointments. So what do you do? Write things down longhand and transcribe them later? Not very efficient. It's tantamount to utilizing Act! as a scheduling tool and then copying the information down in the weekly planner.

To do things right, invest $100 to $300 in a handheld device computer, also known as a personal digital assistant (PDA). You can easily transfer all your contact and appointment data from Act! or almost any other contact management software directly into your PDA. Having done so, trash the weekly planner, though you might wish to retain the leather binder to hold product slicks, your PDA, and candy bars. Check with the software manufacturer or the PDA company to see if it will also accommodate e-mail programs such as Outlook.

Next, transfer all customer information into the PDA, not just contact persons and phone numbers but their entire purchase and payment history. Include copies of attendant spreadsheets and word-processing documents. Yes, all this can be done on a computer that weighs ounces and fits into a shirt pocket! And because of its size, it's practical to use it in a face-to-face meeting or other places where the laptop would be awkward.

Buck had a couple of recent experiences that illustrate the indispensability of his PDA. He was in a meeting with a prospect who was almost ready to buy. We'll go into closing and negotiation in Chapters 7 and 8 respectively, so here we will just touch on the highlights. Essentially, the prospect wanted a discount, and Buck needed to determine what he could ask for in return to confirm agreement and seal the deal. Since he had all his account information in his PDA, Buck made a couple of taps and determined that this customer paid in an average of thirty-five days after invoice. Buck offered a discount under the condition of payment in fifteen days. The deal was done. Without this information at his fingertips, Buck would have had to either call the office in front of the customer, always an awkward situation, or leave without an order and call the customer back later.

Buck's other experience was a situation many professional salespeople can relate to. Products have a base price, but numerous options for accessories and add-ons that can affect that price, so when salespeople are with customers or prospects, they need to be able to quickly respond to inquiries about various alternatives and their attendant prices. Buck has entered all his price lists into his PDA, so it's easy for him to do these calculations on the spot. On this particular occasion, he was in his car when he got a call from a prospect on his cell phone. She had his proposal in front of her and had questions about alternatives. Buck pulled into a parking lot, referred to the information on his PDA, and gave her immediate answers. They reached an agreement on the spot.

Salespeople appreciate the importance of being able to give immediate responses to inquiries from customers and prospects, especially when they appear receptive to making an affirmative buying decision. It can be, and often is, the difference between confirming the agreement or not. These investments in equipment and software pay for themselves in weeks or even days by freeing up time for direct-selling activities. But more than that, as Buck's experiences demonstrate, they can enhance the effectiveness of direct-selling activities and enable you to increase earnings per hour.

The following are some companies and their Web sites that can help you select a PDA which best fits your needs:

Palm Computing <www.palm.com>
Handspring <www.handspring.com>
Sony Clié <www.sony.com>
HP Jornada <www.hp.com>

The following sites can help you find free and for-fee software to help you get the most out of your PDA:

PalmGear <www.palmgear.com>
pdaBuzz <www.pdabuzz.com>
Tucows <www.tucows.com>

Just so you won't forget, try Action Plan Assignment #4.

Action Plan Assignment #4: Dynamic Days

Make all your days dynamic days. As part of your weekly plan for the next thirteen weeks, include activities that will bring you totally up to speed on all the software and hardware you need to be running with technology. Make the commitment. Complete this project within ninety days.

CONCEPT 5: WHAT'S FOR LUNCH AND DINNER? NEW PERSPECTIVES ON WINING AND DINING

One of the more interesting changes in business today is in the area of business lunches, dinners, and other business-related socializing. As in many of the norms we've noted, what were once business-building activities may be today's time wasters.

Of course, some companies and some industries still wine and dine their customers, take them on trips, and provide them with thousand-dollar seats at sporting events. Some still give extravagant gifts of appreciation. More and more, however, customers and their management are coming to realize that when vendors spend lavish sums on entertainment and gifts, that money is coming out of the customer's pocket, not the vendor's. It's simple. Instead of selling me something for $100,000 and spending $5,000 entertaining me and my people, sell it to me for $95,000 and skip the entertainment. I'm the customer, and it's my money paying for all this stuff. Also, as a manager, and especially as a small business owner, I'm very concerned about the ability of my people to make objective decisions when a trip to the Super Bowl is influencing the process. Profits are tough to come by, and you don't want to do anything to increase your vulnerability to a lean-and-mean competitor.

Another factor influencing the nature of business socializing is the nature of the professional environment. In the days of the "organization man," men worked for a corporation and their identity was the company. Women were homemakers and on call for social events as their husbands and their companies required. That world is long gone. In many families today, both adults are independent career professionals, with neither one implicitly obligated to their partner's employer.

But more than anything else, the nature of business socializing has changed because people don't have time for it. The three-martini lunch went out of style long ago, about the time people came to realize they were expected to do something productive in the afternoon. Few busy people want to take two hours instead of thirty minutes for lunch if it means that they have to work an extra ninety minutes later in the day. When you do run across someone happy to have you take him or her to lunch for a couple of hours, it often means that person has nothing better to do and is probably neither a decision maker nor an influencer.

Perhaps the most basic point, though, is that people want to get home to their families. Tomorrow will start very early in the morning, and they'd like to have some time with those closest to them. Thanks to technology, if work must be done, it can be completed in the comfort of their own homes.

All this is not to say there isn't a place for a business meal or other social event to establish an environment conducive to building relationships. And let's face it, a lot of business still gets done on the golf course. Just realize, though, that these activities take you away from direct-selling activities that pay you sixty-five, seventy-five, eighty-five dollars an hour. If a day on the golf course yields that much of a payoff, it's worthwhile. If it doesn't, but you enjoy it, that's fine, too. Just admit to yourself that at least to some extent you're enjoying a little downtime. Don't kid yourself by rationalizing that you're working.

We have noted time required of you by your manager or company as being an inescapable A priority. Some of that time will consist of entertaining customers and social events you're expected to attend. You can live with a little of that—we can't think of anyone who really enjoys it—but not to the extent that it negatively affects your performance and income. Back in his days with the Fortune 500, Bob found himself in a situation in which a company was holding a weeklong convention with extravagant hospitality suites to host its customers after the day's events. These suites featured lavish food and drinks and were to stay open as long as there was one customer present and still standing, which usually meant until around 3:00 a.m. Employees were expected to be there for the duration, then to be up at 6:00 a.m. to get ready for the next day's events. After just a few days of this, you can imagine what these employees looked and felt like and how effectively they were functioning. Bob was one of a handful of employees who dropped in early, said hello and chatted with customers for a couple of hours, then was out the door and in bed by 9:00 p.m. The next morning, he was wide awake and refreshed, bright eyed and bushy tailed. But his absence was noted by management, who expressed their displeasure in no uncertain terms.

If you find yourself in a situation where expectations for unproductive wining, dining, and socializing are having a detrimental effect on your ability to earn a living, you face some interesting choices. If you have sufficient confidence in your abilities and the contribution you make to your company, you can skip some events or at least opt out early, always of course with a legitimate claim of how you wish you could be there or stay, but just can't. In sales, where you get paid for results, you might get away with that, especially if you're a top producer. Seldom does anyone tell the "top dog" how many hours a week to work or what his or her social calendar should look like. Such independence may not endear you to management, which might concern you only if you're looking to get promoted to management at some point. Since the top salespeople earn several multiples of the salary of sales managers, it does seem strange that a good sales rep would actually want to move into management.

In any case, as you work through this chapter's action plan assignments, take a look at how you're doing lunch, dinner, and other socializing, and ask yourself whether many of these traditions are still useful or whether they've become another one of today's time wasters.

CONCLUSION

These first two chapters have laid the foundation for where we're going in the rest of the book. What you've learned so far has provided a perspective for approaching the profession of selling and some ideas for operating more efficiently and more effectively. Now that you have the general picture, we'll move on to specific elements of the selling process in the remaining six chapters. We've noted that sales is high-paid hard work, and it's true that many professional salespeople are earning six-figure incomes in a relatively short time, even before their friends who aspire to be doctors are out of medical school. But conversely, sales is *low*-paid easy work. You can't work half as hard and make half as much money. More likely, if you work half as hard, you'll make one-fourth the money, which means you're out of sales real soon. The flip side is that if you work twice as hard—or, as this book will describe, you can get twice as much done because you're better focused and working smarter—you can make four times as much.

Carefully assess your reactions to the action plan assignments and other materials presented in this book. Our hope is that you'll be excited about doing new things and doing them differently. We want you to think, "Yes, I can do that" and "Hey, that would make me a lot more effective," and wake up every morning genuinely excited about going out to meet with customers and prospects. We do not mean to imply that sales should be your life 24/7/365. As much as you love doing it, you also need time to get away from it. When you set goals and do your plans in this chapter's action plan assignments, set aside time just for you or the family. Lock the cell phone in the trunk of your car. If a customer or prospect absolutely must be dealt with, have a colleague cover your voice mail or e-mail. In turn, you cover for him or her at a later time. Face it, if you have an appendicitis attack this evening and go in the hospital, no one is going to be able to get ahold of you for a couple of days. Ask yourself, "In such an event, who would do what to cover those things which must be done?" Set that up ahead of time, and get out of the loop for a day or two on a regular basis. A couple of times a year, disappear for a few days or a week or more. You'll return refreshed and raring to go. Remember that even the best engine, run continuously at full throttle, eventually burns out. So will you.

Chapter 3

Prerequisite to Getting in the Game: Effective Personal and Professional Communication

In the past few years, we have witnessed fundamental and sweeping changes in how business is conducted, primarily thanks to innovations of information and communication technology. We'll mention some of them in this chapter, but consistent with the theme of what we've addressed so far, the fundamentals of communication are as true as they ever were. Professional salespeople must do all those things as in the past, though perhaps differently, plus more often. It's extremely important to note this, because many businesspeople confuse enhanced information transmission with enhanced communication effectiveness. Yes, we are doing a much better job transmitting information and data. No, most of us are not communicating more effectively and, if anything, are so smothered with messages and overwhelmed with the number of prospect and customer contacts that we are communicating considerably *less* effectively.

We have described the art of selling in the new world of business as a process of developing mutually beneficial strategic relationships and partnerships with other business professionals. And what is that, after all, but interpersonal communication? In a nutshell, effective personal and professional communication is the sine qua non of success in selling, a prerequisite to getting in the game itself. The remainder of this book, in fact, is about various communication themes in networking, presenting, and finalizing agreements. Certainly, technology and other advanced skills will help you achieve your objectives, but it's absolutely essential that you first master the basics of effective personal and professional communication.

In this chapter, we'll go over those basics with the four key concepts for communicating in the new world of business. First, we'll cover eight points for establishing a solid foundation as a communicator. Then, we'll detail the component of communication that is the key to success in selling and describe how nonverbals speak more loudly than words. Finally, we'll explore new technologies and other emerging issues for communicating in the new world of business.

CONCEPT 1: ESTABLISH A SOLID FOUNDATION OF EFFECTIVE COMMUNICATION BASICS

The Major League Baseball season starts in early April. About six weeks before, players report to spring training, and for over a week, they don't even play any exhibition games. Players just practice trivial stuff such as batting, bunting, and fielding. Seems silly. Those guys learned how to do all that in Little League. Why don't they just show up where they need to be the day the season opens and play the game?

The Pensacola Symphony Orchestra and Chorus will be doing nightly performances of Beethoven's *Ninth Symphony* for two weeks. Once they've got it down, they've got it down. No need to practice between performances. And individual members, just leave your fiddles at the cultural center. You know how to read music and play that thing. No need to rehearse on your own at home. Spend the day at the beach.

In sales? You make forty calls a day soliciting appointments. You've got it down cold. Prepare and rehearse a presentation/demonstration? Are you kidding? You can do it blindfolded, and answer all their objections fifteen seconds before they ask them.

Review the basics of communication? Don't need that. Had it in day two of Selling Skills 101. Take me straight to the advanced skills of negotiation.

Starting to get the picture? Whether you're new to sales or a seasoned veteran, the starting point is a reinforcement of the basics. You may have heard some of this before, but pay attention anyhow. You don't want to start backsliding into some bad habits.

Point 1: Listen

"Listen" is *the most important word* in selling. If you remember nothing else from this book, remember "listen."

Professional salespeople don't try to do all the talking. Something that will never happen in sales is for you to run off a fifteen-minute presentation ending with, "So, what do you think?" and have the prospect jump out of his or her chair and say, "I'll take it." We'll discuss this in depth in Chapter 5, but a good rule of thumb is that since your creator endowed you with two ears and one mouth, it was intended that you listen twice as much as you speak. Your objective, then, is not to talk but to get your prospects to talk, because that's the only way to find out what they want, need, and care about. Consider the following dialogue:

SALES REP: Our price is a little higher, but we offer on-site service.

PROSPECT: I don't call ten thousand dollars higher "a little higher."

SALES REP: But think what it could cost you in downtime if you needed service.

PROSPECT: That sort of problem happens very rarely.

SALES REP: Well, our service people are the best trained in the industry.

PROSPECT: When could you have us up and running?

SALES REP: Less than a week. And we have three brands to choose from.

It doesn't take much listening skill to pick up the point of the prospect's first statement, the inevitable price objection. The sales rep then weakly responds by justifying the higher price but fails to substantiate that the value of the service is a benefit worth the price. Then, the prospect states, "That sort of problem happens very rarely," to which the sales rep makes a point about service training. Look at that exchange again and note the sales rep's failure to listen. When the prospect states, "That sort of problem happens very rarely," what does it mean? It happens! If the sales rep were listening, he or she would have seen the opportunity to ask questions about how often it happened, what were the costs and inconvenience, and then sell the value and benefits.

Even worse, the prospect then asks, "When could you have us up and running?" This is a clear indication of interest calling for a closing question. The sales rep responds with a couple of statements and continues the presentation. The closing opportunity is lost.

Always listen carefully. Don't get so wrapped up thinking about what you're going to say next that you fail to hear what the prospect is saying to you. Also, go beyond merely listening with your ears to actively listening with your eyes as well as your ears. Pick up on the prospect's *int*ent as well as the *con*tent of what is being said.

Another benefit of listening is that it helps you set the proper tone in the conversation with your prospect. People hate to be sold, and you probably become defensive when somebody tries to sell you something. But we all love to buy, and we appreciate people who help us make good buying decisions. Salespeople who talk too much are perceived as pushy and trying to sell us something, and our reflex is to escape. By contrast, salespeople who ask questions and listen, trying to help us make good buying decisions, help us feel comfortable.

Point 2: Communication Is a Continuous Flow

Take a glace at a typical communication-arts textbook and you'll see an illustration of the traditional S-R (simulus/response or sender/receiver) communication model. Party A, the sender, encodes a message that is transmitted to Party B, the receiver, who decodes the message. Then, Party B, becoming the sender, gives Party A feedback by encoding and transmitting a message back. Party A, now the receiver, decodes that message.

All well and good. There's nothing wrong with the S-R model except for the fact that it is grossly incomplete and woefully inadequate for interpersonal communication. Yes, it properly describes a conversation going back and forth in a chat room at the time when the respective parties are actively online, but it just won't do for describing face-to-face encounters and ongoing relationships.

First, the S-R model implies that at any given moment, one party is sending a message and the other party is receiving it. Not so. Both parties are *always* sending messages. Party A may not be speaking at the moment, but his or her nonverbal cues may be suggesting boredom, interest, hostility, rapt adoration, or any number of other states of mind. The person's eyes may be saying he or she thinks you're as full of stuffing as a Christmas goose or that he or she has suddenly seen the light and is ready for a close.

It can also be said that both parties are always *receiving* messages, but that's a function of the listening skills we described in Point 1. Of course, the professional salesperson is always listening, on the alert for any messages, however subtle, being sent by the prospect. Communication is a continuous flow. Be actively listening 100 percent of the time, even when you're doing the talking. This is a skill known as multitasking, doing two or more things simultaneously. We've had numerous clients and colleagues tell us it was difficult for them to do if it went beyond walking and chewing gum at the same time. They say they just can't receive a message—listening—concomitant with sending a message—speaking. We then ask whether they've ever watched a television program, read a message scrolling along the bottom of the screen, and spoken to someone else in the room all at the same time. Invariably they answer yes. So, we suggest applying that skill to interpersonal communication. If you can talk and take in multiple messages from the television set, you can certainly talk and take in multiple messages from the other party in the conversation. But probably not with the television on.

But communication is not merely a continuous flow, it's 24/7. You cannot *not* communicate, even when you and the other party are not together. Think about the messages you send when you *don't* send thank-you notes and *don't* touch base between scheduled sales calls, and consider how that lack of communication is being received by the customers and prospects who are being called upon by the competition every day.

Point 3: Write and E-Mail the Same Way You Speak

It's hard to figure out why some of the nicest and most easygoing people revert to such cold formality when they write. Following is an example of being too formal in writing:

> This memorandum is to acknowledge your purchase requisition of Wednesday the 13th. We wish you to know that we consider you a valuable customer. Please do not hesitate to contact us should you require clarification of any kind.

Try a more conversational tone, such as follows.

> Many thanks for your order of Wednesday the 13th. Just wanted to tell you we appreciate your business. Please contact me if you have any questions.

You don't speak, we trust, in such a cold, formal way, so don't write that way. Write the same way you speak, assuming, of course, that you speak like an educated person and not someone raised in a cave by wolves. Be sure to use spell check or have someone look over your work. You don't want to send a customer "congradulations" on a promotion. Along those same lines, be careful to use the correct words. Do you know the difference between "affect" and "effect, "apprise"and "appraise"? A word often misused in recent years is "problematic," which means "doubtful" ("The party will be the first weekend in November, so ice-skating is problematic"). It does *not* mean rife with problems (Do *not* say, "Raising a teenager can be problematic").

Keep written communication brief. Few managers will bother to read *anything* more than one page and will trash without reading an e-mail half that length. If you absolutely, positively can't say it in less, write a brief executive summary and attach a printed appendix or electronic file, which managers can peruse if they want more detail. Remember that with written communication and e-mail, it isn't what you write, it's what they read. Keep it brief. Get it read.

Point 4: Avoid Nonfluencies

We are all guilty of using *nonfluencies,* words that serve no purpose or become annoyingly repetitive. For example, some people can't get through a sentence without saying "you know," or others begin every statement with "Well" or inject "um" or "ah" every fifth word. Bob used to begin every sentence with "Now . . ." After two years, he still falls off the wagon occasionally. Generally, we are not even aware that we are using nonfluencies. But they are verbal bad habits, and tough habits to break. We all need to become aware of our nonfluencies and get rid of them. Since you may not even know which ones you use, ask someone you can rely on to be honest with you and to tell you.

Most nonfluencies are pause fillers that should be deleted in favor of a quarter second of silence. The best cure is every time you say "you know" or start a sentence with "Well," or "Now," stop and say "duh," which is the synonym. For repetitive words such as "exactly," stop and recite an equivalent phrase. So, when you catch yourself saying "exactly," add "I heartily concur with your observation." You may feel like a fool—no, you *will* feel like a fool—stopping in the middle of your conversation to say "duh" or to recite the equivalent phrase, but after a few times you'll begin to conquer the nonfluencies. We suggest initiating this process early in the weekend so you have a couple of days' practice at home before interacting with a customer or your manager.

Point 5: Help Prospects to Buy the Way They Like to Buy

We previously noted that professional salespeople don't try to sell something but help people to buy. Let's take that one step further, since not all prospects are alike and different prospects have different needs and buying motives. Also, different prospects have different styles in the way they like to buy.

The essence of selling lies in getting the prospects to talk so you can discover their unique "hot buttons," then translating features into benefits to demonstrate how your product or service helps them attain what they care about. For example, someone might be interested in an expensive car to impress colleagues, build a client base, attract women or men, or because his or her idea of a good time is a fifteen-hour game of Road Warrior. Sell to the hot button, and don't get distracted talking about features and benefits the prospect doesn't care about. Over time, as you build a personal and professional relationship with customers and prospects, you'll become aware of the benefits and hot buttons that are most important to them personally and address them accordingly.

That's in the long term. Meanwhile, to get things off on the right foot, we need something through which, very early in the relationship—by "very early," we mean within thirty seconds of meeting someone—we can get a general sense of how the prospect thinks and how he or she likes to buy. This calls for a direct application of active listening skills to get a sense of the prospect's communication style. You are looking for two dimensions of his or her relational communication: (1) assertiveness or the level of dominance and control he or she exerts over situations and others and (2) sensitivity or the extent to which a person embraces emotions, feelings, and relationships. Each of these characteristics is readily observable within a short time after meeting someone, particularly in his or her home or office. Combining these, we have the 2 × 2 communication-style matrix, which is illustrated in Figure 3.1.

1. *Low assertiveness/high sensitivity—The amiable:* Slow-paced people whose focus is on relationships. In their offices you'll see many family and group items and pictures. Amiables like close personal relationships and listen more than they speak, so focus on them and their feelings instead of facts, figures, and logic.

2. *High assertiveness/high sensitivity—The expressive:* On-the-go people exuding enthusiasm and loving to work with people. Office is cluttered and disorganized with the million things they're working on at once. There will be awards on the wall and close-contact seating. They're dreamers, so get them talking about their dreams and how you can become a part of them. Talk in anecdotes instead of specifics.

3. *Low assertiveness/low sensitivity—The analytic:* Slow-paced people who deal with facts and tasks. Their office is structured, organized, and functional. Unlike amiables and expressives, they don't like people to touch them, even the family at the holidays. Give them solid, tangible, factual evidence, avoiding opinions and generalities. Keep things in writing, and don't rush them.

4. *High assertiveness/low sensitivity—The driver:* Fast-paced, task-oriented people who want to control and dominate, and will lose respect for you if they succeed. The only touching they'd like, if they could get away with it, would be to hit you to see what you'd do about it. Respond to their intimidating statements with neutral statements or clarifying questions. Ask questions that let them discover the truth for themselves. Let them think it's their idea. Have all the facts, and be sure the facts are right.

The 2 × 2 communication-style matrix is a good starting point for establishing an atmosphere comfortable for your prospects, condusive to helping them to buy. Just remember that this is an issue of the *prospect's* communication style, not yours. Have your four hats and wear the one appropriate to the person you are with.

Closely related to the concept of the communication-style matrix is the principle of common ground. People see and seek in others those things which they are themselves, so help them find a point of similarity on which they can relate to you. Just don't revert to the good-old-boy approach with something such as, "Georgia? Y'all went to

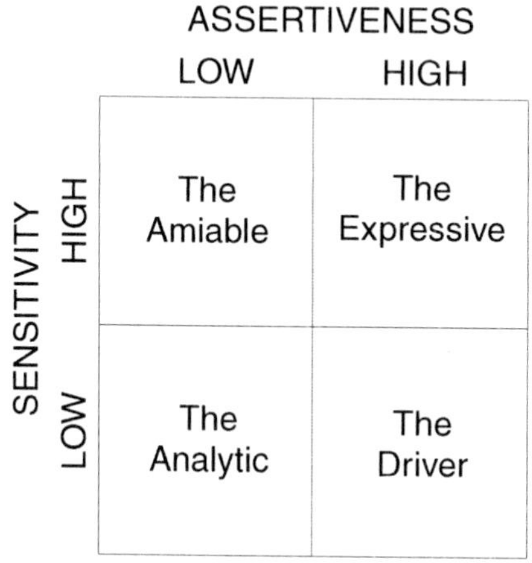

ASSERTIVENESS

	LOW	HIGH
HIGH	The Amiable	The Expressive
LOW	The Analytic	The Driver

(vertical label: SENSITIVITY)

FIGURE 3.1. The 2 × 2 communication-style matrix

Georgia? How 'bout them Dawgs!" Having said that, in some situations with some prospects, it might be the perfect approach. But probably not with an analytic.

Point 6: The Principle of Negatives

People put more weight on negatives. You can do 144 things right and one thing wrong, and you know what they're going to remember. As important as it is to do things right, it's even more important not to make that one big mistake. With analytics and drivers, this can mean having wrong facts, misspelling their names, or being just a few minutes late. With amiables and expressives, it could be an inappropriate or disparaging comment about someone they revere, failing to take time to share small talk, or neglecting to follow up with a trinket you promised to get for their kid.

Everyone makes mistakes. They're a lot like failure. If you never make a mistake, you're probably not doing much of anything significant. What's important is simply not to make the same mistake twice, let alone over and over again. In particular, there is no excuse for negative comments about individuals or groups. This is not an endorsement of political correctness, just a reminder that anything you say may appear at a later time with your name on it. You may have some close personal friends around whom, in a private setting, you can say or do just about anything. That's what close personal friends are for. But in any setting with professional implications or affiliations, always act as though a video camera is recording everything you say or do, and that the tape will be played back to all your colleagues, customers, and prospects. There's a nice benefit to this. You'll never worry about what you said to whom and how you are ever going to keep your stories straight.

When you do make the inevitable mistake, apologize, accept responsibility, and move on. Don't say, "I couldn't help it. It's not my fault," even if you couldn't help it and it wasn't your fault. Your customer doesn't care *whose* fault it is, and as far as that customer is concerned, you *are* your company, which is, after all, the way it should be.

Point 7: The Principle of Selective Perception

It's logical to believe others should see things about the same way you do. Whether you're an extreme left-winger, an extreme right-winger, or somewhere in between, it's natural to believe in the soundness and rightness of your beliefs. The same thing goes with our likes and dislikes. Buck likes Coke and won't go near a Pepsi. Bob likes baseball and can't see how anyone could enjoy basketball. Others, maybe you, feel exactly the opposite, and that's why we have such diverse attitudes and products.

The principle of selective perception proclaims that we literally see different things, not just see things differently. We see what we want and expect to see, filtering stimuli through our beliefs, value systems, and experiences. Selective perception is the basis for stereotyping and prejudice. An individual who has a negative attitude toward a particular group, for example, will see only those negative characteristics that reinforce that prejudice, and won't merely ignore but actually will not perceive good qualities that should be equally apparent. Even though you may be a person who does not stereotype others, it does not stop others from stereotyping you.

Stereotypes are a mixture of negatives and at least some positives. Since you can't eliminate the negatives in the short term, accentuate the positive. For example, if you're an older person, you may be stereotyped as living in the past, an attitude that will take time to change. You may also be perceived as having perspective and wisdom. Accentuate that. On the opposite end of the spectrum, a very young person may be stereotyped as unstable and lacking in social acumen, a perception that might persist for months. However, a young person would also be perceived as having flexibility and enthusiasm, which he or she should accentuate.

It may not be right or fair, but everyone is stereotyped by a large number—dozens—of variables: age, race, gender, ethnic background, social orientation, occupation, hobbies, where he or she lives, etc. Just for fun, jot down twenty or thirty points on which others could stereotype you, and for each one, list one or two positive characteristics generally associated with that stereotype. Let people see those positive characteristics they expect and want to see. It might just help your professional development and also make you a better person without going through all that touchy-feely stuff.

Point 8: *Always Accentuate the Positives in* Your *Proposal*

Don't just accentuate the positives about yourself, but also accentuate the positives in *your* proposal, not the negatives in the *competitor's* proposal. Sometimes your prospect will be considering a competitor whose product is, to put it mildly, lousy. As we'll discuss in Chapter 8, this might merely be a red herring, a ploy to get a price concession from you, or such a product might actually be under consideration.

You may or may not know whether the prospect is seriously considering an inferior alternative to your proposal; in any case, resist the temptation to insult the competitor. Instead, help the prospect discover the truth for himself or herself.

Buck was recently working with a prospect, hoping to develop a bid on a large project. The prospect said he'd already narrowed his search to two competitive alternatives but would hear Buck out. In their meeting, Buck asked the prospect about his needs and the products he was considering. Buck was familiar with one of the competitors and knew the competitor had a viable quality product, but had never heard of the other. After the meeting, Buck researched the other company and its product. As it turned out, the company's sales rep had misrepresented the product, which failed to meet the prospect's specifications, and the rep had also neglected to tell the prospect that the company had filed for bankruptcy.

Buck didn't point out that the product was inadequate and its company in trouble, but when he submitted his bid he included information about all three companies and their respective products to help the prospect compare and contrast. No way was he going to give the prospect the impression that he felt it had been a bad decision to put the other company on the short list. Buck accentuated the positive, encouraging the prospect to examine the specifications and assess the confidence in promises for warranty and service after the sale. Buck did not position himself as a "salesperson" but as a consultant and educator, helping the prospect make an informed buying decision. The result? The short list was still comprised of two vendors, but the other company was off the list and Buck was on it.

Only a few years ago, the information Buck was able to assemble would have been difficult or impossible to obtain, but today it's out there for everyone. Much of what you need to sell against the competition is there for the taking, ready to be gleaned off the competitor's Web site.

CONCEPT 2: RELATIONSHIPS ARE THE KEY TO SUCCESS IN SELLING

Relationships have always been important in selling, but in the new world of business they are absolutely essential. As described in Chapter 1, the only way to differentiate yourself from the low-priced Internet-based competitor is to become a partner instead of just a supplier. To do that, you must master and execute the content component of communication, but your online competitor does that as well as you. The key to your success, which will be a major focus of the rest of this book, will be determined by your ability to establish and develop relationships.

It's time now for a very basic reality check. The fact is that many people just don't like other people. We're not talking about sociopaths or hermits, either. Many intelligent, well-adjusted people love their families and have several close friends but would prefer to spend their working hours writing antivirus software, analyzing spreadsheets, or rebuilding carburetors. They tend to be analytics and craftspeople, and prefer a task-focused rather than a relationship-intense environment. If you're one of these people, you will never love sales. If you don't love sales, you probably won't do very well at it. Therefore, you should avoid sales as a career.

On the other hand, if you're comfortable dealing with a lot of people, the next step is to enhance your relationship skills and develop and execute a plan for building strategic partnerships and relationships (see Chapter 4). This is a simple process.

First, you want people to like you, and you do this by being a decent and considerate person. Be friendly, remember people's names, and give them a warm greeting. Do thoughtful little things to recognize them and make them feel appreciated. When possible, do something for their kids. We know colleagues who give away Beanie Babies, autographed pictures of sports heroes, and mementos for everything from First Communion to eighth-grade graduation. Even the most hardhearted drivers will appreciate your thoughtfulness in the teddy bears they can take home to their children. Don't save these gestures just for principals and others in a position to do something for you, either. Do something for the secretaries, custodians, and receptionists, who, after all, may be your boss someday.

In Chapter 2 we noted a diminished emphasis of wining, dining, and other business expenses designed to influence the buying decision, which were ultimately reflected in the buyer's cost. Those activities may have some place in some situations, but we don't advocate relying on them in the new world of business. Having said that, we strongly endorse business gestures when they are given as a token of friendship with nothing expected in return. For example, Buck has a client with whom he's had an ongoing business relationship for six years. This client is a collector of sorts and one time in passing just happened to mention that for over ten years he'd been looking for a copy of an issue of *The Saturday Evening Post* from the 1950s because of the artwork on its cover. Buck, always an adept listener, picked up on the point and filed it away in his memory banks. Then, months later, Buck was surfing around on eBay and voilà, there it was! He put in a bid, won, paid for the magazine, and sent it off to his client and friend, whose secretary later related what had happened when it arrived on what had been, until then, a bad day. The client was thrilled, not because of the intrinsic value of the gift, but because of its thoughtfulness as a token of friendship.

It's the little things that make people like us, something as simple as promptly responding when people are in need. Fredric G. Levin is one of the most successful trial attorneys in the United States, routinely handling cases in the millions and tens of millions of dollars. He's a highly respected and very busy man, but throughout his career he's lived by a basic tenet: If you're in need and you call him, he'll return your call. Early in his career, in the late 1970s, Levin was working a typical Saturday in his office. Upon returning from lunch, there was a phone message from a prospective client, which he promptly returned. The case concerned a young child who had inadvertently been given medication by a pharmacy at ten times the prescribed dosage, resulting in severe brain damage. Levin helped the family attain compensation in a settlement that gave him significant professional notoriety and helped launch his career. After the trial, the child's father expressed appreciation for the professionalism of Levin's legal services and also related, as the phrase goes, the rest of the story. On the Thursday and Friday before he called Levin, the child's father, desperate for help, had called four other attorneys, none of whom had returned his call. Two never did, and the other two called late the following week. When we asked Levin about this story, he told us: "I had always returned people's phone calls, long before that case. I just think that people call me for a reason that's important to them." Remember Fred Levin the next time you get a call from a customer or prospect and don't feel like answering it right away because it might be an imposition or a hassle. That call means someone needs your help, and it's an opportunity—perhaps an opportunity that could jump-start your career. It will certainly help people to like you and, even more important, respect you.

You build respect by constantly doing some of those things we've already talked about: be competent and knowledgeable, positive and enthusiastic, never saying or doing anything you wouldn't want the world to see. You command respect by doing what you said you'd do when you said you'd do it. Finally, you command respect by respecting confidentiality. Never reveal confidential or proprietary information, even when it might be in your short-term interest to do so. Learn to keep a secret. When someone tells you something in confidence, tell no one, not even your spouse. One of the most important skills in business is the ability to retain a confidence, the product of which is trust. And trust is the basis for a strategic partnership relationship.

The following are some specific points to consider.

Point 1: We Are Always Defining the Nature of Our Relationships

Relationships are similar to any other living thing; they are always changing, growing, or dying, never static. You are getting closer or drifting apart. You are building trust or losing it. The minute your competitors begin taking a customer for granted, they've opened the door for you to take that customer away from them. The minute you start to take your marriage for granted, it's heading for the rocks.

No one cares what you did for them last week or last month, let alone a year ago. All anyone wants to know is: What have you done for me lately? As in baseball, last year Cy Young, this year sayonarra. The New Age Willy Loman, whom we met in Chapter 1, was expecting the skills, achievements, and relationships of the past to keep carrying him along, not unlike the boxer a few years past his prime or the thirty-something guy in the college bar. Unlike the boxer or the barfly, though, the professional salesperson has it within his or her control to maintain a position at the pinnacle of professional competence and to do those things that continuously add value to the business relationship.

Early in a professional relationship, as in a personal relationship, the parties assess whether this is likely to be a one-night stand or if it has the potential for a long-term relationship. A vendor positioned as a supplier is tantamount to a one-night stand. You have something I want and I'm ready to close the deal on the spot, provided the short- and long-term costs are sufficiently low. By contrast, a vendor positioned as a partner is proposing a long-term relationship. The cost is more, but there may be more value and benefits for the money. We're not going to close this deal here and now, but we can engage in dialogue, see how much we like, respect, and trust each other, and take it from there.

Buck was very fortunate on the proposal we previously described because at the outset he was able to do something for the prospect, helping him avoid the pitfall of considering an inferior product from an unreliable company. Don't expect that sort of thing to happen that early that often. Generally, openness and trust must develop over time, just as in a personal relationship. The courtship takes time, and you have to earn respect.

Point 2: In Relationships, People Communicate in Similar or Differing Modes

Relational communication can get pretty complex, and it's absolutely essential to evaluate its different modes and determine whether you and the other party are engaging each other similarly or differently. The most important component mode is power. We'll lay the foundation here and get into numerous applications later, particularly in Chapter 8.

The bottom line is that you never want to go into any selling situation in an inferior power position. You'll never close a profitable sale if the prospect knows you're desperate for an order. You'll never get a good job offer if the prospective employer knows you've been out of work for a year and are about to be evicted from your apartment.

In any conversation, be alert for dominant, one-up, assertive statements, and avoid the temptation and natural tendency to respond with one of your own, because the following can happen:

JOE: I'm sick and tired of you people messing up deliveries.

SUE: It's not us. We sent it where we were told to send it.

JOE: It went to Cairo. I told you personally it was supposed to go to Metropolis.

SUE: And your guy in Marion called the shipper and diverted it to Cairo.

JOE: Here's the order form. Look, Metropolis!

SUE: What am I supposed to do when *your* people call the shipper?

This conversation is not contributing to a healthy, growing relationship. What do you do? Instead of responding in kind, respond to a dominant, one-up, assertive statement with a neutral statement or clarifying question:

JOE: I'm sick and tired of you people messing up deliveries.

SUE: What happened?

JOE: It went to Cairo. I told you personally it was supposed to go to Metropolis.

SUE: That's right, but then your manager in Marion called the shipper and diverted it to Cairo.

JOE: Here's the order form. Look, Metropolis!

SUE: I'm sorry it happened. In the future, should we tell the shipper to verify any changes with you personally, or do you just want to talk to the manager in Marion?

JOE: That guy in Marion just does whatever he wants.

SUE: Then we'll tell the shipper that in the future no changes should be made without talking to you first.

JOE: That would be best. Thanks.

Notice how in the second scenario, Sue responded to the one-up statements with either a neutral statement or a question about how to deal with the issue. Here, as will happen in most real-life situations, the other party finally responds with a neutral statement of his or her own.

In addition to the power component, there is also the emotional mode of communication, and it, too, can be similar or differing. At different times, people operate in one of three emotional modes: adult, parent, or child. A productive relationship state between adults is adult-adult, a state of similarity you should seek to develop and maintain. Just as you would not wish to deal from an inferior power position, you will not build a viable partnership relationship without the adult-adult mode, even though one party or the other might occasionally revert to the parent or child state. Dominant, assertive, one-up statements, such as those of Joe in the prior scenarios, are indicative of a child state. In the first scenario, Sue responded in kind and the conversation degenerated into a child-child interchange. By contrast, in the second scenario, her neutral statements and clarifying questions were adult mode and guided the conversation to an adult-adult dialogue. In doing so, Sue took control of the communication environment.

If you are a young person, particularly a young female, you may encounter a parent state, with the other party making patronizing statements suggesting you are not being taken seriously. This is an example of the principle of sterotypes, which, though it may rightfully irritate you, still must be dealt with. Comments along the lines of "Did you learn that in school?" or "After you've been around for a while . . ." or "Do you like our industry?" suggest that they're dealing with you in a parent-child mode, which is very unproductive for establishing a partnership relationship. Accept the fact that the person's parental attitude may persist in the short term, play to the positive aspects of your youthful sterotype, and consciously do those things which demonstrate your competence and help engender an adult-adult relationship. If you have success stories of achievements with persons or companies the person is familiar with, note them, without, of course, revealing any proprietary information.

Point 3: The Power of Attitude

Success is the result of skills, hard work, and knowledge. But take 100 people approximately equally matched in skills, work habits, and knowledge, and their results will spread out on a bell-shaped curve ranging from extraordinary to deplorable. Some of that is due to pure random chance; most of it is due to attitude.

You may have gathered we're not too hot on those rah-rah "motivational" sales seminars that pump everybody up but don't address the underlying problems of expertise, skills, and personal management. What we mean is that no one should *rely* on those programs as being sufficient in and of themselves; they're not. Attitude and confidence might account for 5 percent of the formula for success in selling. The other 95 percent is what this book is about: skills, hard work, and knowledge. But just for the moment, let's take a look at the 5 percent which is attitude and confidence.

To use another sports analogy, the effect of attitude and confidence in selling is similar to golf. If you're a typical weekend hacker, you may shoot a 114 instead of 115 for eighteen holes if you think positively and keep telling yourself you're a winner and you can do it. In sum, don't expect your friends to compliment you on how much your game has improved. But if you're one of the top money winners on the PGA tour, one stroke a round equates to four strokes a tournament and that's an immense difference in money winnings and endorsements. Tiger Woods has great skills, but his unique attitude and confidence have given him a tremendous edge at crunch time.

If, and the operational word is *if,* you have done all the right things in the areas of skills, work habits, and knowledge, that extra boost from attitude and confidence can make a *very* significant difference in your success in selling. In a recent sales training seminar, Bob was asked by one of the participants what to do if he encountered a sign in an office building that read "Absolutely no soliciting." Bob's answer was "That's for people there to sell something. You're not there for that. You're there to talk to people about forming a strategic alliance." The idea is a subtle but important difference to take into the sales encounter.

Your attitude can dramatically affect your power in selling and negotiation. You must believe that you yourself represent value worth paying for and that the prospect would benefit from working with you. A rejection, then, does not mean "no"; it means only that you have not yet managed to communicate what you have to offer.

The power of attitude is not the traditional, "I can do it. I can get this sale." It's just the opposite. It's more like an ambivalence. You've done all you can do, and you hope prospects will want to work with you, but if not then that's fine. You convey, in everything you say and do, that you want to have the opportunity to build a relationship with them, but you also convey, without arrogance, that if they choose not to do business with you, you'll go find someone else. If you're competent, this attitude of quiet confidence makes people more comfortable with you and more likely to consider you, whether in a professional or a personal environment.

In the previous section we pointed out that in communication the participants operate in similar or different power modes. Traditionally, sales professionals have entered the sales encounter with the perception that the prospect held a superior power position. If you truly believe you're there to develop a mutually beneficial partnership, such an assumption is patently erroneous; nevertheless, even top salespeople will go into a meeting with the belief that the prospect holds all the cards. Such an attitude is detrimental to the ultimate result. You *must* truly believe that you have a product or service your prospect needs, and you *must* truly believe it's to his or her advantage to do business with you instead of the competition. If you *don't* truly believe these things, you'll be operating from an inferior power position, and you will not be successful in sales.

Point 4: Seek Out Coaches and Mentors

A lot of what makes sales fun and exciting is that every day is different and you'll never lack opportunities to learn and grow. Age is no barrier, as long as you're willing to keep learning and adapt to change. But whatever your age, and especially if you're relatively young, seek out those persons who can help you as a coach and mentor. Learn from those people who have been there before and want to take an active role in your career.

Coaches and mentors are where you find them, especially in your own organization, but they're also in your community or at the university. Buck has had considerable success developing mentors among his customers as part of his partnership relationships. These customers helped him better serve them, and subsequently have generated numerous referrals to their peers and colleagues.

A contemporary football coach and motivational expert pointed out three things to look for in a person you'd have as a coach or mentor: you respect that person, that person is committed to excellence, and that person cares about you. On the other side of the coin, you must have credibility with the coach and the coach must trust you. Another thing not to overlook is to be sure that your coach or mentor has credibility with the buying organization he or she is helping you with. You don't want to tell a prospect that Fred Frump suggested you give him or her a call, only to have the prospect express astonishment that Fred is not yet in jail.

In seeking out someone to be your coach and mentor, we suggest an approach basic to sales: be direct and ask. When you do so, do it the right way. Do *not* ask him or her to put in a good word for you or to influence a buying decision. That's an improper imposition on the person. He or she may say that he or she will tell Mr. Chavez what a cool person you are and urge him to send business your way, but he or she won't actually do it. And the person won't give you any coaching, either. Instead, go on up to someone you'd like as a coach and mentor and use three of the most disarming words in the language: "I need help." You will be pleasantly surprised how often the person will be receptive to helping you when the request is made that way. Then say something along the lines of: "I'm going to be calling on Mr. Chavez next week. Is there anything I need to know about him and his operation that would help me develop a better proposal?" When you phrase it in these terms, chances are good you'll get coaching and mentoring. Also, you won't know when it happens, but you're also probably going to get a referral when your coach is talking with Mr. Chavez and happens to mention helping with a proposal, noting the care you're taking to see that it's right for him and his operation.

Point 5: Be a Back Door Sales Rep

Every book on sales, including this one, will tell you the importance of meeting in person with the individual with the authority to buy. The most direct route to that person's office is through the front door and past the receptionist, so it's the path many salespeople take. That's a mistake. Go through the back door. This will allow you to get to know everyone in the day-to-day nuts-and-bolts operations of your prospect's company. You'll be astonished how much you can learn and how many lightbulbs will start turning on in your head. This is plain and simple bottom-up thinking, and it's the first step in developing strategic plans. The American automobile industry would be out of business by now if they hadn't figured out that the only way to build a quality product was to talk to the workers on the factory line, and the only way to generate consumer loyalty was to talk to dealers and their service department managers, who were dealing with customers every day.

Naturally, we're not suggesting that you start snooping around some place where they've never heard of you. Security will not think highly of that, and it's not the way you want to introduce yourself to a prospect. Remember that your objective is a long-term relationship, not a one-night stand, so you're not out to close a sale on your first meeting with a prospect. At your first meeting, express an interest in getting to know more about the person and his or her business. Get the names of people in all the operational levels and, from then on, enter through the back door, meet them, and find out what's *really* going on.

Bob's friend Dave sells flooring and carpeting in large commercial building projects. In his business, traditionally, sales reps would meet with decision makers to develop specifications and, upon closing the sale, turn the project over to other parties who would handle all the details of installation which, out of necessity for customer convenience, was done between midnight and 6:00 a.m. Dave did things a little differently, showing up on site at midnight dressed in jeans and a T-shirt. No sales rep had ever shown up on a worksite before, and at first the crew was very apprehensive, asking if he was there to spy on them. Dave laughed and said no, he just wanted to learn how to lay flooring and carpet. They set him to work, and at the end of the shift, he took the crew out to breakfast. What Dave learned was invaluable and has enabled him to develop proposals that better address his prospects' needs at a net savings in costs. It's a great example of being a back-door sales rep and what partnership is all about.

CONCEPT 3: NONVERBALS SPEAK MORE LOUDLY THAN WORDS

Written and verbal communication are superior for the content component of communication, which is only logical since written and verbal communication have formal structure, language, and rules. As previously noted, relationships are the key to success in selling, and it's nonverbal communication that is superior for the relationship component. For feelings and relationships, nonverbals not only speak more loudly than words, they are the vehicle through which a majority of meaning is conveyed. Overall, in fact, studies have indicated that no more than 10 percent of a message is content whereas as much as 40 percent is voice, especially tone of voice, and in excess of 50 percent of what we convey is through other nonverbal channels. What nonverbal communication should you consider in the art of selling?

The most important factor in selling anything—a product, service, or yourself—is enthusiasm. People are just naturally inclined to do business with someone who is genuinely enthusiastic. Enthusiasm is the number-one factor in the hiring decision, and will enable a candidate to prevail over someone with better grades and credentials. In the selling environment, enthusiasm communicates confidence and a sincere belief in the product or service you represent. If you truly feel so strongly about what you can do for them and their business, prospects will hear you out and be more amenable to entering into a partnership with you. By contrast, a lack of enthusiasm will make them skeptical and reluctant to agree, even if a proposal looks a little better on paper. Enthusiasm is an intangible, an attitude that comes from within, but it can be consciously conveyed through nonverbal channels.

Vocal communication is the key channel for enthusiasm. It describes *how* you speak, not *what* you say. Make a point of varying your volume, pitch, and rate of speech, avoiding flatness and nasality. Avoid speaking too fast or too loudly, as this will indicate anxiety and aggressiveness. Also, be aware of regional differences. Speaking loudly at a relatively fast 180 words a minute might be appropriate for the retail trade in New York City, but it will turn folks off in southern

Alabama. Use pauses appropriately. When you get to an important point, pause and then continue. The pause will help your prospect pay attention to that key point you'll make next.

Gestures and posture are also important for communicating enthusiasm. It's often said that you can spot a winner when he or she walks in the door. Stand up straight and stride confidently, seeking people out with your eyes and making gestures that appear spontaneous, unrehearsed, and relaxed. If you can do so naturally, smile. As you speak, use head and hand gestures to emphasize points and to convey emotions, but be aware of different audiences. You'll employ more gestures dealing with Southrn Europeans, and fewer dealing with Asians.

The eyes are *the most important* channel for defining and establishing relationships and feelings. The face is the mirror of the mind, and the eyes are the window to the soul. Make a point of sustaining eye contact. Look directly at the person you're speaking to, and don't look down or away, which will negatively affect your credibility. Lyndon Johnson was a master of this. When he addressed U.S. Congress, he had in his notes specific persons with whom to make eye contact at specific times. By the time he finished any address, all of the influential senators and representatives felt the president was speaking directly to them.

Norms for clothing are rapidly changing, and who knows what "dress for success" means anymore. Many anchormen on the cable financial networks no longer wear sport coats, and chief executive officers (CEOs) of newly emerging companies show up for interviews in polo shirts. Companies have dress-down days, though the dress code seems to be becoming more formal than the one it replaced. There are major regional differences. For example, if you wear a suit in Seattle, you're either a banker, a lawyer, or an FBI agent.

One thing hasn't changed, however. You still dress for your audience and dress for the job you want, not the job you have. If you err, do so on the conservative side and be a little overdressed. Generally, an older audience calls for more conservative attire, whereas a younger audience prefers something less formal. If you wish to convey authority and expertise, overdress your audience. In a financial planning seminar, the audience may be casual but the certified financial planner should dress up. But don't overdo it. If you're meeting a blue-collar prospect, a suit might be intimidating. Go with casual slacks, shirt and tie, but no coat.

Often, women or persons who are younger or small in stature will want to overdress in darker colors to enhance authority. By contrast, big hulky guys might emphasize lighter shades to appear less intimidating and more approachable. Don't forget the accessories: new belt and new shoes in matching colors.

Attire is mostly common sense. Think about your audience and the impression you wish to convey, and go with it. One other thing you might wish to do, however, is to keep a record of what you wore to each business occasion. Even if it's three or four weeks between meetings, you don't want to visit a customer wearing the same clothing. Vary something, even if it's only your tie or accessories.

Closely related to clothing are such recent considerations as tattoos and piercings, which, outside select audiences, have a demonstrated negative impact. Also, be aware of proper grooming, especially superfluous hair and your teeth. Hair must be done daily around your nose and ears. Teeth should be brushed, flossed, white, and complete. If they're not and you need dental work, spend the money. It's a good investment.

You should have no scent. Shower a little more often than once a month, and leave the cologne or perfume at home. If your scent arrives ahead of your handshake, it's a negative, and you remember what we said about making mistakes.

Be aware of distance and space, known as proxemics. Be especially careful not to get too close to people or invade their spaces. Some audiences want you to get close to them and like touching, but others don't want anything beyond a basic handshake. Getting too close and getting even a little touchy makes many people, especially analytics, very uneasy, and in these days of plentiful sexual harassment suits there can be other negative repercussions as well.

We've quickly hit upon the highlights of effective nonverbal communication and its numerous components and channels. Do not look at individual nonverbal cues in isolation but rather at all of them as a collective whole. Be aware of all channels of nonverbal communication, and take care to have all your messages working synergistically to achieve your objectives. In particular, have a plan for the first seven seconds of any encounter. Recall what we said about your daily plan and how it remained intact only until the first shot was fired. That's true for an in-person meeting of any kind. You can plan the sales call as well as possible, but the instant the first words are spoken you'll have to modify that plan and improvise. But you *can* plan the first seven seconds, and that initial impression is extremely important to setting the tone and getting things off on the right foot. The first seven seconds are almost exclusively nonverbal and relationship intense, so make positive eye contact, stride confidently toward the other person, smile (or at the least don't look like a grouch), and give a firm hand-shake. Don't crush his or her hand, but, even worse, don't give the person a limp fish either. Use his or her name, and say it's nice to see him or her. The first shot has been fired, and you were on target.

We also mentioned the principle of negatives, and although you can't score a win in the first seven seconds, you can chalk up a loss and be out of the game. Bob and many of his colleagues have had years of experience hiring people and being called upon by sales reps, and they consistently find that about one time in four, the person making the call was excluded from consideration within the first seven seconds. In some of those situations, the sales call or job interview went on for as much as twenty to thirty minutes, but no matter. The decision had been made within seven seconds: No, this is not someone we're going to do business with.

At first, you might deem it inappropriate to exclude someone from consideration so quickly without so much as talking to them. But think about it: You do it every day, sizing up people on the spot and instantly deciding whether this is a person you're inclined to deal with. As the old saying goes: You never get a second chance to make a first impression. Plan those first seven seconds, and make a positive impression the first time and every time you encounter anyone.

CONCEPT 4:
EMERGING ISSUES FOR COMMUNICATING IN THE NEW WORLD OF BUSINESS

So far, this chapter has addressed traditional issues in communication. Now let's get to new and emerging issues. If you've been in the business world for more than a few years, you've certainly noticed how much the pace has picked up. Technology is here and middle management is gone, with the net result that professional salespeople have many more contacts to make every day, necessarily briefer, with a smaller proportion being in person. Even in person, the prospect who used to give you thirty minutes is so busy that you need to be able to cover your business in fifteen. Technology lets us get more done in less time, but many people seem so caught up in the technology that they've forgotten the basics. For example, individuals would not normally bring pornographic magazines to the office and leave them atop their desks for management to see. Yet these same people wouldn't think twice about checking out Web sites and downloading files they'd never want their manager to know about. It's as if they believe that there's complete anonymity between them and their computer screen, which couldn't be farther from the truth. Courts have ruled that everything that goes in or out of your company computer is the property of your company, and that the company has a right to monitor all your activity on the Internet. Employees had best be aware that management has a complete folder on them at the main server, documenting every message in, every message out, with a complete history of Internet activity.

In the same vein, most employees would never send out an inappropriate personal message on company letterhead. Bob remembers a former colleague who had a dispute with people at a local service station and later sent a scathing letter on company letterhead to the company CEO. A few weeks later, when top management from Bob's company made a call on the oil company, the CEO pulled out the letter and declared, "If this is the kind of person you have working for you, we're not doing business with your company," and terminated the meeting on the spot. Bob's colleague was not fired for this indiscretion, but things were never the same. His career was finished, and he resigned soon thereafter.

Similarly, you would never write up an off-color joke or compose a patently offensive diatribe on company letterhead with your name included, and send it off to a few thousand of your closest friends. Yet many people do exactly that with e-mail every day. Your e-mail address is tantamount to your company letterhead. Once you send it out, you've lost all control over that message. It can be forwarded, modified, and circulated, similar to gossip around the coffee machine. And as with gossip, it will find its way to your customers and your management with your name on it, on the company letterhead.

A few more points on e-mail and voice mail, both of which can be valuable contact tools for a skilled salesperson. There's nothing like a face-to-face meeting, but to get that first meeting and as a follow-up between calls, it's important to get the most out of e-mail and voice mail. The main reason they present such an opportunity is that, contrary to a phone call, e-mail and voice mail are seldom screened, thus giving you a one-on-one contact with the prospect. Both should be to the point and have a reason to be read or heard. As in all written communication, e-mail should be well written and correct in all aspects. Voice mail should have a prepared script or, if you prefer, a point-by-point outline so as not to be wandering or stammering.

If you're sending e-mail, it's essential that it not be viewed as spam or junk e-mail. Writing an initial e-mail to introduce yourself, noting a referral, and identifying a benefit is fine as a prelude to a phone call requesting an appointment. But some people send a message or a newsy item twice a week for a month or two, thinking they're warming you up, before finally getting around to popping the appointment question. But to a busy prospect facing 100 or more e-mails a day, such messages are nothing but annoying spam. With a typical e-mail program such as Outlook or Eudora, the recipient is going to quickly filter you by having all your messages sent directly to trash, which means you'll never get another e-mail through to the individual.

There are a few other considerations for people who contact you by phone or e-mail. For starters, there's something to be said for the old adage "call yourself up," to experience what your customers and prospects have to go through. What does your voice mail say, and is it properly updated? You look very bad when someone calls you on Wednesday the 15th and the message tells them you'll be out of the office until Monday the 13th. You also don't shine when you stumble over words recording the message. There's no excuse for that message being anything less than 100 percent polished and perfect, even if it takes you ten tries, which, after all, is only about five minutes. How often do you check your e-mail and voice mail—twice a day?—and is there a system for getting other messages to you promptly? How can your customers and prospects get ahold of you, and what's the maximum time before you get back to them? Good customer service departments respond to e-mails within fifteen minutes, and not with an automated form letter, either.

Take a serious look at your Web site and ask yourself what it's telling your customers and prospects about your company. Pages on the site should be clean and uncluttered, and they should load quickly. Whether users come directly onto your site or indirectly through links, they should always be able to figure out where they are and how to get back to the home page and other key locations.

Get some outside eyes to take a look at every page of your site and how to move through it. Have them tell you whether everything is easy to understand and confirm that every page says or does what it's supposed to. Borrow ideas from other sites. Check out a wide variety of others in and out of your industry to glean ideas of how your site could be more effective. Don't undertake this effort haphazardly. Your Web site is one of the most—if not *the* most—important communication tools in the new world of business. Invest the time and effort to ascertain what your Web site is now and what it could be. Chances are very high there will be significant opportunities for improvement.

Be sure that all employees are familiar with every aspect of the site. There is nothing quite as embarrassing—or inexcusable—as a prospect asking about something he or she saw on the site and you or any other employee not knowing what the person is talking about. That's tantamount to what happened a few years ago when a major motel chain launched a promotion by direct mail but neglected to inform employees at their properties. Customers arrived in response to the promotion, and motel staff didn't know what they were talking about.

Also be sure that messages on the Web site are consistent with other company communications, especially pricing. Buck was in a training class with salespeople from a company that had one set of prices posted on its Web site, but a better set of prices available through its sales force. When a prospect called the company to order in response to the Web site, the secretary told them to call one of the sales reps to get a better price. Really bad. Selling the same thing under the same conditions to different people at different prices is guaranteed to antagonize anyone who pays the higher price, and it may be illegal to boot.

In the new world of business, even the smallest company can have a Web site as effective as that of the big guys, and it can't afford not to.

CONCLUSION

In this chapter, we've addressed issues of effective interpersonal communication, to help you convey the messages you wish to send and to pick up on all messages being sent to you. Now, let's put these ideas to work to create an impression of professionalism in those initial contacts with those persons who might be candidates for your network of professional colleagues and customers.

Chapter 4

Networking and Prospecting: Developing Professional Relationships and Strategic Alliances

To this point, we've laid the foundation for being a professional salesperson in the new world of business. With that foundation in place, now we'll get into action. Before you can ever make use of communication and negotiation skills, you've got to identify and get an appointment with a qualified decision maker. In this chapter, we will discuss the four key concepts for networking and prospecting, and developing the professional relationships and strategic alliances essential for success. Prospecting is your most important activity and we'll review some of the tried-and-true prospecting strategies. You'll need a strategy for building professional relationships and strategic alliances, and we'll describe some innovative approaches to prospecting and networking. We'll also note the importance of qualifying prospects and referrals. Finally, we'll give you some points about getting the appointment and improving the proportion of prospects who agree to meet with you in person.

CONCEPT 1: PROSPECTING IS STILL YOUR MOST IMPORTANT ACTIVITY

If you ask someone relatively new to sales what he or she considers to be the most important activity, he or she will usually say presenting, closing, or negotiation. Ask successful sales professionals and invariably they'll say prospecting, especially networking. That's because in the numbers game of sales, once you get face to face with a qualified prospect, assuming you've developed the attendant communication and negotiation skills, you'll close a certain proportion of those prospective opportunities. The challenge is not what you do when you're face to face, but getting face to face in the first place with the people you need to see. Consistent with our approach in prior chapters, let's first look at some of the principles of prospecting that were true a generation ago and are still valid today.

Point 1: Referrals from Satisfied Customers

Repeat business and referrals from satisfied customers are fundamental to success in selling. The longer you work in sales as a professional person committed to treating your customers right, the higher and higher will be the proportion of your business emanating from repeat business and customer referrals. By contrast, think about the stereotype of the person we would generally consider the antithesis of professionalism in selling, the used-car salesperson. Of course, there may be some used-car salespersons out there who are professional businesspeople, but by and large their reputation is not exemplary. The reason? We believe it has a lot to do with the fact that the person selling on the used-car lot sees the prospect as an opportunity for a one-time transaction. Seldom will a customer return to that same used-car lot for a repeat purchase, and the used-car dealer virtually never has service facilities for developing an ongoing relationship after the sale. Used-car buyers rarely refer friends and colleagues to the dealer they bought from. When they do, it's because of the availability of a particular vehicle rather than the dealership per se. Compare that with successful new-car dealerships, especially those at the high end, who want you as a long-term customer that will refer friends and colleagues to the store and its salespeople. If you've ever dealt with a dealership like that, you've enjoyed a personal relationship with your salesperson and the service department reps, which is well worth paying for. You'd certainly agree that your salesperson does not fit the stereotype of a used-car salesperson. It's just one illustration of a business which appreciates the fact that its survival is contingent upon repeat business and customer referrals.

It's no different with you and your customers. If your approach to sales is to dump and run, either you won't be in sales long or your next job will be at Billy Bob's Used-Car City. The close of the sale may be the end of the process for you, but it's the beginning of the relationship between you and you customer. Never forget it's customer satisfaction that generates repeat business and referrals, and customer satisfaction is entirely a product of what happens *after* the sale.

The professional salesperson builds customer satisfaction by always delivering more than the customer expects. Please note that we did not say you met your specifications. Customers couldn't care less about your specifications. All they care about is whether you met their expectations, and professional salespeople never *meet* their customers' expectations. They always *exceed* them. If you promise delivery by Wednesday, get it there by Tuesday. If they expect a room, give them a suite. If you quoted a job for $900, either invoice them $880 or throw a little something in for free.

When a customer calls you at 4:00 p.m. on a Friday afternoon or at 4:00 a.m. on a Monday morning with a problem, rejoice! It's an opportunity to augment customer satisfaction and your value in the business relationship. Whenever they ask, "Is there any way you can help me?" the answer is always, "Let me see what I can do." When Ed Koch was mayor of New York, he regularly went out to meet with his constituents to ask, "How'm I doin'?" Do the same thing with all your customers. You may not be thrilled to hear that some things aren't perfect, since it means more work for you, but would you rather let a small dissatisfaction fester under the surface? Keep doing that, though, and sooner or later the customer is going to tell you that everything is fine and that he or she appreciates all you've done. At that point, you might be inclined to smile and sit back, feeling good about the job you've done. Don't! This is the moment you've been waiting for. The customer is expressing satisfaction. Ask for a referral!

Yes, every time customers express satisfaction, ask for a referral. Use a prospect-focused phrase such as, "Great. I'm glad it's working out so well. Tell me, can you think of any of your associates who could benefit from a program like this?" If the person can't think of someone right off the top of his or her head, narrow the focus. "How about some of your colleagues in the marketing association?" or "You mentioned your friends in the civic club. Do you think some of them . . . ?" Asking for referrals from satisfied customers is as essential as asking for the order.

Point 2: Stay in Touch

Often you'll have customers with whom you'll conduct numerous transactions over time, but with whom you have no ongoing contacts for service and follow-up between sales. In this situation, remember the point about communication being 24/7 and the fact that you cannot *not* communicate. Between meetings, stay in touch, but of course don't annoy. Send an occasional e-mail on a point of interest and cards for birthdays and holidays or other important events.

Some customers buy on a regular repurchase cycle, often at a certain point in the fiscal year. Have your time management program alert you in the appropriate time frame in advance of those purchases, and make contacts or take other timely actions accordingly. For customers who have purchased top-end products or services on the cutting edge, contact them whenever there is a significant product enhancement or a leap in technology. Innovators don't wait for things to wear out. They want the latest and greatest, and they want it now.

For sales organizations that do not have assigned geographic territories, especially those with significant sales-force turnover, circumstances may arise in which a sales rep leaves your company and thus leaves existing customers with no one to service them. If it's to your advantage to do so, immediately talk to your sales manager to see whether it would be possible for you to assume responsibility for handling some or all of those accounts. Given the time required to hire and train a new rep, your sales manager may be very receptive to the idea, especially since the departed rep likely had not been providing optimal customer service in the days and weeks before leaving. That means the accounts you take over may not be all that happy with your company and its service at the moment, which is a great opportunity for you. Think of what an improvement you'll be compared to the rep you replaced, the number of problems you can address, and the number of referrals you can generate when it comes time to ask the customer, "How'm I doin'?"

Later in this chapter, we'll discuss building a network of business professionals who generate and share referrals with one another. A closely related concept, involving a fee-for-service rather than a strategic alliance, is the bird dog. Depending on your industry, and assuming that such tactics are ethical and proper, bird dogs can be found almost anywhere. The process is simple. You give the bird dog a bunch of your business cards, which he or she signs on the back. This person, in turn, gives your card to prospects who bring it to you for the best deal. The prospect buys, and you pay the bird dog a referral fee. You can have individual bird dogs or get groups to bird dog as a fund-raiser. Whether or not this prospecting tool is effective varies considerably by industry, so determine for yourself if it's appropriate for you. It can be very useful in real estate or new car sales, of little value for small-ticket items infrequently purchased, and illegal or unethical in fields such as banking.

There may be good opportunities for bird dogging by servicing the service department. For example, if you sell televisions, stereos, and other electronic equipment in a retail store, you might want to enlist bird dogs among those businesses that service such items. A customer comes in, or a service call is made, on a fifteen-year-old television set that will need $200 in repairs, and the service department tells the customer it's not worth fixing but, hey, take this card in to Lee Anne at Circuit Circus and she'll give you a great deal.

Point 3: Mine All Viable Prospects

After you've been in sales awhile, you'll find that virtually all of your business is generated from long-term customer relationships, referrals from satisfied customers, and your network of professional colleagues. This is all well and good, but you have to meet those people in the first place. To get started, you'll need an organized and effective system for locating viable sources of prospects. As discussed in Chapter 1, the Internet makes that job much easier, enabling you to do in fifteen minutes what would have taken half a day at the library. Speaking of the library, don't rule it out. Librarians tend to be analytics, mixed with a touch of the amiable, and they can be very helpful to you. They might be able to help you identify sources of prospects and point you in directions you never would have found on your own.

Another potential source of prospects are newspapers and business and professional publications, most of which can be found online, though hard copies may be more complete and comprehensive. Buck subscribes to six Sunday newspapers, from all the major markets he covers. He peruses the classifieds, public notices, and local business sections. His fourteen-dollar-a-week investment has had a phenomenal return on investment, keeping him apprised of what businesses are up to and which people are making news.

Depending on your industry, the Yellow Pages <www.yellowpages. com> or reverse directories might be useful. Reverse directories, listing phones by address rather than alphabetically, enable you to identify prospects you wish to target in a specific geographic area. Bob knows an insurance salesperson who goes through the obituaries every day, looking for death notices of persons aged thirty to fifty-five. He then sends letters to everyone living within one block of the deceased, introducing himself as a prelude to a personal contact. Naturally, discretion being the better part of valor, he never mentions any awareness of their departed neighbor, but he's found that prospects contacted through this strategy are significantly more receptive to sitting down with him to talk about insurance and estate planning.

If you market through a direct distribution channel, mailing lists can be a valuable source of prospects. If someone has purchased a certain type of product, or supported a certain type of organization in the past, they're disproportionally more likely to do so again. Remember the dishware you ordered from a catalog in July and how your mailbox was full of catalogs for similar products at the holidays?

Many industries hold conventions, fairs, and trade shows at least once a year. Look into them. The investment of your time and expenses may be insignificant compared to the payoff. You'll have the opportunity to update yourself on trends and issues, and learn about everything affecting your industry. What a perfect place to learn everything you need to know about the competition and its products. But mostly, it's an opportunity to meet other business professionals in related but noncompetitive industries, the perfect kind of persons to become partners in a mutually beneficial business relationship. Just be sure that when you're at events such as this you're in the proper mind set. These fifteen-hour days are for business, not just for a good time.

Other potentially viable sources of prospects are government agencies and licensing bureaus. If new businesses are prime prospects for your products or services, the first day they open, you call on them to introduce yourself and your company's offerings. The only problem is by the time they open the doors, they've already procured those products and services from someone else. Yes, you can get ahead of the curve by reading about the opening in the local newspaper, but even then it may be too late. A better idea is to jump to the head of the line by being the first one in the know, when the principals apply for building permits and business licenses. Close the sale before your competition even hears about the impending event.

CONCEPT 2: THE OLD WATERING HOLES JUST AIN'T WHAT THEY USED TO BE

To this point, we've described some of the traditional prospecting methods, many, most, or all of which can help build your base of prospects. Much of what we discuss from here on, though, advocates another tack. So far, your research has helped you identify key individuals you've noted as potential prospects or as people who might be candidates for a strategic partnership. You have information about their interests and affiliations. Now it's time to get out and meet them where they are. If you meet and get to know prospects and candidates first, the cold call will be a lot warmer.

We need to make one thing abundantly clear, however. We are absolutely, positively *not* suggesting that you join their country club, start working out at their gym, attend cultural events they frequent, or buy tickets to the charitable balls they support. Yes, you may be at those places and socialize with them there *after* you've met them. No, you will not go there *to* meet them.

We've all seen some of the puppies in these environments, there to rub elbows with the influential people, just waiting for the opportunity to introduce themselves, flatter the person, get in a few lines about what they do, and hand out a business card. It's pitiful. Such people are never taken seriously, they never impress, and they always annoy. At best they get a patronizing comment before being unceremoniously dismissed. Are we talking about you?

Along the same lines, there may have been a day when the business-after-hours happy hour was a viable networking activity. No longer. You may have fun at such events, but make no pretense about them being a worthwhile environment for meeting candidates for a strategic partnership. Arguably, they never really were all that useful in the first place. Go to any so-called networking event and watch the show. Mostly, people are standing around with people they know, socializing. A little business might be getting done, but generally people are interacting with their own circles of friends and colleagues, people they deal with on a regular basis. Occasionally, someone actually tries to use this event as an opportunity to meet potential clients. He or she will walk around from group to group, smiling, adding a comment or observation to something someone said, then declare, "I don't believe we've met. I'm Bubba Bullwinkle from Gulf Breeze Feed Store." This forces everyone else—all of whom know one another—to introduce themselves to Bubba, who goes on to pass out business cards to them all, informing them: "Gulf Breeze is hog-raisin' heaven, and all the happy hogs get their feed at Gulf Breeze Feed Store." Everyone patronizes Bubba, hoping he'll go away. They smile and say that the next time their hogs are hungry, they'll be sure to look him up. If this scenario sounds a bit familiar, it should. It's a variation of the puppies at the social event. This approach will not work. No one is interested in having a stranger come up, give his or her speil, and pass out a business card. People don't like to be sold, remember?

The business-after-hours happy hour is one of the last vestiges of what is known as the good-old-boy style of selling: love me, love my product. It was in its heyday in the late 1940s and early 1950s, performed to perfection by Willy Loman and his cohorts. At that time, it may have been an appropriate mode of doing business, as the business environment was very different from today. After World War II, Germany and Japan were devastated. The Soviet Union was technically a winner, but lost 20 million people with virtually nothing left standing west of Moscow. Great Britain and France were on the winning side, too, but lost their empires. So, for five, seven, or maybe ten years following World War II, the United States, alone unscathed in the hostilities, had essentially no competition on the world's markets. Ever see a 1943 Chevrolet? How about a 1944 Ford? A 1945 Chrysler? No, you haven't, because there weren't any. Or any refrigerators, washing machines, or dryers, either, because all production capacity was diverted to the war effort. Once World War II ended, you didn't have to be a good marketer or a professional salesperson. All you had to do was produce the goods, and customers were lining up to snatch them off the shelves. With plenty of demand and no foreign competition, people had the luxury of doing business with people just because they liked them. Persons of influence could stand around drinking cocktails and smoking cigarettes, holding court, inviting the puppies to come over to shower them with compliments and laugh at their jokes. If you could sell yourself as a "good guy" with the "right" beliefs and the "right" proclivities, you were on the road to success. In the global economy of the new world of business, those norms of fifty years ago won't get you far.

Contributing to this change are the emerging attitudes about mixing alcohol and business. In this era of attorneys and the media, individuals and companies simply cannot afford problems associated with events that can spark inappropriate behavior by their employees. Bob remembers a retreat at a golf resort when an inebriated employee drove a golf cart through a leading customer's sliding plate-glass door. Buck tells of an employee who closed down the hotel bar, staggered to the elevator and got up to his floor, but then could not remember which room was his, so proceeded to pound on all the doors as he walked down the hallway. One of the doors was answered by a rightfully indignant gentleman who demanded to know what was going on. The drunk muttered some epithets about the gentleman's ethnic background and parentage, apparently unaware he was speaking to the new vice president of human resources. The drunk was fired on the spot and put on a plane the next morning, his seven-year career with the company over.

All this goes hand in hand with our earlier points about changes in wining, dining, and business socializing. The bottom line is forget about prospecting at happy hours. Many of the decision makers you wish to target won't be there in the first place, and those who are won't be receptive to your advances.

CONCEPT 3: NEW PERSPECTIVES ON NETWORKING AND PROSPECTING

We previously described the necessity for you to position yourself as a partner instead of a supplier. Those people perceived as suppliers, we proposed, were fighting it out on price against their online competitors and were condemned to frustration. By contrast, people perceived as partners were consultants, experts, and helpers who generated business-building ideas equating to value worth paying for. Some of those business-building ideas are composed of your expertise in marketing and management strategies and tactics. The key to getting this process started, as you're about to see, lies in prospecting, networking, and referrals. These fundamental changes of how business is conducted in the new world of business give you an opportunity to employ innovative approaches that have the potential for an immense payoff, especially if your competition and your peers have yet to embrace them.

Point 1: Become the *Prime Referral Source*

Set a goal of becoming the "referral expert" throughout the business environment in which you work and the community in which you live. Position yourself as the person who can send customers, colleagues, and friends to the person or business that can meet their needs for whatever product or service they're looking for. Whether they need a software company, a lawyer, a printer, an answering service, or a plumber, you be the person who sends them where they need to go.

Technology makes it easy for you to create a referral database. For everyone you know—personally and professionally—maintain this database and keep it up to date. It should have two classes of information: first, their areas of expertise and specialization, including what they're looking for in a prospect; and second, products and services most important to them, which they're either currently buying or are in the market for. On an ongoing basis, match what people are looking for and who might best meet their needs. Then, send them each a referral, with your name on it.

Whenever you're engaged in conversation, get people talking and remember to listen. Here, though, you're not in a selling situation. Well, let's say you're not in a *formal* selling situation. Find out what people want, need, and care about with the objective of sending them somewhere as a referral, not as a prelude to a sales presentation. It should not matter whether their hair is falling out or their septic tank is backing up. Perhaps you can think of someplace to send them on the spot. Maybe you have to check the database and call or e-mail them the next day. Or you might have to enter the information into the database and get back to them when there's a match. Unless it was a bird dog, you don't get anything for this, but ultimately you may gain more than a bird dog would have ever been paid. You've made a meaningful gesture to two people, the person to whom you sent the referral and the prospect whose needs will be satisfied. If they get the chance, most people would want to reciprocate for a gesture such as that, which, of course, is the whole idea.

Don't just limit yourself to business referrals. Remember that you want to become *the* prime referral source. Buck recently referred a friend to a car dealership, Bob a colleague to an air-conditioning contractor, no bird dogs. Neither of these may ever result in a payoff per se, but no matter. It's all part of the numbers game of sales. If you become *the* prime referral source to more people in more environments, ultimately it will pay off.

Point 2: Always Qualify Your Prospect

Back in Selling Skills 101, we were introduced to the sales pyramid (not to be confused with the sales triangle noted in Chapter 1). The sales pyramid was used to illustrate the essence of prospecting. The base of the pyramid—suspects—was very large, consisting of names on a list. You first narrowed that down to prospects—those with a need for your product or service—and further narrowed it to qualified prospects—those who could afford it—before going into action seeking an appointment with the decision maker.

Qualifying is pretty basic stuff, or at least it should be. Yet every day salespeople are showing million-dollar palaces to couples who should be in starter homes and giving test drives in Corvettes to people who can at best afford the Cavalier. Perhaps there's something in the water that has salespeople so caught up fantasizing about how they're going to spend the commission check that they think only about closing the sale and live in denial of the fact that the financing won't go through. This should never happen to you. Right up front, ask qualifying questions to determine whether the prospect can buy and what he or she can buy. You can do this in an unobtrusive way as part of the opening information gathering we'll describe in Chapter 5, positioning it as a way to help facilitate the paperwork and get the person the best deal.

In the B2B environment, take this one step further to estimate how long it will take to get paid, if you get paid at all. Dealing with firms without a proven track record or businesses in financial trouble, you might insist on cash up front or that the transaction be applied to a credit card, guaranteeing that you'll get paid by the issuing company. If they default, it's between them and the credit card company. You got paid.

Let's add one more consideration to qualifying, a point often overlooked. Sometimes a prospect is fully qualified but it's just not worth your while to mess with it. Why would you drive 200 miles to call on someone who, at most, might yield fifty dollars worth of business a year? Before soliciting anyone for an appointment, go through these four simple steps:

1. Estimate how much you'll earn in a given time period if you make the sale.

   Example: $4,000

2. Multiply that by the probability of making the sale. We understand you don't know exactly, but give it a good guess. Make the process a little easier by using a five-point scale—10 percent, 30 percent, 50 percent, 70 percent, and 90 percent—ranking an account from not-at-all likely (10 percent) to very likely (90 percent).

   Example: 50 percent, which, multiplied by the $4,000 you earn if you get the sale, equals $2,000. This is your estimated gross earnings.

3. Subtract all the expenses of pursuing and servicing the account in the given time period.

   Example: $500 in expenses, subtracted from the $2,000 estimated gross earnings, equals $1,500. This is your estimated net earnings.

4. Divide estimated net earnings by the number of hours required to pursue and service the account in the given time period.

   Example: 20 hours. Dividing $1,500 estimated net earnings by 20 hours equals $75 per hour. This is your net estimated earnings per hour. Is this account worth pursuing? If there's nothing else to do that will net you $75 bucks an hour, go for it. If you have plenty of other qualified prospects who will net you $100 an hour or more, let it ride.

We fully appreciate that these four steps require some educated guesses, but it's essential in setting priorities and doing your plan that you have such a system to help you focus on activities that have the greatest payout. A few years ago, Bob was given a referral to a prospect in the Midwest. The company was undergoing massive restructuring at the time and, in doing the four steps, Bob was able to determine that although the potential gross was significant, probability of consummating an agreement was low, expenses would be substantial, and extensive time would be required for proposal development. As a courtesy to the person who had given him the referral, Bob called the prospect and they chatted for a few minutes, but he did not actively pursue the account. You are probably already going through the four steps, albeit informally, to help focus on qualified prospects with the greatest potential. We urge you to quantify the process as best you can. If you can sharpen your focus a little bit, you'll optimize the process of setting priorities, and that will have a big payoff.

Point 3: Always Qualify Your Referrals

There's another dimension to qualifying, and we're making special mention of it here because some of the best professional salespeople don't give it proper attention. As we've stated, you want to develop a reputation as the referral expert. This is all well and good, but don't get so carried away that you neglect to qualify those referrals. Whenever you refer someone to a colleague, be sure to qualify the person in advance. Don't just send all the suspects you can find and expect your colleague to do the qualifying. One of Bob's friends at the university was referring graduating seniors to a leading realtor in the area. Although their futures looked bright, these twenty-two-year-olds had no money and bad credit and could in no way afford the realtor's upscale listings. Instead of being perceived as a business gesture, these referrals were awkward and an annoyance to the realtor.

In addition, be sure to qualify the person you send someone to. That is, have confidence everyone you send business to will do the job right at a price that is a good value. Buck learned this lesson when he referred a friend to some new colleagues he'd met at a professional organization he'd recently joined. Unbeknownst to Buck, these people were full of stuffing, but he sent his friend to them without checking into the reputations of them and their companies. The experience was a disappointment for Buck's friend and an embarrassment to Buck, who never again sent anyone to a person or business he hadn't already checked out thoroughly. Beyond that, he now follows up on all his referrals to make sure the beneficiaries of the referral are fully satisfying the expectations of the party being referred. Up front, he tells parties receiving referrals that he'll be touching base with them to be sure everything is being handled properly. And Buck will contact the party he referred to confirm that his or her expectations were met or exceeded.

Point 4: Regularly Send Qualified Prospects to Your Current Customers

We've already drilled you on the importance of positioning yourself as a partner rather than a supplier, and it's on Point 4, more than in any other way, that you implement this strategy. Send qualified referrals to your current customers. When you consider the concept of helping your customers develop business-building ideas, can you think of anything that better epitomizes this objective than you directly involving yourself in helping them obtain customers? This literally puts you shoulder to shoulder with them as a partner in achieving their sales and profit targets. Now you're in it together, splitting the profits. Sure, your competitor is going to show up sooner or later, proposing to undercut you on your products and services. So what? The value you provide your customers by sending referrals and directly generating sales is far greater than they could ever save by going with someone else. When you become directly involved in helping them build their business, you have become tantamount to one of their best employees, a top field rep they don't have to pay commission or benefits.

Take this a step further and get involved in your customers' operations. Look over all their vendors and service providers, and seek out opportunities to refer them to some of your colleagues who can provide superior value in the products and services they utilize. There are two big benefits for you. First, you help your customers to obtain good values for their operations, further developing your partnership. Second, you enhance your role as the referral expert, sending business to qualified colleagues.

Point 5: Take a New and Different Approach to Networking

To be a partner, not a supplier, you must create an adult-adult dialogue as peers with an equal power component. To succeed, you must sell yourself to them as a competent, knowledgeable, achievement-oriented person first, *before* you approach them about any partnership. Eventually, you may be able to socialize with them as a peer. Until you attain that status, limit social environments to scenarios in which you present yourself professionally, greet them, and let them talk about themselves a little. Don't expect them to remember your name. They won't. Don't be all that concerned about handing them your business card. They're just going to trash it, probably before they go home.

Instead of trying to schmooze your way to success, we suggest *demonstrating* that you're an achievement-oriented person by getting involved in achievement-oriented environments where you can work as a peer with those people you believe would be good prospects or candidates for a partnership. Those people are leaders and get involved in their industry and community. You must do the same! There may be a professional or community organization out there that has all the personal resources it needs to accomplish its mission. We just don't know about it. And there may be a professional or community organization someplace that can rely on all its officers to do everything they said they'd do when they said they'd do it. We just haven't heard from them yet. There are opportunities for you to take a leadership role in every professional or community organization you wish to target. The very few people in them who are doing the vast preponderance of the work are exactly those people you wish to cultivate as prospects and partners. Get in with them shoulder to shoulder and create that peer relationship. Think of the different atmosphere at the social hour when it was you who organized the program. Think of the different atmosphere at the charity fund-raiser when it was you who managed all the publicity with the newspapers and radio and television stations. No, these commitments to professional and community organizations will not yield the instant gratification of a one-night stand, but in an amazingly short time they will put you on track to generating prospects and creating partnership relationships.

As you become involved in these organizations, commit yourself to doing your assigned tasks and doing them well, and at the same time get the lay of the land and study the players on the stage. Early in the process, it will become apparent who are the movers and shakers, the centers of influence. You were probably aware of who most of these persons were when you targeted the attendant environment in the first place, but several more may come to light.

The movers and shakers are your targets for establishing strategic alliances and partnership relationships. They are professional people who are regularly involved in a circle of 100 or more other business professionals with whom they strive toward mutually shared objectives. Your goal is not merely to do business with them but to become a part of their inner circle of 100.

So, let's take it from there. You take an active role in achievement-oriented environments in your profession and in the community where you regularly encounter persons who might be candidates for a partnership. As you do so, take it slow and easy. Don't come on too strong. Let them discover you. There's an old saying about courtship: you let them chase you until you catch them. Keep that in mind. Do your job and do it well. Be friendly, courteous, and professional. Don't try to sell these potential partners, but help them to buy into you.

Eventually, a situation will arise in which you have an opportunity to engage one of your candidates in a casual conversation. At this point, you've already established yourself as a professional person in the candidate's mind, and you have a bond of common ground from your work and achievements in the professional or community environment. What a difference from the stranger who walks up to butt in! You have a scenario in which both parties can establish rapport and engage in dialogue. This is a great opening, the perfect stage on which to meet those persons you might want to get to know better. Professional salespeople long ago discovered that this was the way to prospect for strategic alliances. Unfortunately, many of these sales pros fail to take optimum advantage of this opportunity.

When you find yourself in this situation, it's very tempting to start telling this person about yourself and what you do, but that's not the way to go. It's at this point that otherwise successful professional salespeople forget one of the most fundamental principles from Selling Skills 101: Don't put the focus on yourself and your product. Get the prospect to talk, listen, and concentrate on need-satisfying benefits.

Instead of talking about yourself and what you do, get the person to talk about himself or herself and what *he or she* does. As Dale Carnegie pointed out almost seventy years ago, people will think you're an excellent communicator when you shut up and let them talk about themselves. Also, keep in mind that your primary objective is to position yourself as the referral expert.

It's not difficult to get others to talk about themselves, especially achievement-oriented people who rightfully like to brag a little. Listen carefully and at some point be sure to ask the critical questions: "What do you look for in a prospect?" and "How do you know when someone is a good prospect for you?" Again, these people will gladly talk about the kinds of clients they look for and how they determine whether a person or business is something they'd like to target. In the course of this conversation, ask for their business cards. Don't be at all concerned about talking about yourself or giving them *your* business card. When you ask for theirs, they might ask for yours in return as a courtesy, but don't expect them to do anything with it before they throw it away.

Now you're ready to get to work. Check out this person and his or her business, utilizing the many information sources we've already described. Be sure you're comfortable about referring prospects this person's way, and confident that this is someone you'd like to have as a strategic partner.

Keep in mind that your intelligence gathering can get you only so far and that at some point you'll have to go with your gut. Is this someone I want to affiliate with or not? When it gets to that point, your gut must respond with a resounding "Yes!" If you're not quite sure, if there are any lingering doubts, that means "No." Remember, you're not looking for large numbers of partnerships. A few really good ones are all you need. Ultimately, you're going to assemble a small group of highly competent and motivated business professionals where there's no place for anyone who isn't one of the best. And, of course, it's not as though you're formally rejecting someone's application to join an organization. A person who doesn't make your cut has no reason to believe he or she was under consideration for anything in the first place. If at some future time a person you're not sure of now demonstrates that he or she is indeed a consummate business professional, you can always develop an alliance then. What you *don't* want to do is to bring the person inside the tent and then have to figure a way to get him or her out.

For those people you select as objectives for partnerships, your next step is to get them to discover you. Remember our analogy about courtship and another basic principle from Selling Skills 101. It's not enough to help them to buy; you want to make them think it was *their* idea. You should employ tactics designed to get *them* to seek out a partnership with *you*.

Some books on the market hypothesize that everything you needed to know about life you learned in kindergarten. We agree with the basic premise but would modify it to say high school. Think back to the days when you had your first really serious crush. There was someone in whom you felt an interest, and at some point someone casually introduced you to each other. Unless you were one of those beautiful people that no one could resist—and this book is neither written *by* them nor *for* them—the other party was cordial but no sparks were flying and no relationship was initiated on the spot. If this sounds similar to what we described the first time you meet someone who might be a candidate for a partnership and strategic alliance, it should.

What you did next was to find out more about the person, exactly what we described for a strategic partnership, and then you worked out situations in which you could happen upon this person and then proceed to establish the first stages of communication and dialogue— no different from forming a relationship in sales.

When you next see your candidate in an achievement-oriented environment or an informal social setting, make a point of greeting this person by name. Remembering people's names is one of the most important selling skills and, yes, it's a learned skill. The fact that you remembered a person's name is a compliment and makes him or her feel important. It's subtle and sincere, a contrast to flattery. The first time you do this, chances are the other person will have forgotten your name, so it doesn't hurt to mention it. "Rosa. Nice to see you. Beth Belfry." Or, certainly on a second or later encounter, just say hello without using your name to see whether the person will come up with it on his or her own. Whether or not he or she happens to remember your name at this stage isn't all that critical, anyhow. The person recognizes you and perceives you to be a decent and friendly person. If you've rubbed shoulders with the person in an achievement-oriented environment, you'd like to think he or she at least knows who you are and what you've done in that setting, and he or she should. But the person may not, and you can deal with that.

The next thing you did over that first high school crush, and the next thing you need to do here, is to find a legitimate reason for contacting the person on an informal matter. Please note that contacting the person on an informal matter absolutely does *not* mean a sales call. You're not there yet.

Some sales trainers suggest you just send a friendly, handwritten note.

> Dear Frank:
>   Nice seeing you at the seminar. If I hear of anyone looking for an accountant, I'll send them your way. Look forward to seeing you again soon.
>   Regards, Jenna

We most definitely advise you *not* to send anything similar to this. For one thing, if you're like most people you probably place little credibility in someone telling you they're going to do something for you, especially if that person has never done anything for you in the past and has no sense of obligation to reciprocate for something *you've* done for *them*. We also urge you not to send the basic happy note.

> Dear Frank:
>   Nice seeing you at the seminar. Look forward to seeing you again soon.
>   Regards, Jenna

It serves no useful purpose. It's junk mail, and it makes you look like a puppy.

Instead, find a legitimate reason to communicate with the person. During your informal conversations, be alert for opportunities to exploit. For example, if the person mentions that his wife is looking for an English teapot, you might be able to say that you know of a distributor who handles them. This, then, gives you a legitimate reason to write or e-mail the person with the information he's interested in. Or, even better, since you're the referral expert, refer him to someone he's looking for:

Dear Frank:

Nice seeing you at the seminar. Here's the guy to contact to handle the problem you were talking about: Hector Lopez, 555-7158. Look forward to seeing you again soon.

Regards, Jenna

Doing things this way, you're establishing adult-adult dialogue and now, finally, people know who you are.

Back in high school, the next step in the courtship was to find a way to do something nice for that other person, a gesture without a demand for reciprocation, and it's your next step here, too. In high school, there may have been numerous alternatives for gestures, but for the professional salesperson in the new world of business, the tactic is simple and straightforward. Send the person a referral without expecting anything in return. You don't want a bird dog, and in no way will you imply that you expect reciprocation. You want appreciation, and you want the person to perceive you as someone who can be helpful to him or her and his or her business. That, of course, is what partnership is all about. It also should not escape your attention that this person now will probably be inclined to send referrals to you, especially since you made a gesture without asking him or her to do so. No, not everyone will so respond in kind, but most professional businesspeople will want to, particularly when they think it was their own idea. At the least, people will now be considerably more predisposed to consider your request for an appointment.

What a difference when you encounter these people now. You greet each other, socialize, and interact professionally as peers. Now, and only now do you propose getting together to meet and talk about ways you might work together in the future. One of those ways, of course, will involve them becoming customers of your products and services, all part of an evolving relationship and partnership.

This innovative approach to networking and prospecting in the new world of business is fundamental and obvious, so it's astonishing that so many salespeople are spinning their wheels in the tactics of fifty years ago. As you develop your long- and short-term plans, be sure to include your personal strategy for taking this new and different approach to networking.

Point 6: Organize a Swap Shop of Professionals in Related but Noncompeting Businesses

To this point, we've talked about one-on-one relationships in which principals work together and, in the course of things, occasionally give referrals to one another or to people known and respected by the referral expert. In addition to this, we suggest you put together a swap shop, a networking group of people in related but noncompeting businesses that meets on a regular basis with the express purpose of exchanging leads. Such a group might include, for example, a realtor, an appraiser, and a home-repair contractor. Set a specific time to meet each week, say 7:00 a.m. Monday at the breakfast bar, with the understanding that everyone is expected to show and everyone is expected to bring leads. The swap shop is one more example of a partnership relationship, so take care to evaluate candidates thoroughly before inviting them to join. Just one leech could drain all the energy and ruin the group. So before formalizing the relationship and having new members join, work with them informally for awhile, giving and getting referrals.

Swap shops function most effectively when they are fairly small in size, maybe five or six people. Start small, perhaps two or three, and add new members slowly and carefully, seeking the one new person at a time who can bring in a special synergy that exponentially augments the effectiveness of the group.

If your business deals with diverse types of clients, you might benefit by being a member of multiple swap shops, each specializing in a particular market segment. There is no reason you couldn't attend a different swap shop several days or every day every week. This gets the day started right, and it sure beats cold calling.

Point 7: Develop Your Own Benefit Statement

Whenever anyone asks you what you do for a living, always respond in terms of the benefits you provide, not the functions you perform. Thus,

- do *not* say: "I sell insurance and also handle stocks and bonds."
- Instead, say: "I help people attain security and financial independence through a wide variety of products, including insurance, stocks, and bonds."

Similarly,

- do *not* say: "We are a personnel outsourcing firm specializing in staff support."
- Instead, say: "We help companies improve their effectiveness and professionalism by providing trained and qualified staff support."

It's just one more variation of translating features into benefits. Start with the *benefits* you provide, putting the focus on the prospect:

- "We show people how to . . ."
- "We help people to . . ."
- "We save companies money by . . ."
- "We help companies make more money by . . ."
- "We show companies how to enhance their . . ."

Then, talk about the *features* that make those benefits possible, describing your competitive advantage:

- "We're able to do this by . . ."
- "We've been successful because . . ."
- "The reason people like doing business with us is . . ."
- "We offer our customers more because . . ."

If you don't already have a twelve-second personal benefit statement, take a quick break and do it now so you'll have it ready the very next time someone asks you what you do. Also, it's perfect for those occasions when a whole bunch of people around a table take their turn introducing themselves. If you hadn't noticed, most of those intros are pretty bland and don't hit on a single benefit of interest to anyone. You'll be an interesting contrast.

As you undoubtedly noticed, Concept 3 has covered almost half of this chapter. We hope it's provided some insights about how you could adopt new and different approaches for achieving your objectives. In any case, it's time for Action Plan Assignments #5 and #6. Do them now, again in about six months, and at least once a year after that. Quantify and assess your prospecting and networking activities on a regular basis, and formally include them in your weekly and daily plans.

Action Plan Assignment #5:
Prospecting and Networking Assessment

Do this now (note date): _____

Do again in six months (note date and record on calendar): _____

_____

Do again every twelve months thereafter (note date and record on calendar): _____

Step 1: List every prospecting and networking activity you are engaged in. Break down to the smallest possible elements. (Example: One particular organization you work with may include several separate and distinct activities.)

Step 2: For every item in Step 1, quantify the number of hours invested in the activity. Use hours per week, per month, or per year—whatever is easiest for you.

Step 3: For every item, quantify the earnings you have generated as a direct result of that prospecting or networking activity.

Step 4: For every item, divide earnings (from Step 3) by hours invested (from Step 2) to calculate earnings per hour invested.

Step 5: (This is the critical step.) We realize it can be difficult to specifically quantify earnings from a particular activity or to isolate the impact of one element from another, especially different activities within the same organization. That said, considering what you calculated in Steps 2, 3, and 4, rank every item on a scale of 1 to 5.

    5: an extremely effective activity
    4: overall, an effective activity
    3: a marginally effective activity
    2: an activity of limited effectiveness
    1: an activity of little or no effectiveness

**Action Plan Assignment #6:
Integrating Effective Activities
and Eliminating Ineffectual Activities**

Formally integrate specific prospecting and networking activities into the weekly and daily plans you generate with Action Plan Assignment #3. Make time for those activities ranked 5 (extremely effective), and eliminate activities ranked 2 (limited effectiveness) or 1 (little or no effectiveness).

The purpose of Action Plan Assignment #5 is for you to identify those activities that are effective—which you'll continue to do—and those that are not—which you won't. Of course, since you may be adopting innovative approaches to prospecting and networking, you may find that certain environments will become more effective, and that's why we urge you to repeat this process in six months and at least every twelve months thereafter. After completing the assessment, go to Action Plan Assignment #6.

CONCEPT 4: GETTING THE APPOINTMENT— CONVINCING PROSPECTS TO SEE YOU IN PERSON

As you can readily see, we dedicated considerably more space to Concept 3 than we will to Concept 4. The reason is namely that through innovative approaches to networking you establish communication and dialogue with persons in a manner that makes them receptive to meeting with you by the time you finally get around to popping the question. Still, you'll find numerous prospects outside the networking environment. Some will be referred to you in the swap shop, by current customers or strategic partners, and elsewhere among your circles of business professionals. Also, especially if you're relatively new, you'll be making a certain number of dreaded cold calls.

Once you establish the proper prospecting and networking habits, you're going to find it will take fewer phone calls to obtain an appointment. If it now takes an average of twelve calls to get an appointment now, it might be down to eight for one a year from now. In addition to that, you can embrace simple procedures to reduce that ratio even more, immediately.

Point 1: Get All the Information You Need Before Speaking to the Prospect

We've described how, in the new world of business, it's far easier to obtain this information. If you're still not sure who the decision maker is, speak with the receptionist to confirm the name/spelling/title of the decision maker, and then research him or her carefully.

Point 2: Cover Your Bases with All the Buying Influences

Let's take the point of being a back-door sales rep one more step. Generally, we've been concentrating on the so-called decision maker, the person who gives final approval to buy and releases the dollars to buy. This is the only person the front-door sales rep thinks about, but that may be a mistake. Sure, the decision maker is your primary focus, and you're wasting your time talking to a person without authority. But there may be other people in the background who influence the buying decision, and you ignore them at your peril. The back-door sales rep learns who they are, understands their roles, and puts them in the spotlight.

The user buying influences are those people using or supervising the use of your products or services. They're going to be affected by it day in and day out. Sure, the decision maker can issue an edict ordering their compliance, but the back-door sales rep knows that everything will go a whole lot more smoothly by getting them on board and showing them how it will work for them. Leave them out of the loop and don't be surprised when your plans go awry.

The technical people evaluate the measurable, quantifiable aspects of your proposal and screen you out if you don't meet the specifications. You're out of the running if your fat content is 30 percent and their specs say no more than 28 percent, your proposed computer is a billionth of a second per hour too slow, or your mutual fund includes a corporation they consider environmentally unfriendly. Find out who these people are, what their criteria are, and whether you can have your technical people consult with their technical people *before* you submit your proposal.

Point 3: Introduce Yourself with a Brief Note

The operative work is *brief:* a few lines in a letter or e-mail identifying a referrer, a reason for contacting the person, and informing him or her you'll soon be in touch:

> Chan Ho Kim suggested I give you a call. We've been helping him with tax-sheltered annuities, and I've got some ideas I believe you'd be interested in. I'll call you early next week to arrange a convenient time for us to get together.
> Regards, Sue Ella Bradley

If you prefer, call at some odd hour when you know the person won't be in and leave a message on his or her mail. If you do so, however, be prepared for the possibility that the person just might happen to be there, in which case you'll move directly into asking for an appointment. As a rule, it's best to send nothing else in advance of an appointment. The person is just going to trash it anyhow, and it gives him or her an excuse to say, "Yes, I looked over what you sent me [which they didn't] and I'm not interested." In any case, you're not trying to sell the person through the mail, with files attached to an e-mail, or over the phone.

Point 4: Use Telephone Calls to Get a Face-to-Face Appointment

This book is not about telemarketing. Never lose sight of the fact that your objective is to meet with prospects in person. The more you talk to a secretary, the less likely it is he or she will let you through to the prospect. The longer you're on the phone with the prospect, the less likely it is you'll ever get an appointment. If you as much as begin to make your presentation over the phone, you're through.

An effective tactic for avoiding the secretary altogether is to call very early in the morning or late in the day, when the office staff is not around to screen your call and the decision maker may pick it up directly. If you do encounter a secretary, get his or her name. For one thing, it's just common courtesy, but in addition, there may come a time when you need his or her help. Then, state your name and company, a referrer if there is one, and convey that the decision maker would want to talk to you (*not* that you would like to talk to the decision maker).

SECRETARY: Mr. Murton's office.

YOU: Hi, this is Stan Bennett. And you're . . .

SECRETARY: Cindy Smith.

YOU: Cindy, I'm with Metro Particleboard. Stew Forrest suggested I speak to Mr. Murton. Is he in, please?

SECRETARY: What does this concern, Mr. Bennett?

YOU: We've been doing some contracting with Mr. Forrest and his company. I have some information I believe Mr. Murton would want to know about.

SECRETARY: We already have a supplier for particleboard, Mr. Bennett. Mr. Murton is very busy today.

YOU: I know that, Cindy, and I'm not going to waste his time. I need to talk to him for two minutes. Is he in now?

SECRETARY: Just one moment, Mr. Bennett.

You get the idea. If you convey that what you have to say is important, that the prospect would want to talk to you, and that all you need is a couple of minutes, you have a good shot at getting past the secretary, assuming you've shown him or her respect. By the way, we mean it when we say "a couple of minutes." As we'll discuss later, two minutes is the optimal time frame for getting an appointment.

Once you are past the gatekeepers, it's on to the decision maker. At this point, it's just possible you'll get his or her voice mail. If you hadn't previously sent a note, e-mail, or voice mail message introducing yourself, now's a good time to do it. If you *have* previously done so, don't be redundant. Say you called to set up a convenient time to get together. If you wish, leave a number at which the prospect can return your call, but don't sit by the phone all day expecting him or her to do so. In any event, give yourself permission to call *him or her* back. "I'll be at 555-7159 until four this afternoon. If you can't get back to me, I'll give you a call later in the week." Do this *once!* No repetitive voice mail messages. If you get the person's voice mail on a subsequent attempt, hang up. If after ten or fourteen days of being unsuccessful in getting ahold of the person, you might leave another voice mail to let the person know you're still trying to reach him or her, but by this point you should be asking yourself whether you're just spinning your wheels.

So, you finally reach the decision maker. Now, go into your eight-step "script" for getting the appointment. It's "script" with quotation marks because you will not actually read to your prospect. Having said that, you *will* be thoroughly prepared, you *will* have rehearsed what you're going to say, and you *will* have the eight steps, with attendant notes, in front of you to cue you as you go.

Step 1. Greet the prospect, identifying yourself and your company. "Good morning, Mr. Le Blanc. This is Pam Pierson with Amalgamated Widget."

Step 2. Note a referrer if you have one. "John Schultz from Consolidated Bromide suggested I give you a call."

Step 3. State the reason for your call. Here, you should note something you've been doing which relates to the prospect and his or her company and which is something you wish to discuss with the prospect in person. "We've been working with them on a new process for enzyme extraction . . ."

Step 4. Identify a primary benefit, a specific benefit you've achieved that should also be a benefit important to this prospect. ". . . which has given them a twenty percent savings in production costs."

Step 5. Confirm this benefit to get a "Yes." Be careful! Don't ask an obvious, manipulative question such as, "Tell me, do you want to make more money?" Instead, use tie-downs such as "isn't it," "wouldn't you," or "aren't they" to make this a casual statement the prospect will readily confirm. "I'll bet that kind of savings could really help your bottom line, wouldn't you think?"

Step 6. If confirmed, close for the appointment. Do *not* use the choice technique ("Would Monday at ten or Tuesday at four be better for you?"). Instead, suggest a time and shut up. Let the prospect suggest an alternative time. "It will only take me about twenty minutes to show you some of these ideas. Would nine-thirty on Wednesday be good for you?"

Step 7. If not confirmed, ask questions and probe to uncover some unmet need or dissatisfaction. "How much downtime are you experiencing?" or "How do you feel about your packaging costs?" (What you do here will closely parallel how you handle questions in the presentation, which we'll cover in Chapter 5. First, you should not move into your presentation over the phone, even though some pertinent benefits may be right on the tip of your tongue. Remember that your *only* objective is to get the appointment. Most important, though, is to be alert for some expression of interest you can grab ahold of.)

Step 8.   When you confirm some interest or a benefit, bring in the witness, cite a success story, and again close for the appointment. Let's expand on the dialogues from Step 7.

YOU: How much downtime are you experiencing?

PROSPECT: It's below industry average.

YOU: Fred Lewis was telling me that. He's been working with our people for a month and we have him down to six percent. Getting down to six percent would really improve your operations, wouldn't it?

PROSPECT: Hmm . . .

YOU: I can show you this in about ten minutes. How's Tuesday at eight?

PROSPECT: Can you make it seven?

YOU: How do you feel about your packaging costs?

PROSPECT: They're going up a little, along with everything else. But I think we're getting a good value, and we're completely satisfied.

YOU: Interesting. Bob Davis at Metro told me that. They're one of our customers now and are saving more than ten percent. Every dollar you can save is important, isn't it?

PROSPECT: Can you send something in the mail?

YOU: There are things you'll need me to go through, and you'll probably have some questions. Is Monday at ten good for you?

PROSPECT: You know where we're located?

YOU: Sure do. See you then.

Notice how the sales rep uncovered some interest and closed for the appointment and how, in the second example, the rep declined to send something in the mail. By the way, depending on your business, you might send something in advance of the appointment. Just don't agree to send anything before confirming the appointment. Another thing you may have noticed is that the rep closed on very subtle cues. As you'll see in Chapter 7, prospects almost never give you obvious and direct cues, so you always have to be alert for any expression of interest, and close on the spot.

Before moving on, get your appointment script down pat with Action Plan Assignment #7.

Action Plan Assignment #7: Appointment Script Outline

On a sheet of paper write out the eight steps and, for each, an outline of what information you need at your fingertips and points you're going to cover. Have it in front of you every time you make a call for an appointment. Customize it to include all necessary information at each step: name of referrer, success stories, specific results and benefits achieved, target time for an appointment, etc.

CONCLUSION

In this chapter, we've explored the four key concepts for networking and prospecting in the new world of business. As in the past, prospecting is still your most important activity, and we described many of the traditional approaches to prospecting that may be useful. One thing has changed, however. The old watering holes just ain't what they used to be. You're no longer going to get much accomplished hanging around business-after-hours cocktail parties and so-called networking social events. Instead, become the referral expert, helping current customers and others rely on you for getting them in touch with all the right people for all the products and services they need. Take a leadership role in achievement-oriented environments for your profession and your community, where you can meet the kinds of people with whom you'd like to form a partnership and strategic alliance. Send then referrals without expecting something in return, though it should come as no surprise that they'll want to get to know more about you and will be inclined to do business with you and send referrals your way. Most important of all, regularly send referrals to all your current customers. In addition, form a swap shop of business professionals in related but noncompeting industries that meets regularly to exchange leads.

Finally, use discussed strategies for getting through to prospects and an eight-step process to efficiently move you to the sole objective of the phone call: getting an appointment with a qualified prospect.

Chapter 5

The Professional Presentation: Making It Effective

Colleges and universities used to offer communication arts courses in sales communication in which students, as the sole activity of the course, would make two twenty-five-minute presentations during the semester. They did a twenty-five-minute "informative presentation," a twenty-five-minute "persuasive presentation," and they spent the rest of the time listening to classmates make *their* presentations. Courses such as this were still around as recently as the early 1980s. Although it seems somewhat hard to imagine, communications arts instructors were under the illusion that in sales, people stood up in front of a group and talked for twenty-five minutes, finishing up with something along the lines of, "Well, that's the end of my presentation. Since you don't seem to have any questions for me, I have one for you. Can I have your order?" As anyone who has ever endured a non-stop twenty-five-minute presentation knows, there were no questions because those few people still awake were fantasizing about something not remotely related to the matter at hand. Returning from daydream to earth, all the audience could say was, "Thank you so much. That was very interesting."

Sales professionals know that a sales presentation is not a presentation per se but an engaging dialogue with the prospect. As is true in all other aspects of selling, though, there are new and innovative ways of making the presentation more effective, and in this chapter we'll go through the five key concepts for making an effective presentation/demonstration. One thing is as true as ever. You must be thoroughly prepared, not only having all the facts and information, but also using technology to establish backup systems for everything. Then, control the environment and set the agenda, employing a sequence of questions to get prospects to talk and discover the truth for themselves.

CONCEPT 1: BE PREPARED

You have scheduled a face-to-face meeting with the prospect. Even after many years of sales experience, you feel just a little apprehension, with one or two butterflies in your stomach. But you have a sense of quiet confidence because you've done all you could do to get ready. You're fully prepared to give it your best shot. Or are you?

Every day of the year, salespeople go into meetings only to have something unanticipated go wrong. Often, there's nothing they could have done to prevent it. A bolt out of the blue has hit the prospect's company, and they're no longer in a position to act on the proposal. A new purchasing manager has just taken over and is shifting business to his brother-in-law. It happens. Random probabilities guarantee that a certain proportion of the time you don't get the sale, despite your best efforts, and that's just part of the game which, as long as you can maintain your sense of humor, makes sales fun. Sometimes, though, things don't work out because, quite simply, the salesperson was not properly prepared, and there is absolutely no excuse for that.

Point 1: Set Goals for the Sales Call

Incredibly, salespeople actually go into sales calls without setting objectives, apparently thinking they'll just see what evolves and try to make the most of it. Such an approach virtually guarantees failure or, at best, a less-than-optimal outcome. Decide in advance exactly what you want to achieve on the call, and also have a secondary fallback position if the primary objective proves unattainable. Traditionally, that would mean something such as the primary objective of a sale of 200 units in all four of their offices; the secondary fallback a trial of fifty units in one of their offices. As we've discussed, however, if your ultimate objective is the development of a partnership, the objective for this call might not be the confirmation of an order but the agreement to move to the next step of the relationship. Thus, the primary objective might be an agreement to undertake a feasibility study to explore opportunities for the respective organizations to work together; the secondary fallback could be to convene a team that would be charged with determining the parameters and timetable for such a study.

Point 2: Procure All Necessary Information

We've described how technology makes it easier to obtain all the information available and have it at your fingertips. In addition, be a back-door rep and learn everything you can about the prospect's relationships with your competition, not just who they are but how satisfied the prospect has been with their products and services. What does the prospect like most and like least, and what kinds of good and bad experiences has he or she had? If there is a contractual relationship, when does it expire, and is there a penalty for premature termination? The answer to *that* question might tell you, before you invest any more time, that the prospect is not qualified at this time.

Become familiar with the prospect's buying and bidding procedures and whether he or she practices reciprocity and barter, which we'll discuss in Chapter 8. Know the names and roles of all buying influences, and details of any technical evaluation criteria.

Finally, prepare the presentation itself, employing some of the considerations we'll describe in this chapter, and get a coach to help you plan your overall strategy and specific tactics.

Point 3: Build in Backup with Online Storage

Everyone is occasionally subjected to four very irritating words: "The computers are down." It's especially annoying, and absolutely inexcusable, when we've phoned in to a business, spent twenty minutes listening to a recorded message tell us that all available representatives are busy at the moment, only to finally reach a human who says those four words and apologizes for being unable to help us. Understandably, we are frustrated and angry, wondering why on earth this business couldn't have at the least changed the opening recorded message to inform us of the situation so we could have hung up and called back later.

There may not be much we can do about it when someone's server, or our server, is down, but let's consider a related situation. You're on the road with all your information and your PowerPoint presentation contained in your PDA and/or your laptop and they're lost or stolen. Or, say your laptop just ups and crashes. You're 100 miles from the office and you have an appointment to make that presentation in ninety minutes. What are you going to do? Tell the prospect your computer is down? Or lost or stolen? Not acceptable.

After the World Trade Center bombing in 1993, enlightened companies understood the need for redundant computer systems. When those buildings were destroyed by the 2001 terrorist attacks, despite horrendous losses of life and property most tenants retained continuity in their operations since all records were intact. It's no different for a small business in Oklahoma that might be subject to flood or tornadoes. And it's no different for you on the road. Redundancy and backup are not luxuries, they're a necessity. And especially for sales professionals and smaller companies, the solution is online storage.

Simply put, online storage, or virtual storage, is a Web site you rent to store files on, and whereas many service providers don't provide twenty-four-hour-a-day access to their networks, with online storage you have access at all times. Let's say, for example, that your computer is stolen. All you need to do is buy or rent a new computer, download the presentation and files you backed up onto your online storage site, and you're back in business. Many hotels have rentals available or can lend you a computer for your presentation.

If your marketing staff is revising a presentation and proposal while you're on the road, you can simply download it when you get to your hotel. This is a lot more convenient than having them overnight a disk, plus you won't have to worry about that disk being crushed en route. And whereas e-mail often has file attachment size restrictions, online storage offers almost unlimited space and few compatibility problems among varying disks and drives.

Companies can store entire libraries of product literature, brochures, and other materials online, providing access for employees, prospects, and customers from any Internet connection, twenty-four hours a day. You can even access these files wirelessly from your PDA. Passwords enable you to restrict access and maintain confidentiality, so you can store proprietary files and presentations at the site. Therefore, if an important principal was unable to attend a presentation, you can post it online and give that person the attendant URL.

Consistent with other services we've noted, online storage is an excellent value at around $350 a year for a gigabyte of space. These services may be available through your Web host or independent suppliers. The following are a few of the leading companies in the field:

bigVAULT: <www.bigvault.com>
IBackup: <www.ibackup.com>
i-drive: <www.idrive.com>
My Docs Online: <www.mydocsonline.com>

Point 4: Check Out All Equipment and the Room

We don't want to turn this into a horror story, but some sales presentations turn into, well, horror stories. Many of these can be averted with proper planning.

Let's start with equipment. If you're going to utilize the prospect's computer to show your presentation on the Web, do your homework to be sure that everything is compatible. We said in the previous section that with online storage there were few compatibility problems. That does not mean there are *no* compatibility problems. You could run across glitches such as bandwidth considerations which preclude data retrieval. Check things out in advance.

If you're making a multimedia presentation to a large group, make sure you have a color LCD projector of high power and hook up the stereo sound. Be sure to carry spare bulbs for all equipment including the overhead projector, LCD projector, and the lamp on the podium. If there is any equipment for which you don't have a spare bulb, make sure you have printed backup in case of failure. Or, in the case of the podium lamp, always carry a flashlight. Know the limitations of your equipment. If you have an older laptop with a blurry screen, don't even think of trying to run video through it.

Check out the lighting of the room to be sure that it's adequate and, if necessary, can be dimmed. Be sure you have power outlets where you need them. If you don't, bring extension cords and duct tape them to the floor.

Most sales presentations will take place at the prospect's place of business, in an office, boardroom, or meeting room. Occasionally, however, you'll meet at a hotel, conference center, or other outside location. Let's cover a few additional points about these.

Always check out the meeting room in advance. We don't just mean the night before the meeting, either. You or a person you can rely on should thoroughly scope out the proposed meeting location before contracting for it in the first place. You're simply up the creek without a paddle if you show up the night before and find the room is far too big, far too small, won't be quiet because of building repairs or the fact that there's only a curtain between you and a meeting next door, or there's no curtain at all covering glass doors overlooking the swimming pool. Given the choice of your PowerPoint or checking out the pool, what do you thing your prospects will be watching?

Double-check all meal and beverage services the night before *and* very early the day of the meeting. Confirm everything with management *and* catering itself, since there is almost always miscommunication with one, the other, or both. Negotiate for the right to give them final numbers the day of the event. If, for example, you contract lunch for twelve, they will bill you for twelve even if just ten show up. Instead, contract for an anticipated number of twelve with the stipulation that you'll give them a final number by, say, 9:00 a.m. Then, if you have only ten there, you pay for only ten.

Most facilities will not permit you to bring in your own food and beverages, but it doesn't hurt to ask. You can save a lot of money by bringing in your own doughnuts in the morning and having an outside delivery of pizza or Chinese for lunch. Just don't be penny-wise and pound-foolish. If it adds the right touch of class to be served lunch in the dining room, pay the money.

Do save a few bucks on the ancillaries such as pencils and paper. The facility will charge for these, so bring your own. Not only will you save a little, but you can give out your own pencils and paper, with your name and advertising message on them. Or take it one step further: your name *and* the prospect's name on them. That's class.

A couple of quickies on timing. Never, for any reason, dim the lights right after lunch, even to show a bells-and-whistles, shoot-'em-up-bang-bang action video. You know why. When the lights go back on, half the audience will be asleep. Instead, first thing after lunch, give everyone something to do that gets them up, moving around, and interacting with one another. Likewise, do not even think of conducting any serious business, let alone an overnight assignment, after cocktail hour. The first drink, the only one that counts, is the end of productive activity for the day. If you must address an audience after cocktail hour, limit it to three minutes. Tell a joke or two and, with voice rising to a crescendo, let them know you think they're the greatest. Then quickly retreat to avoid any thrown dinner rolls. Do not use this as an occasion to remind them that business is tanking and soon you may all be out of work.

CONCEPT 2: SET THE AGENDA

In any selling situation, social or professional, you are consciously attempting to achieve your objectives by persuading others to act in a manner conducive to the attainment of those objectives. This does not mean that you are an evil person manipulating others, which is not a productive approach to building partnerships or generating repeat business and referrals. It does imply, however, that you are taking control of the environment, guiding events toward the outcome you're looking for. It's confidence and an appropriate level of assertiveness, but not being overly aggressive and pushy. It always has you focused on the best interest of customers, collaborators, and all others in your network. Consistent with that, you need to take command of events in a proactive manner. All that started with the call or personal contact in which you asked for and got a face-to-face appointment. Now, you take it to the next level as you meet with the prospect in person. The first thing to do is put yourself at the center of the process, and set the agenda.

We suggest that you go into the selling presentation with a different mind-set, not just thinking about how you can close the sale but seeking ways to position yourself as the person who will lead prospects in the process of making decisions that are in their self-interest. As long as you're at the center of that process, you and the prospects are going to do business together. The only question is defining the parameters and negotiating terms and conditions. That's the good news and the easy part. Now here's the bad news and the hard part. This approach to the sales call means that your presentation might not get you a close on the first meeting, and the presentation itself may extend over weeks and months. It can be tough keeping the process in focus over a protracted period, and it is easy to lose sight of your objectives. Discussions can get off track and wander aimlessly unless you remain alert about exactly where you are now and where you're directing the course of events. Think of it as a cross-country drive. Sure, it can be a long and tedious drive across Kansas, but you're always aware that your ultimate objective is San Francisco and you're not going to get distracted and take a turn toward Santa Fe. And remember our analogy about courtship and a long-term relationship. This marriage isn't going to be consummated until you really get to know each other and feel comfortable being together, communicating openly.

It has been said that opposites attract, but in professional partnerships it's more likely that similar persons and organizations will make the best fit. We are not talking about diversity here and, in fact, there are benefits to forming a strategic alliance with an individual or company that is socially and culturally diverse since they contribute knowledge and understanding of people and marketing opportunities you might otherwise lack the expertise to address. We *are* talking about allying yourself with people and companies with whom you share similar values within the framework of a similar organizational culture. Everyone talks a good game about this sort of thing, so it's up to you to take some time to get to know them and determine whether they really walk the talk. Likewise, they're going to need some time to make the same assessment of you. Depending on the situation, this could take several meetings with people not familiar with you before you contacted them. More time will be needed for a purely cold call, perhaps a little less when referred by someone who has a high level of credibility with the prospect. But don't automatically expect to jump right into things even with people from your network. They may recognize you as a professional person in an achievement-oriented environment. You may have even sent a referral or two their way. But now you're taking this relationship to a whole new level. Expect them to have some apprehension.

Perhaps we should clarify a few points to be sure that the subtleties of our new approaches to prospecting and networking have not been lost on you. Yes, you have become actively involved in professional and community organizations. Yes, you have become the referral expert, sending business to customers and prospects and helping them obtain the products and services they need. These and other gestures are thoughtful and, in general, will be appreciated. But make no mistake about it: You are not doing this out of a sense of altruism. You are doing it as part of a strategy to help you attain your objectives by meeting with qualified decision makers and persuading them to buy your products and services. You are consciously attempting to get the money out of their pockets and into yours. We trust you know that. The person you're meeting with most certainly knows that. And since you're going to be selling your products and services at a price higher than the lowest-price competitor, you're going to have to sell the value you personally bring to the transaction. This may take some time.

In addition, many or most of the prospects you call on will not become formal partners and join your swap shop. Your relationship may be limited to providing products, services, and follow-up that provide them with important benefits well worth the money. You're a competent professional they like doing business with, but, though your relationship is more than a one-night stand, there are no chances of it leading to marriage. It's a good friendship, and that's fine. In fact, most people have more colleagues with whom they're friends than to whom they're married. In these situations, you need not be as concerned about the compatibility of culture, though you will need to demonstrate that you understand them, their needs, and how they do business.

What we're leading to with all this is to point out that every sales call is different. Every buyer is different. Every buying organization is different. We will address the sales call step by step, but you must adapt this to each unique situation and modify it so you are personally comfortable with it.

As you set the agenda, take control of the environment, and move through the sales presentation, you must be sure you've covered each point adequately but not lingered on it too long. Help the prospects buy the way they like to buy, and make them comfortable with the process. An example of this, which you do at the very opening, is establishing rapport. You spend a lot more time socializing and rapport building with an amiable than with an analytic. With an amiable, if you cut him or her off after only two minutes of looking at baby pictures, he or she hasn't made the necessary bond with you. By contract, if you babble on about football for two minutes with an analytic, he or she perceives you as wasting time and will tune you out.

Once rapport has been established, formally set the agenda, clarifying why you're all there and what the meeting is all about. Remind the prospect why he or she gave you the appointment in the first place: "When we spoke on the phone, you said that you might want to learn more about online storage if it could eliminate compatibility problems with your field sales reps."

Outline the process and formalize the agenda.

First, I'm going to ask you some questions about your company and its operations. Then, I'll tell you a little about us and our services. Finally, we'll decide whether there's a reason for us to continue our discussions about possibly working together. Does that sound all right to you?

That last question is the key because you should always get a "Yes," granting you permission to proceed into the sales presentation. Should you get a "No" or a "Well, not exactly," a red flag should go up. You didn't do your job with the phone call requesting the appointment, or you're a day off on your calendar.

Given a yes, proceed to ask questions about the prospect's culture and values. As we noted, this is less important for a friendship than for a marriage, and it's predictable that the person will tell you how committed he or she is to his or her customers, animals, and the environment. But if you get the person to talk, and you listen, he or she might give you insights about how he or she does business, insights that will be important later in the presentation as you formulate feature-benefit statements. One thing that's predictable is that he or she will say that he or she has a commitment to customer service. Later in the presentation, you will bring that up in discussing and demonstrating *your* company's customer service. That's important, since even companies that aren't 100 percent as good as you are with customer service still want to rely on others to provide it to *them*. And you can make a casual lead-in with something along the lines of, "You were mentioning customer service. Let me tell you a little about what you can expect from us." Naturally, if you're contemplating marriage and not just friendship, you'll thoroughly investigate the person's reputation for customer service before even considering offering an engagement ring.

CONCEPT 3: DON'T PRESENT TO PROSPECTS— GET THEM TO PRESENT TO YOU

Once you've established rapport, talked with the prospects about their company and how they do business, outlined the process, and confirmed the agenda, you're into the presentation. This is not a sudden and dramatic shift. You do *not* say, "Well, get a load of this," and move into your spiel. In fact, if you do it properly, prospects will never even perceive that the presentation has begun. Although you are consciously moving into Step 1 of the presentation, from the prospects' perspectives you are simply continuing with an orderly sequence of questions. *You* know, however, that you have shifted away from general inquiries about their company and its operations, and have shifted to specific discussions about the products or services you hope to sell them.

We will outline all the steps of the sales presentation in detail, but first, let's lay the foundation. For starters, maybe we shouldn't talk about a sales "presentation" at all since it should be more of a sales *interview*. Just as a television host controls the interview and guides the guest, so should you control the dialogue with prospects. This is difficult to do if you put the focus on yourself and tell them things. It's easy to do if you remember that the sales call and the sales interview are all about the prospects. Put the focus on them and ask questions that enable them to discover the truth for themselves.

You are going to learn a "canned," scripted sales presentation, and yes, we know you just cringed when you read that. Let's explain what we mean. No, you're not going to read anything to anyone, and you're not even going to work off an outline in front of you as in the phone call. Yes, you will have everything so perfectly internalized and memorized that you can respond verbatim to any cue. We're going to provide the framework with the ten steps of the sales presentation. You, then, will need to do two things:

1. Compile and know absolutely everything you need to have at your fingertips at every step.
2. When you're in front of a prospect, be aware of which step you're at, and be sure to cover every little detail which must be covered at that step. When completed, move to the next step.

Handled properly, this should move you smoothly to the close and negotiation of terms and conditions. Remember, though, that all this might take ten minutes or four meetings or more, depending on the complexity of the transaction and the implications for a partnership relationship.

Previously, we discussed multitasking, simultaneously performing two or more activities. In most selling situations, your sales presentation is another example of multitasking. No, this will not be the case in a simple transaction such as the purchase of a refrigerator at an appliance store. There you would move through most of the ten steps in a matter of a few minutes, concluding with a closing question to finalize arrangements. For a more complex selling situation, however, there are potentially a very large number of points to address in defining and formalizing your business relationship, requiring you to go through the ten steps on each point. Instead of selling them a refrigerator, you are selling them on potentially dozens of parameters that will ultimately define your agreement. Generally, you will move them through the respective steps more or less concurrently. That is to say, if, for example, there were twenty parameters to your proposal, you would tend to initially have all twenty in the early steps, progress to having all twenty in the middle steps, and then proceed to move all twenty toward the latter steps and an agreement. You do not take each parameter and move it through the ten steps separately and independently. That's called "piecemealing" and is a negotiation no-no (see Chapter 8).

Not to get ahead of ourselves, but also in Chapter 8, we'll address the concept of constantly searching for variables that can provide points of agreement in a negotiation. As you progress toward finalizing terms and conditions, when all parameters currently on the table are in the latter steps of their respective sales presentations, it's likely that the respective parties will unearth a variable that can be injected into the proposal as a new parameter in the agreement. In such a case, the presentation on this parameter is at Step 1, whereas discussions on other parameters are at Steps, 8, 9, or 10.

You've likely already sensed that our approach to the "sales presentation" is fundamentally different from the traditional "pitch," especially as we describe twenty "presentations" going on concurrently. It *is* different, with you multitasking numerous dialogues on a wide variety of points. You are fully aware, however, of which step you're at on each and every one of those points as you move the discussion toward its conclusion, when you tie the whole package together, finalizing agreement on all terms and conditions. To the prospect, all of this is a back-and-forth dialogue in which he or she discovers the truth and decides to become involved with you in a business relationship. As the consummate professional salesperson, you help him or her to buy.

All that said, let's look at this innovative approach to the sales presentation, step by step.

Step 1: Ask Closed-Ended Questions to Get Facts and Information

Closed-ended questions are used to get specific responses addressing factual points of information. This is the starting point, where you get prospects talking about every aspect of their current situation. In many situations, particularly with prospects who are potential partners in a strategic alliance, you've done extensive research before the meeting and already know the answers to most of the questions you pose. It's similar to a lawyer asking questions of a defendant on the stand, in which it's often said that the attorney never asks a questions to which he or she doesn't already know the answer. In a trial, the question is not asked for the purpose of providing information for the attorney, but for the edification of the judge and jury. In a selling situation, such questions are not asked to enlighten the professional salesperson, but to help the prospects become engaged in the process of thinking about their current situation and opening them up to considering the possibility that it might be to their advantage to do things differently, namely doing business with you.

To illustrate these steps, we'll walk through the process with three very different examples: selling a refrigerator in a retail store, a pharmaceutical sales rep presenting a new drug to a doctor, and a representative of a company specializing in the outsourcing of professional services, in this case the payroll function in a presentation to the owner of a small business.

Refrigerator

> "What kind of refrigerator do you have now?" (If the answer to this is "We don't have one," we trust you have sense enough to skip down to asking questions about their family, their needs, and which benefits would be important to them, then going directly to Step 7 with a summary and paraphrase.)
> "How long have you owned it?"
> "How large is it? What color?"
> "How large is the freezer compartment?"
> "Does it have an ice maker?"
> "How many people are in your family?"

Pharmaceutical Rep

"Do you have any patients who suffer from acid reflux? How
many? What ages, men/women?"

"What are you currently prescribing to them? In what dosage?
Taken how often?"

"What other health-related problems are these patients experiencing? How are you treating them?"

Payroll Services

"How many employees do you have? How has this changed
from a year ago? How many do you anticipate having a year
from now?"

"How do you do payroll now? Who does what and at what salary, including benefits?"

"How many forms and reports do you prepare? How long does it
take to get them done?"

"How do you handle reporting requirements of the IRS [Internal
Revenue Service]? Have you ever been audited? What happened?"

In the simplest case, the refrigerator, you probably had no information about the prospects before they walked in the door, so you're asking what they have now and getting information about their families
to get an idea of their needs and what features and benefits might be
important to them. The fact that they came into the store implies that
they are amenable to making a purchase. In this single-task presentation, your objective is straightforward. You should guide them through
the presentation and convince them they get a better value, though not
necessarily a better price, from you than at the store down the street.

The pharmaceutical rep is also getting information, though in this
scenario he or she may have already known many or most of the facts
in advance. This situation is considerably more complex. The rep
must ascertain which patients might be viable candidates for the drug,
and whether other health-related issues might affect a recommenda-
tion or open the doors to another product the firm markets. Perhaps
most important of all, the doctor is presently prescribing a competi-

tor's product and may have a business relationship with the competitor's rep.

The situation with the payroll services rep is most complex of all, and typical of those meetings we've described in which the objective of the call is not merely a sale but the proposal of a partnership relationship. Here, the rep will propose a major upheaval in the way the prospect conducts his or her payroll function, shifting from conducting it internally to outsourcing it to a specialist. The presentation will be a multitask dialogue that will explore numerous service options to customize a package for the prospect's unique needs. In this example, the rep is proposing to become an ongoing partner who will play a critical role in the prospect's business, so much more time will be required to develop a trust-based relationship.

Once you have all the information you need to get on the table for a given line of dialogue, move on to Step 2.

Step 2: Ask an Open-Ended Question to Find Out How They Feel About What They're Doing Now

Open-ended questions are not seeking specific information but instead invite the prospect to respond as he or she sees fit. The question asked would be similar in all three scenarios.

"How do you like what you've got/what you're doing now?"
"How's it done for you?"
"Overall, how do you feel what you're doing now is working for you?"

Only in a straightforward transaction situation, such as with the refrigerator, will this elicit a response indicating a dissatisfaction with the present product or service. That's precisely why the prospect walked into the store in the first place. It's too big, it's too small, it's the wrong color, it doesn't have an ice maker, or the old one just went beat. Again in this situation, since the prospect is sending out buying signals, go straight into needs and benefits and the summary/paraphrase of Step 7.

In many straightforward transactions, though, prospects will tell you they're essentially satisfied with what they have or what they're doing now. Of course, you know better. If they really were satisfied, they wouldn't be there in the first place. But simply nod to acknowledge their statement before moving into Step 3.

With the pharmaceutical rep or payroll services outsourcer, though, Step 2 is virtually guaranteed to get a response along the lines of "Great. Everything's fine." Of course that's what the prospect will say! To state, "I'm really not all that satisfied," is tantamount to saying, "I'm an idiot because I haven't done anything about it." And that's all right. No professional salesperson says or implies that the prospect is wrong, because that will only succeed in making the prospect get defensive and be *less* likely to change.

Remember that your objective is to help prospects discover the truth for themselves, then help them to buy. That's the process you initiate in Steps 1 and 2. You put the focus on the prospects, getting them to talk about themselves and what they do. Then, you let them tell you they're happy and doing fine. You're in no way applying high-pressure tactics, and the prospects are comfortable. You build rapport and establish a positive flow of interpersonal communication, which continues as you move into Step 3.

Step 3: Ask Closed-Ended Questions to Identify Important Features and Benefits

Your strategy in Step 3 is similar for each of the scenarios. Again, put the focus on the prospects and get them talking about all the specifics of why what they're doing now is so great. And keep them talking. At first, you might think that would be detrimental to your objective of persuading them to do business with you, since after a few minutes of telling you these specifics and why they're so happy, they might reinforce their feeling of satisfaction and be disinclined to change anything. But encourage them to keep talking. Listen! They're telling you all the needs, features, and benefits you'll want to address later in the presentation.

Refrigerator

SALES REP: What do you like most about the refrigerator you have now?

PROSPECT: The freezer's on the bottom. I love having the freezer on the bottom.

SALES REP: Anything else you really like about it?

PROSPECT: The kids love the ice maker.

SALES REP: Any other things that you've enjoyed?

PROSPECT: Well, it keeps the food cold most of the time.

Pharmaceutical Rep

SALES REP: What do you like most about what you're prescribing now?

PROSPECT: Efficacy. I know it works.

SALES REP: Any other reason you like it?

PROSPECT: No problems with upset stomach. Never had a patient experience upset stomach, as with with some other drugs for acid reflux.

SALES REP: Anything else?

PROSPECT: Doesn't interact with other drugs. None. Nada.

Payroll Services

SALES REP: What do you like most about your current payroll system?

PROSPECT: We can design all the forms and reports. Whatever we need them to give us, we can get.

SALES REP: Anything else it does well for you?

PROSPECT: They handle problems. If something's wrong with an employee's paycheck—and it happens—they know who to contact.

SALES REP: Other reasons you like it?

PROSPECT: We've been doing it this way for twenty years. If it ain't broke, don't fix it.

Keep the conversation going until you have the complete and comprehensive list of everything they're getting now in essential features and need-satisfying benefits. Remain alert. Often a statement of satisfaction holds the seeds of an unmet need or dissatisfaction. For example, the statement that the refrigerator keeps the food cold most of the time suggests it does not keep it cold *all* the time. And the comment that they've been doing payroll the same way for twenty years suggests that their system may be antiquated and grossly inefficient.

Step 4: Uncover an Unmet Need or Dissatisfaction

This is absolutely critical. If you can't identify some unmet need or dissatisfaction with what they have or are doing now, you are dead in the water. They have no reason to change. At the very least, you must be able to demonstrate that you can do the same thing cheaper, but as we've discussed, there's not a lot of money to be made in trying to market the same thing for less.

There are three stages of probing questions to uncover an unmet need or dissatisfaction. First, simply ask whether there is anything they would like to see altered or improved in their present product or service. If that is unsuccessful, raise the intensity of the question by asking, "If there was one thing you could change, what would it be?" Finally, if nothing has been identified, directly point out a disadvantage of the competitor's offering or the way things are being done now.

Should you need to directly point out a disadvantage, be sure to do so properly. Never be perceived as bad-mouthing the competition or telling prospects they are wrong. You achieve that objective by phrasing your point as a question rather than a statement.

- Don't say: "Those engines burn out if you run them hard for twelve hours."
- Instead, say: "Some of our customers who formerly used those engines have told us they burned out if run hard for twelve hours. Has that been your experience?"

- Don't say: "It would take your computer thirty minutes to download that file."
- Instead, say: "I've heard that model is slower than some of the new ones. How long does it take to download a file like that?"

- Don't say: "That compressor leaks Freon."
- Instead, say: "Have you had any problems with Freon leakage?"

Approach this crucial step in an easygoing and informal manner, taking your time and helping the prospect begin to realize that perhaps he or she really *isn't* all that satisfied after all. Let's look at our examples.

Refrigerator

SALES REP: Is there anything you'd like to see altered or improved in your present refrigerator?

PROSPECT: Oh, it could be a little bigger. We have three kids now.

SALES REP: Anything else?

PROSPECT: I wish they didn't keep the door open so long when they get ice.

Pharmaceutical Rep

SALES REP: Is there anything you'd like to see altered or improved in the medication you're prescribing now?

PROSPECT: Nothing I can think of.

SALES REP: If there was one thing you could change about it, what would that be?

PROSPECT: Oh, maybe side effects on blood pressure.

SALES REP: Blood pressure . . .

PROSPECT: It can tick it up ten or twelve points in older patients.

Payroll Services

SALES REP: Is there anything you'd like to see altered or improved about your present payroll system?

PROSPECT: No, I'd say it was doing okay.

SALES REP: If there was one thing you could change about it, what would that be?

PROSPECT: Like I said, we've been doing it this way for twenty years. I think we have all the bugs out of it by now.

SALES REP: Many people I've talked to in companies similar to yours have told me it takes between twelve and twenty hours every week to prepare all required paperwork for the IRS. Has that been your experience?

PROSPECT: Sounds about right.

Notice that with the refrigerator, the nature of the selling situation is such that the prospect is already inclined to buy. Thus, all the sales

rep needs to do is get the prospect to talk about needs and buying motives. Initially, the rep encouraged the prospect to talk about important features and benefits in his or her present refrigerator. Now, the
rep is helping the propect describe features and benefits he or she
doesn't have now but would like to have. In this most basic scenario,
the rep listens carefully to determine which models will best suit the
prospect's needs. He or she will then help the prospect make the specific buying decision, and finalize the terms and conditions. This is an
example of efficient order taking.

The pharmaceutical scenario is more complex, since the rep must
convince the prospect to switch from a competitive product. To do
this, the rep must be careful not to imply that the prospect's current
choice is wrong. Rather, he or she must help the prospect discover
that an alternative might be better. It's not an oxymoron to say that
you still accentuate the positive, even when pointing out a competitive disadvantage. In this case, the rep had to go to the second stage of
probing by asking about whether there was one thing that might be
changed. Notice, then, in response to the prospect's statement identifying an issue about blood pressure, the rep employed the echo technique, saying, "Blood pressure . . ." The echo technique encourages
the prospect to continue talking and be more explicit about the disadvantage. In lieu of the echo technique, the rep could have inquired
directly, "What kinds of side effects have you had?"

The situation with payroll services, the most complex, necessitated
that the rep go all the way to the third stage of probing since the prospect has no awareness that there's anything wrong with the way things
have always been done. Here, too, notice the phrasing. The rep talks
about situations in similar companies, acting as a consultant and
helper, encouraging the prospect to confirm that the circumstances are
similar. Of course, as with the good attorney, the sales rep knows the
answer to the question before asking it and also knows that such a system is grossly inefficient, but will help the prospect discover that truth.

Step 5: Get the Prospect to Spell Out the Specific
Negative Consequences of the Unmet Need
or Dissatisfaction

When we began the dialogue, the prospect said that he or she was
basically satisfied with the current situation, but now we've uncovered an unmet need or dissatisfaction. Keep the prospect talking, de-

scribing how that's affected him or her. This is elementary with the refrigerator, where we are just obtaining information we'll paraphrase in Step 7. We pick up where we left off.

Refrigerator

PROSPECT: I wish they didn't leave the door open so long when they get ice.

SALES REP: Does that happen often?

PROSPECT: At least six times a day.

SALES REP: How does that affect you?

PROSPECT: By the end of the day, everything in the freezer has thawed out.

Pharmaceutical Rep

PROSPECT: It can tick it up ten or twelve points in older patients.

SALES REP: Has that ever been a problem?

PROSPECT: For patients with high blood pressure.

SALES REP: What do you do for them?

PROSPECT: Watch it carefully, and maybe modify their blood pressure medication. I don't want to raise their risk of stroke.

Payroll Services

PROSPECT: Sounds about right.

SALES REP: How much does every hour cost you, including benefits?

PROSPECT: Oh, I'd say about twenty bucks.

SALES REP: So, it's costing you two hundred forty to four hundred dollars a week just for IRS paperwork . . .

PROSPECT: That's the cost of doing business.

SALES REP: Accuracy pretty good?

PROSPECT: Pretty good. Some weeks are better than others.

At this point, you might be feeling fairly confident, having uncovered an unmet need or dissatisfaction and getting the prospect to specify an attendant consequence. It might seem reasonable to move into the formal presentation right about now, since you have plenty of ammunition for feature-benefit statements. But not so fast. The prospect is talking about negative consequences of his or her present product or service, convincing himself or herself that maybe it's time to consider an alternative. Why cut him or her off now? Go to Step 6 to keep the prospect talking.

Step 6: Use a Turn-Denying Regulator and Invite the Prospect to Continue Talking

A turn-denying regulator may be a nonverbal cue such as a nod or the raising of eyebrows, a "hmm," a simple phrase, or use of the echo technique that shows the prospect you are declining to speak and would be interested to hear him or her further discuss the consequences of his or her unmet needs or dissatisfaction.

Refrigerator

PROSPECT: By the end of the day, everything in the freezer has thawed out.
SALES REP: It has?
PROSPECT: Yes, I had to throw away five pounds of hamburger last week.
SALES REP: Five pounds?
PROSPECT: Thaw it and refreeze it every day for a week, it goes bad.

Pharmaceutical Rep

PROSPECT: I don't want to raise their risk of stroke.
SALES REP: No, of course not.
PROSPECT: One lady's ninety-five.
SALES REP: Is she really?
PROSPECT: I have to monitor her carefully.

Payroll Services

PROSPECT: Pretty good. Some weeks are better than others.
SALES REP: How so?
PROSPECT: People are human. We all make mistakes every once in a while.

SALES REP: [nodding] Hmm . . .
PROSPECT: But the IRS has zero tolerance for mistakes.

Keep the prospect talking until you feel confident that you have the complete picture of all the features and benefits that are important to him or her, you've identified some unmet need or dissatisfaction, and you have had the prospect elaborate on its consequences. Now the prospect has begun to realize that maybe he or she really isn't all that satisfied with what he or she has now, and might be amenable to a change. In the fundamental scenario of the refrigerator, you had a good idea of what the prospect was looking for soon after he or she walked in the door. You might think now is the time to get into the formal presentation and start the feature-benefit thing. Well, almost but not quite. There's still one more thing you need to do first, Step 7, and that is to get the prospect to confirm that he or she *wants* you to make the presentation. It's a very important initial "Yes" in a series of little agreements that will ultimately lead to an affirmative buying decision. In this step, you confirm agreement on the benefits the prospect is seeking as a prelude to the formal presentation, when you will demonstrate how you can provide those benefits. But again, don't tell the prospect. If you tell him or her, the prospect may still doubt you. Do this in the form of a question, and get *the prospect* to say it. Then it has to be true.

Step 7: Paraphrase the Prospect and Confirm Benefits

Restate to the prospect what he or she has stated are the current benefits as well as the unmet needs or dissatisfactions. Phrase this as a question by using a tie-down to get a "Yes." "So from what you're telling me, you want a product or service that gives you this-and-such a benefit [which you're getting now] and that-and-such a benefit [which you're also getting now], but will also do this-and-such [which you're not getting now and I've helped you realize you wish you were], is that about right?" Since you're paraphrasing the prospect's statements to this point in the sales interview, this question gets an almost guaranteed "Yes" if you're playing it straight and not putting words in the prospect's mouth. Let's look at the examples.

Refrigerator

SALES REP: So, from what you're telling me, you want a large capacity refrigerator, with an ice maker, which has the freezer on the bottom. And you'd like to stop having your food thaw and refreeze all the time, is that about right?

PROSPECT: I'd say so.

Pharmaceutical Rep

SALES REP: Let me be sure I've got this right. You want an efficacious product that won't interact with other drugs and doesn't cause upset stomach. But you'd also like something without the side effect of raising blood pressure, is that it?

PROSPECT: That's about it.

Payroll Services

SALES REP: You're saying, then, that you need a system that you can customize to meet your needs, with a point of contact to quickly resolve problems, and you'd also like to reduce or eliminate errors in reports to the IRS, is that what you're telling me?

PROSPECT: You got it.

Now, and only now, do you get into the formal presentation. That's right! To this point, all you have done is to get the prospect to talk, confirming his or her needs and buying motives and helping him or her realize the need to act to address an unmet need or dissatisfaction. In Step 7, responding positively to your paraphrase/tie-down, the prospect indicated an interest in having you continue.

Step 8: Move into the Formal Presentation

As a prelude, make a prospect-focused statement stating that you have something to say that would be of interest to him or her. Then, do the feature-benefit review, personalizing the benefits to address the specific needs the prospect raised earlier in the sales interview. Conclude with a tie-down to confirm agreement.

Refrigerator

SALES REP: I believe this model is what you're looking for. It has a large capacity, which will give you all the room your family needs. The freezer is on the bottom, so you'll have the same convenience you're looking for. And also, its ice maker is on the door, so now your kids won't have to open the freezer to get ice. You'll have a lot less spoiled food, won't you?

PROSPECT: That's nice.

Pharmaceutical Rep

SALES REP: I think you'd be interested in these clinical trials. Take a look at this. Our drug provides comparable efficacy with no side effects or interactions. But its unique benefit is that it does not affect blood pressure. That would be very important for those older patients at risk for stroke, wouldn't it?

PROSPECT: Hmm . . .

Payroll Services

SALES REP: I have some ideas on how we can help you. Our payroll services offer flexibility, which means we can fit them to your specific needs. I'm the person who will be personally responsible for your account, so you can contact me directly to resolve any issues. And our system has been thoroughly tested, so you should never again have reporting problems with the IRS. But in the rare event that there were a problem, we would cover all costs and penalties to resolve it. You'll never again have to worry about reports to the IRS, will you?

PROSPECT: Guess not.

In the next segment, we'll touch on some considerations for enhancing the quality of your presentation. First, let's hit a few basics:

Point 1: Casually move along in a dialogue in which you continue to encourage the prospect to talk. During your conversation, it is entirely likely that new issues will arise, for which your presentation will revert to Step 1 on that point. As you multitask this process, perhaps over several meetings, move the discussion through all the steps on all the points until, as we will address in the remainder of the book, you achieve agreement in principle and finalize all terms and conditions.

Point 2: Give the prospect a part to play in the formal presentation, even if just looking at or holding something. Involve all of his or her senses. Just as you do in conversation, help the prospect discover the truth for himself or herself in the context of your formal presentation.

Point 3: Be aware of all needs and buying motives of every individual involved in the decision. Those individual needs may be different from, or in opposition to, the needs of the organization. We will discuss this in more detail in Chapter 6.

Point 4: Always be alert for closing cues or indications of agreement, and whenever you encounter them, ask a closing question, even if only a little decision point on a peripheral issue. We'll hit this in Chapter 7.

Point 5: Steadily progress toward tying the plethora of individual issues into a comprehensive agreement addressing all points, terms, and conditions. And, yes, we'll discuss that in Chapter 8.

The last two steps of the sales call get into closing and negotiation, which, as previously noted, we'll cover in Chapters 6, 7, and 8.

Step 9: If You Get an Affirmative Response to Step 8, Follow with a Closing Question

Refrigerator

SALES REP: You'll have a lot less spoiled food, won't you?

PROSPECT: That's nice.

SALES REP: It comes in a standard model or energy-saving model. The energy saver is only forty dollars more, and will save you that much every year in electricity. That's a pretty good investment, isn't it?

PROSPECT: Well worth it.

Pharmaceutical Rep

SALES REP: That would be very important for those older patients at risk for stroke, wouldn't it?

PROSPECT: Hmm . . .

SALES REP: How many patients do you have who might benefit from this?

PROSPECT: Three . . . no, four.

SALES REP: When will you be seeing them?

Payroll Services

SALES REP: You'll never again have to worry about reports to the IRS, will you?

PROSPECT: Guess not.

SALES REP: What kinds of reports do you need prepared on a regular basis?

Step 10: Confirm All Details, Terms, and Conditions

This is a no-brainer with the refrigerator. "When will you want it delivered? Right or left door handle? Cash, check, or charge?" It's a little more complex for the pharmaceutical rep, confirming which patients are candidates and when (not if) the physician will be seeing them and writing the prescription. It's still very early in the process for the payroll services rep, but there appears to be sufficient agreement in principle for the rep to proceed with assumptive statements about how (not whether) they can work together. To put the ten steps of the sales presentation to work for you, take a quick time-out for Action Plan Assignment #8.

Action Plan Assignment #8: Customize the Ten Steps

Now you can customize the ten steps for your specific selling situation. To prepare for every sales call you make, write out, in advance, the specific questions you will ask for each of the ten steps on all issues of inquiry in the call. If, for example, you must multitask the questioning sequence for three points of agreement, preplan and write out all ten steps for each of the three points. When you make the call, be sufficiently prepared on all steps for all points so that you will need, at most, a quick glance at your notes in the meeting.

CONCEPT 4: USE TECHNOLOGY
TO ENHANCE YOUR PERFORMANCE

No matter who you are or what you sell, technology can turn a good presentation into a professional performance. We trust that you already customize the title page of a proposal, but think how much sharper it would look if it included the prospect's logo. It's easy to do. Just go to the prospect's Web page, right click on the logo, and "save as" to your hard drive. Then insert the image into your Microsoft Word, WordPerfect, Publisher, or CorelDRAW file. It adds a nice touch of professionalism for just a little effort.

We've already described how technology enables you to obtain a huge amount of information about companies and individuals: annual reports, press releases, and newspaper articles. Yes, all that was helpful for identifying qualified prospects and preparing you for the call. In addition, integrate this information, as appropriate, into your proposal. It will convey the impression that you've done your homework and have customized your proposal to the prospects' unique situations and opportunities. Technology can also enhance the presentation itself, whether it be low tech, mid tech, or new tech.

Low Tech

Even if you present with a "pitchbook" (a three-ring binder with pictures, text, or other graphics), you know that having quality color materials is superior to black and white. The operative word here is "quality." Unfortunately, many salespeople have the color but not the quality. This is patently inexcusable now that high-quality color printing has become affordable for everyone. Quality color-inkjet printers now cost less than $200, and color laser printers are under $1,000. A little short of cash at the moment? Then run your proposal down to the local copy shop and have them run it off on their equipment for five or six bucks. It's inexcusable for poor quality documents to reach your customers and prospects. Do it right. It's a good investment.

Mid Tech

There have been numerous changes in computer-based face-to-face presentations. Notebooks are lighter with longer battery life and a crisper screen. PowerPoint lets you generate slide presentations that are inexpensive, easy to use, and reliable. Avoid getting so carried away with showmanship that you lose sight of your objective. You're there to sell something, not merely to provide the halftime entertainment. Use graphics in motion and sound effects if they add something to the presentation; delete them if they're just clutter. And please do not think you're the first one to incorporate the spinning dollar sign or the screeching car. We know of one prospect who has reached the point that he gets up and walks out of the room without saying a word if he sees either one of them in a presentation. Buck was in a meeting recently when the sales rep stopped the presentation for five minutes while he tried to get a sound effect to work, which completely destroyed the meeting's continuity. Care to guess whether that rep made a sale that day?

New Tech

Naturally, nothing beats a face-to-face presentation, but sometimes logistics get in the way. Maybe you need to make a multimedia presentation to sixty people in thirty markets simultaneously. Perhaps half a dozen members of a project team, each of them seated in front of their personal computers, need to study an architect's proposal. Or two managers, speaking on the phone, want to walk through a PowerPoint presentation. In these situations, the solution may be Web conferencing.

Don't confuse Web conferencing with Webcasting. Webcasting is merely the streaming of audio and video over the Internet, perhaps to a large audience, but with little or no interaction. Web conferencing, by contrast, is interactive in a wide variety of modes including online document sharing and annotation applications, though it is most often limited to an audio connection by telephone while simultaneously viewing a PowerPoint presentation on a computer screen. More sophisticated users can expand its applications to chat, polling, or whiteboarding. When time or cost constraints make person-to-person meetings impractical, Web conferencing can be a viable alternative, with the added benefit that presentations can be left on a site for future visits by persons wishing to review materials or whose schedule makes it more convenient to view them later. Virtual storage, which we described early in this chapter, makes this possibility practical and inexpensive.

Before launching a Web-conferencing program, be sure to double check to be sure that all participants are, literally, up to speed. Most major companies have the bandwidth (generally T1 and T3 lines) for a positive Web-conferencing experience, but if you're on a T1-connected computer and your prospect is dialing in at 56k, your full-motion video is garbage. Make sure you know what technology all participants are using and how they're connecting before you schedule the show. To learn more about Web conferencing and its many potential applications, check out the following sites:

Genesys Conferencing <www.genesys.com>
Netspoke Conferencing <www.netspoke.com>
Salestool <www.salestool.com>
Webex <www.webex.com>

CONCEPT 5: THE CLOSE
IS JUST THE BEGINNING, NOT THE END

When you finish the presentation and get the order, this is the beginning of your relationship with the prospect. You made promises to the prospect in order to get the sale. We trust you have written them down so you won't forget them. One thing is for sure: your prospect will remember them, especially at referral time or when speaking to 5,000 of his or her closest friends at the industry chat room. Do what you said you'd do, plus a little bit more.

CONCLUSION

In this chapter, we've looked at the five key concepts for making an effective presentation/demonstration, emphasizing that this is not synonymous with a stand-up oration in which you do all the talking. Just the opposite. Good presentations are similar to sales interviews in which the professional salesperson gets the prospect to talk, building agreement and helping him or her discover the truth for himself or herself. As you move through this process of building agreement, it's inevitable that there will be some objections and other impediments to deal with. Working through those obstacles, you'll look for closing cues, subtle indications that the prospect is predisposed to do business with you. You're getting toward the endgame, that moment of truth when you discover whether all your hard work will pay off.

Chapter 6

Objections Have Not Gone Out of Style: Dealing with Objections, Barriers, and Other Impediments

We hope that Chapter 5 opened your eyes to a new and innovative approach to the sales presentation: get prospects to talk, and help them discover the truth for themselves through an organized, preplanned sequence of questions. We suspect you may now be engaging in fantasies of rolling through the steps, reaching the crescendo when prospects jump out of their seats, embrace you, and shout "Yes! Yes! Yes!" Sorry, but it's not going to work out that way. Unless you're an order taker at the five-and-dime or Hamburger City, you're almost certainly going to encounter objections, stalls, or other barriers and impediments to your objectives. Indeed, objections have not gone out of style.

Professional salespeople might easily delude themselves into thinking that "objections is objections," believing that there isn't much difference to handling them today than in the past. Although it's true that many of the principles and techniques for handling objections remain applicable, subtle but very important changes have occurred in the new world of business. Just as in every other aspect of the selling process, this new world requires salespeople to go beyond the traditional approaches to overcome all those inevitable barriers to the sale.

In this chapter, you'll discover the four key concepts for dealing with objections, barriers, and other impediments, starting with that magic word again: listen. Get the prospect to talk about the objection and, as you listen carefully, determine what type of objection you're dealing with. In the new world of business, where your objective is to establish long-term strategic alliances as a consultant and helper, it's more important than ever to identify and manage the relationship-based visceral objections. Of course, you'll always get a price objection; in Concept 3, we'll describe how to answer that objection or any other content-based objection with questions that will not only get you past the barrier but nearer to the close. Finally, we'll remind you to get back on track after handling the objection, rejoining the ten-step sales presentation.

CONCEPT 1: LISTEN, ASK QUESTIONS, AND LISTEN SOME MORE

Let's get this up front. By now, we trust that you appreciate the importance of getting prospects to talk and listening to what they have to say. That's a basic skill of professional selling, one which every successful sales pro agrees on. So why is it that these same people *fail* to listen when they hear an objection? Too many otherwise successful salespeople completely undermine their sales presentation by responding prematurely to objections. Don't fall into that trap.

It's easy to stay focused on listening early in the sales presentation. At that point, you're concentrating on asking questions to get prospects to open up, guiding them through the ten steps toward agreement. With objections, though, prospects have moved outside the path you've paved for them and have popped up with something you hoped wouldn't happen, though deep down inside you knew would happen: they've given you a reason *not* to buy. Your natural instinct is to immediately respond. Wrong.

Objections are inevitable. You cannot ignore them or wish them away. If you are smoothly rolling through the ten steps getting nothing but polite nods or other implicit nonverbal cues of agreement, a red light should go on inside your head. Something is wrong. Nothing is that easy. Instead of starting to daydream about how you're going to spend your commission check, it might be a good time to pause and ask the prospects if there are any reasons why they might *not* be inclined to do business with you. Of course, when you directly open up that line of dialogue, you will probably hear loud cracks as the dam breaks and you are engulfed in a flood of objections. *Darn,* you might think, *I should have just continued on with my assumptive closes until it was time to pull out the order form.* But, in reality, you knew better all along. There are going to be objections, barriers, and other impediments to the sale. Better to have them out in the open instead of festering under the surface where they will ultimately be a fatal toxin to the sale. When they do come up, resist the temptation to respond right away. Get prospects to talk and elaborate on the objection.

Have the right attitude when prospects are giving you an objection. Sure, they're telling you why they don't want to do business with you. You're too expensive or you don't fit their needs. They're completely satisfied with what they're doing now. And it's easy to perceive that you're hearing things you don't want to hear. Adjust your attitude and modify your perspective. If you get prospects talking, you can uncover what they really do care about and what really does concern them. If your attitude is that the glass is half empty, all you hear is how inadequate your company and its products and services are. If you see the glass as half full, you're learning about what prospects will weigh in the buying decision and what their hot button is. You're loading up on ammunition that you'll target through feature-benefit statements later in your meeting.

When an objection surfaces, ask prospects to elaborate on the objection and seek out the reason behind the objection:

- "Why do you feel that way?"
- "How would that be a concern for your people?"
- "Is there anything in particular which makes you think that?"
- "What is it that has you see ABC company as a better source?"
- "Why do you think we wouldn't be as good?"
- "What makes them your first choice?"

Give prospects ample time to describe the objection in detail, and then paraphrase the objection to confirm understanding, in a manner similar to Step 7 of the sales presentation.

- *Example 1:* "From what you're telling me, then, you have no alternative other than to go with the low bid . . ."
- *Example 2:* "So, you're saying that XYZ company is better able to customize services to your unique needs. Would that be right?"
- *Example 3:* "Let me be sure I've got this right. You're concerned that our people might not be able to handle that sort of complex data application. Is that it?"

As in Step 7, a summary/paraphrase statement, followed by a tie-down to turn it into a question, confirmed agreement. By the way, note the alternative to a formal tie-down in the first example, where summarizing and pausing had the same effect. In dealing with objections, however, you would not now move directly to a feature-benefit statement. Instead, first neutralize the negativity of the objection with a disarming phrase to acknowledge prospects' concerns:

- *Example 1:* "I can appreciate that. Profits are tight. There's no reason to pay more than you have to, is there?"
- *Example 2:* "I see why that might concern you. If a system couldn't address your unique applications, it wouldn't be much better than what you're doing now."
- *Example 3:* "That's a good point. If we couldn't handle those, it might set you back several days."

Through a summary/paraphrase, followed by a disarming statement, you have communicated to prospects that you understand and appreciate their concerns. You've smoothed down the negative edges and eased into a productive dialogue. Now you can move on to classifying and answering the objection, as we'll describe later in the chapter. Just a few quick points before getting into that.

Point 1

Prepare for objections as part of your preparation before the call. Put yourself in the prospects' shoes and think about every reason why they might be disinclined to buy and every objection, barrier, and impediment they might put in your way. We know you hate having to think about all the possible horror stories you might run into, but why live in denial and hope they won't come up? You *know* they *will* come up, all or most of them. After more than three weeks on the job, you should be able to come up with at least 90 percent of the objections you'll come across, maybe more. Get your head out of the sand, figure out what they'll be, and prepare your response in advance. There will be no reason to be apprehensive about objections since you already know what your prospects are going to say and how you'll respond. You're way ahead of your prospects, who don't know what either one of you are going to say.

Point 2

You will also encounter objections when you are soliciting appointments by phone, but the situation is different. As you'll recall, the purpose of the phone call is solely to procure an appointment, never to get into your presentation. Therefore, when prospecting for appointments, close for the appointment whenever the prospect confirms any sort of agreement. In Chapter 4, we noted how you always close for the appointment whenever the prospect confirms a benefit, unmet need, or dissatisfaction. Let's add to that. Close for the appointment immediately after responding to an objection with a summary/paraphrase and disarming statement. Do *not* answer the objection, that's getting into the presentation. Going back to the scenario of Example 1:

> There's no reason to pay more than you have to, is there? (Whether prospect confirms agreement or remains silent, continue.) I have some ideas that would actually increase your productivity and save you eight percent. That would look nice on the bottom line, wouldn't it?

See where you are now? Right back to the point of closing for the appointment from Chapter 4. If prospects confirm the benefit, suggest a time for the appointment and shut up. If not, bring in the witness, probe for a benefit or unmet need, etc.

Point 3

There's an objection you'll almost always get when prospecting for appointments, one form or another of "I don't have time" or "I'm too busy" to talk to you. Expect and prepare for this objection by considering the difference between what prospects are saying and what they really mean. They are saying they're too busy and don't have time to see you, but what they really mean is, "I don't have time to waste talking to the fifty idiots who call me every day asking for an appointment. Convince me you're not an idiot and that I should take time to see you." Hit this objection up front.

- "I know you're busy. That's why we need to get together. I have some ideas that can save you time and make you money. We need twenty minutes. How's Tuesday morning at seven?"
- "I know you don't have any time to waste, and I'm not going to waste your time. This will take fifteen minutes, and I'll make those fifteen minutes worth your while. How does Wednesday morning at eight look for you?"
- "If you weren't busy, you wouldn't need me. I've got some ideas on how we might work together on a promotional program that can significantly increase your distribution. Twenty minutes max. What about Thursday morning at eight?"

Your primary objective is to procure an appointment that gives you enough time to accomplish the call's goals. However, a secondary fallback position might be merely to get prospects to agree to meet with you face to face. Period. Nothing more. Just get your foot in the door and make eye contact. And that can be done in ninety seconds.

We don't recommend you do this on your initial contact, but if you keep getting the "I'm too busy to see you" objection over a protracted period, it's worth a shot. Say, "I need ninety seconds of your time. No more. Just give me ninety seconds. I'll make it worth your while." And, of course, close for the appointment: "How about seven fifty-eight Wednesday morning?" More often than not, prospects will agree, if only to see what you can possibly do in ninety seconds and whether you will be true to your pledge not to go over time. And if they do agree to see you under such an understanding, it's critical that you not exceed the promised time. After all, this is the first opportunity for them to confirm that you'll really do what you say you'll do.

If you get a ninety-second appointment, greet the person, shake hands, and cut to the chase. "Thanks for agreeing to meet with me this morning. I know I have only ninety seconds, so let me get to the point." That just took you six seconds. Now, about the only time you will ever do so in a selling situation, you'll deliver an oration that summarizes, in 140 words or less, why the prospect should talk to you further.

> Mr./Ms. Prospect, we've been working with several companies similar to yours which specialize in aftermarket automotive parts for rare and antique vehicles. Our clients include large distributors such as ABC and smaller firms such as XYZ. We've

helped them develop a system for inventory control and parts procurement that has increased their sales by forty percent and reduced expenses for shipping, warehousing, and carrying inventory by ten to twenty percent. We've developed a database that has identified owners of over twenty-two thousand vehicles in your target market, and we can help you market to them directly. We also have a comprehensive list of every manufacturer in the country that makes parts for those vehicles. I believe we could work together to develop a system customized to you which would pay for itself in six months or less.

The oration will take sixty seconds max, so now you're at sixty-six seconds and counting. Conclude by acknowledging that you're running out of time and asking permission to continue, now or later.

Mr./Ms. Prospect, I know my time is almost up. It will take about thirty minutes to go over a few things to see if this could work for you. Is now a good time to do that, or should we make an appointment to do it later?

And shut up. Bingo! Ninety seconds or less. You got your foot in the door and, hopefully, have initiated the process. This is a good time for Action Plan Assignment #9.

Action Plan Assignment #9: Develop and Memorize Your Own Ninety-Second Presentation

Develop your own sixty-second, 140-word presentation and learn it cold for a ninety-second presentation. Develop as many of these as needed for different situations with different types of prospects.

Only ask for a ninty-second meeting if you just can't get a meeting of the length you needed. And, of course, your objective of the ninety-second presentation is to procure an appointment of the needed length. If a prospect still declines to meet with you, even for ninety seconds, gee, they must be awfully, awfully busy. Or, more likely, they're unwilling to consider meeting with you at all and are just making up a cheap excuse to blow you off. Probably time to stop spinning your wheels and move on to greener pastures. You're dealing with a visceral objection.

Point 4

Classify the objection as content-based or visceral. Not all objections are alike, so as you listen, ask questions, and listen some more, ask yourself what type of objection you're dealing with. Content-based objections are based on facts and logic, an openly expressed legitimate reason not to do business with you. These are the easy ones, and, as we'll see in Concept 3, will lead you directly into a close. More difficult to get your hands around are visceral objections, based on feelings, emotions, or relationship issues. In the new world of business, visceral objections have taken on an even greater significance than ever since your objective is to establish strategic alliances and partnerships that are, by definition, relationships. By contrast, in a more fundamental selling situation, as with selling the refrigerator or a basic call that covers all ten steps, you'll focus primarily on feature-benefit statements and successful handling of content-based objections.

There are numerous reasons why you might encounter visceral objections, many of which are downright illogical. Prospects might not like you. You may be too young, too old. You're a man or you're a woman. You're wearing blue, you're not wearing blue. They're uncomfortable with your pierced tongue. They might not like your company. They heard something bad about it before, yes, it must have been that company, I wonder exactly what it was I heard. They may simply not feel like making a decision or doing anything today. No, you won't run across a lot of people like that in smaller and mid-sized companies, but they are out there. They may have preconceived attitudes or opinions not based on facts. Or they may have established relationships and friendships they're comfortable with. The worst is that you may be perceived as a threat to them, their territory, or their security.

After you ask prospects to elaborate on the objection, listen carefully for subtle cues that help you differentiate between content-based and visceral objections. The following is an example of a visceral objection: "There's no reason to make that available to my employees. I don't know any small business owners who offer it, and none of my employees has ever mentioned it." This is an objection based on pre-conceived attitudes and opinions. Next is an example of a content-based objection: "There's no reason to make that available to my employees. Fred's company tried it and dropped it. It cost him a bundle, and none of his employees thought it was worthwhile."

Generally, you will take objections at face value and deal with them as content-based objections. If, however, every time you answer an ostensibly content-based objection you immediately get hit with another one, you are likely actually being confronted with visceral objections. A red light should go on. Pull in the reins. Stop presenting and start probing. Uncover and deal with those visceral objections before proceeding further.

CONCEPT 2: UNEARTH AND HANDLE ALL VISCERAL OBJECTIONS FIRST

The operative word here is "first," as in well before you even think about formulating any feature-benefit statements and moving prospects toward a buying decision. Simply put, if you encounter significant visceral objections after the first two or three steps of the sales presentation, you got way ahead of yourself and failed to cover all the proper bases in the opening. Remember that visceral objections are usually concealed. Don't expect prospects to come right out and tell you there's a problem with the relationship component of communication, and don't delude yourself into thinking everything's peachy if prospects haven't told you otherwise. Ignorance and denial won't serve you well in sales.

It is essential to sell yourself before starting to sell your product or service. This goes far beyond a good appearance and other basic verbal and nonverbal communication skills. A little small talk and rapport building is all part of an effective opening, but don't assume that prospects will be inclined to do business with you just because you shared some friendly banter and found a few points of common ground. Throughout the early steps of the sales presentation, encourage them to discuss their reservations about changing what they're doing now, reservations about your company, and reservations about you personally. These are words you don't want to hear, but they won't go away unless you bring them to the surface.

If you're a young person, many prospects will believe you couldn't conceivably know more about their operations than they and their people do. A twenty-four-year-old information technology whiz kid encountered that when talking to a veteran manager in an established company. In the opening steps of the sales call, she sensed that the prospect was resistant to working with her and her company. His patronizing statements suggested he was not perceiving her as a professional peer, so instead of moving further into the sales presentation, she continued to probe about points of concern and issues that needed to be addressed. Every answer she gave helped demonstrate that she was a competent professional. As the conversation progressed, the prospect stated: "We're not there yet, but when we want to do it, our information technology [IT] people can manage it. They know everything about our database and the company's information needs." Finally, the visceral objection was out in the open: the prospect was uncomfortable with the thought that a twenty-four-year-old might be more competent than his people. Our colleague resisted the temptation to say, "Well, if your IT people can manage it, why haven't they done it yet, dummy?" Instead, she responded with the feel/felt/found technique. "I understand. It's interesting. I was meeting with Spunk Newnan a couple of months ago and he said about the same thing. We've cut their processing time by eighty percent and they're saving over four thousand dollars a month. Let me show you this . . ."

Once you get visceral objections in the open, the feel/felt/found technique helps you shift the conversation to facts and content. Please do not apply this technique literally—"I know how you feel. So-and-so felt the same way. But they found whatever."—unless you want prospects to jump out of their seats and exclaim, "Oh, wow! The feel/felt/ found technique. Where did you learn that, puppy?" Instead, do it very casually. "Feel" is any variety of disarming phrase, "felt" cites someone prospects can relate to who expressed a similar reservation, and "found" describes the success story, shifting the discussion to content.

Sometimes a visceral objection has nothing to do with you personally but is a halo effect from those who came before you. Buck called on a large plumbing company to consult on their computer system, and the first thing out of the president's mouth was, "I don't trust salespeople." *Fair enough,* thought Buck, *I don't trust plumbers.* By asking questions, Buck learned the president had purchased a system from an unethical vendor who had neglected to tell her that the software was pirated and the equipment had no warranty. Fortunately for Buck, this prospect was up front about her visceral objection. He had another situation, though, where he kept hitting his head against a wall, getting nowhere. Executives and field managers alike were giving him one objection after another. Buck sensed he was dealing with a visceral objection, but he just couldn't uncover it. Finally, a regional manager confided to him that the last outside consultant the company hired had gotten drunk and openly used illegal drugs at the post-session cocktail hour. Subsequently, Buck was able to convey that he was aware of the prior situation and state directly how that was not the way he conducted himself. From that point forward, he made progress toward the sale, having eliminated a visceral objection the managers may not have even been conscious they were harboring.

You may also encounter visceral objections in an established business or social relationship. Think about the relationship you have with a significant other when there's an unresolved emotional issue. Until that issue is addressed, you won't get far attempting to deal with facts and content. The same is true in a business relationship. Be sure there are no unresolved problems or customer dissatisfactions before moving into your sales presentation, or you are virtually guaranteed to get bogged down in visceral objections. And don't assume your customers will bring up these dissatisfactions on their own. Ask direct questions to confirm that they're completely satisfied. If there are problems, get all the details and let them know when you'll get back to them. As previously noted, be sure to follow up on those promises. If you don't do what you said you'd do, when you said you'd do it, you will be, and you will deserve to be, up to your eyeballs in visceral objections.

If your company is relatively new or not the major player in a segment, you're also going to have to sell your company. In such circumstances, visceral objections mean, in essence, that prospects need more information. Listen carefully and read between the lines to ascertain the difference between what they say and what they really mean. When prospects say they're sticking with your competitor because "They've been around for twenty years and have a nationwide service and support network," what they really mean is, "Show me that you're a stable and reliable firm, and that you can take care of me when I need help." Paraphrase that back to prospects, not as what they said but what they meant, and shift the discussion to content by addressing the points of concern.

Similarly, when prospects say they plan to expand utilizing your competitor's service because "We're thoroughly familiar with how they operate, and their newer systems are fully compatible with the old," what they really mean is, "Tell me how long it's going to take to get us up to speed and how you can integrate all our systems." Again, paraphrase what they meant, and move into content.

Always be on the lookout for visceral objections about your company when they suggest that prospects want and need more information. When they confirm your paraphrase, it's an open invitation to proceed with the sales presentation.

The situation is different when you encounter a visceral objection that indicates prospects have an openly negative attitude toward your company. Once again, it is unpleasant to hear all this, but permit them to fully vent their feelings and rage before answering the objection. And, of course, then first paraphrase their comments to confirm understanding of their feelings. It's possible that your prospects have had a bad experience with your company in the past. Although their feelings may be fully justified and based on factual events, this negative attitude still constitutes a visceral objection since it is relationship based and precludes a willingness to consider the content of your proposal. There is only one thing to do here. Convince them that although your company was lousy before, it's great today. That won't be easy, but there's one thing going for you. Help them to develop a more favorable attitude toward your company by letting them see you as a competent professional they can respect and trust.

One thing to keep in mind when you encounter negative attitudes based on past experiences is to air your dirty laundry only as much as necessary. Sure, you'll have to do a comprehensive mea culpa if your company messed up in the past, but consider an objection such as this:

> When we opened three years ago, I called you people to ask for a proposal. I was promised that someone would call me back the next day. I've been sitting by this phone day and night for three years waiting for that call. Now here you are, asking for an appointment. Sorry, pal, you're a little late. I got tired of waiting for you and called your competitor. They do it all for us now.

This prospect is understandably negative and deserves an opportunity to vent his or her anger. You need to apologize, but there's no need to go into the "We were lousy then but we're great now" scenario. Accept accountability, but don't blame the office staff or answering service for losing the message. Simply adapt the feel/felt/ found technique to express the point that you've *always* been great and the experience was an aberration. "I can appreciate why you wouldn't think highly of us. There's no excuse for us failing to call you back. I don't know why it happened, but that's not an example of how we do business. We pride ourselves on customer service, and in the future, I'll personally be available to you twenty-four/seven. I work with several companies in your industry who will tell you I do what I say."

Don't assume that your personal credibility is automatically transferable to a different environment. Buck relates the story of a friend who is a mechanical engineer, describing a salesperson who had called on him.

> This guy sold janitorial products and did a fine job for us. He was reliable and we liked doing business with him. But then he changed jobs, and a week later came by selling cutting tools for my assembly line, high-end tools costing thousands of dollars, tens of thousands if a mistake was made. There was no way I was going to buy from him.

In this prospect's mind, the salesperson was going to have to demonstrate experience and expertise in his new, more complex product line, not a quick process that could be glossed over because of prior positive experiences. The door was not permanently closed, but the process would require time. Anyone new to a job should expect a similar visceral objection. Just because you did a bang-up job raking their yard when you were a student doesn't mean they'll contract with you for financial services immediately after you graduate.

Visceral objections may also arise when people and their territories feel threatened. We both encounter this when discussing sales training activities with potential clients. Though unspoken, there is often an undercurrent of apprehension that procuring the services of an outside expert implies that the prospect's work is somehow inadequate or unsatisfactory. In some cases, the prospect's work *is* inadequate *and* unsatisfactory, which means you probably should be talking to that person's boss instead of him or her. Whichever the situation, you don't want to appear to threaten anyone, be they supercompetent or super-incompetent, and you most certainly don't want to get involved in the prospect's office politics or personnel matters.

Bob ran across a superincompetent manager who spent his day hand-drawing graphs of product sales and plastering them on his walls. Though tempted to call this person an imbecile and inform him that anyone who wanted such charts could generate them in four mouse clicks, Bob was careful to compliment him on recognizing the need to track sales and discuss ways in which his employees could best implement a similar tracking system.

Buck was working with a client on instituting a location and tracking system for its service vehicles. Rollout of the program was repeatedly delayed because test vehicles in a prototype project consistently failed to report properly, so Buck spent a day in the field to find out why. As it turned out, the equipment was working perfectly. The problem was a manager who believed the system indicated his company didn't trust him and wanted to spy on him, so he was disconnecting the units or covering the antennas with aluminum foil. Unfortunately, this manager was adamant, and no one could convince him that the system could actually help him do his job. Ultimately, this twenty-year employee was fired for insubordination. Buck was wise enough not to embroil himself in the internal turmoil, but full-scale implementation had to be delayed until the impediment could be removed.

You will not often encounter superincompetent or totally irrational prospects, but still, expect a certain discomfort level when you propose changes. The more significant the changes, the greater the discomfort. Convey to prospects that what they're doing now isn't bad and in no way represents a failure in judgment on their part. Help them to see that over time things have changed and new opportunities (specifically, you, your products, and your services) are at hand. Use the questioning sequence in the ten steps of the sales presentation to help them reach the truth for themselves. Once they perceive changes as opportunities rather than threats, you can begin to move into the content of your proposal.

You should most definitely expect to run into visceral objections when selling against an established competitor. Recall what we said about relationships in Chapter 3. They are always being redefined, either growing or dying, never stable. That may be true, but there's still a problem that can cause visceral objections. The relationship may be dying, but your prospect may be living in denial, deluding himself or herself into thinking everything is hunky-dory. Please don't dismiss this idea as far-fetched, confident that, of course, a person would be aware when a relationship was on the rocks.

To illustrate our point, we need only ask that you take a look back at the last time one of your close personal relationships went south. If you're like most of us, by the time you woke up to reality, that relationship had already been dead for weeks, months, or more. It happens the same way in business. Your competitor won the prospect in the courtship, took great care of the company over the honeymoon, and has taken it for granted ever since. You know, of course—we remind you one more time—that satisfaction began at the close. They were happy then and have tried to be understanding or were not even consciously aware of the slowly but steadily diminishing attention since the end of the honeymoon.

That being the case, initially you may encounter a visceral objection at the very thought of divorcing your competitor and marrying you. But as you walk them through the ten steps, help them come out of denial and realize they're really not that happy after all. The visceral objection dissolves as you sell yourself and shift the discussion to content. Utilize a similar approach when bidding against a competitor with whom the prospects have a close personal relationship. Don't tell them they're wrong to make a decision based on friendship, but gently shift the discussion to content. Consider the following situation:

SALES REP: You're leaning toward Acme Realty? Could you tell me why?

PROSPECT: They've been around for twenty years. Experience!

SALES REP: Anything else?

PROSPECT: Well, their fee is only three percent. That's half what you people charge.

SALES REP: There's no reason to pay more than you have to.

PROSPECT: Money doesn't grow on trees.

SALES REP: Any other reason you're inclined to go with Acme?

PROSPECT: Well, the agent is my daughter's soccer coach. Our families are friends.

Notice how that with a few questions the rep has uncovered the ubiquitous price objection and two visceral objections. The first one means, "Give me information about your company and its experience," which is straightforward. The relationship-based "There's a friend in the business," is a bit more challenging. "Give me information about your company and its experience" can be dealt with by introducing facts and content. However, the purely visceral "There's a friend in the business" must be dealt with first.

SALES REP: It's nice doing business with friends. I think of my clients as friends, too. But if it were really in your best interest to do business with someone else, your friends would want you to do what was best for you, wouldn't they?

PROSPECT: I guess so.

SALES REP: Now, as you were saying, we charge a seven percent commission whereas they only charge three percent. But is that really important?

PROSPECT: Of course it's important! That's several thousand dollars!

SALES REP: You're right, but what I meant is, what you're looking at—bottom line—is the cash you'll receive at closing, isn't it?

PROSPECT: That's how I figure it.

SALES REP: Would the number of qualified buyers who saw the house affect that?

PROSPECT: Of course.

SALES REP: How about the ability to put together packages of creative financing?

PROSPECT: Yes, certainly.

SALES REP: So, from what you're telling me, your objective is to maximize cash at closing, with the sales commission as one of the points to be addressed. Is that about right?

PROSPECT: I'd say so.

SALES REP: Let me show you some ideas about how we can maximize the cash you'll get at closing.

Notice how the sales rep in no way criticized the prospect for considering friendship in a business decision but instead gently guided the conversation to issues of content. Also note the attention-getting statement the rep used to lead into the price objection. "Yes, we cost more, but is that important?" leads you directly into feature-benefit statements which demonstrate that although you're not the lowest price, you are the best value.

Perhaps one of the most frustrating causes of visceral objections are prospects who won't, or can't, make a decision. Even in the new world of business, some people still insulate themselves from doing anything all day for fear of making a mistake. Some bureaucrats want to go to committee on anything and everything, shielding themselves from any possible blame and avoiding accountability at all costs. Some bosses and organizations permit this to go on, hoping the company goose will keep laying enough golden eggs to get them into retirement before, to continue the barnyard analogies, the chickens come home to roost. Every community has a few companies like these. Though it's tempting to want to feed on the carcass, the time required to get a decision should make you wonder if your time might not be better spent elsewhere. It's one thing to face visceral objections you can address through points about yourself, your company, and its products and services. It's something else to be suffocated in visceral objections caused by organizational ineptitude.

Even in the best companies, though, there can be a reluctance to make a buying decision if prospects believe a better deal may be down the road. We'll go into closing in Chapter 7, but just a tidbit here. Always have a compelling reason for prospects to make a decision in a timely manner. At the outset, cut off the "I've got to run this by my boss" stall by qualifying at the time of confirming the appointment and again at the beginning of your meeting. Ask directly if anyone else will be involved in the decision. If they want you to talk to a subordinate, confirm that person has the authority to make a decision, and reconfirm that understanding when you talk to the subordinate. Should you be fool enough to make a presentation to someone without authority, just remember we told you so when you drown in visceral objections as you try to locate the elusive decision maker.

Finally, don't bog down in visceral objections by creating unnecessary objections. This can happen in one of two ways. First, the sales rep can misinterpret a statement of astonishment for an objection. For example, "Two million dollars is a lot of money for a house" is not a price objection and should not be treated as such. A simple "You're right. It's a significant investment," will suffice. Consider the following dialogue:

SALES REP: We're proposing that you buy full positions advertising on *Temptation Atoll.*

PROSPECT: Advertising on *what?*

SALES REP: *Temptation Atoll.* It's the new reality program.

PROSPECT: I know what it is. People actually watch that garbage?

SALES REP: It's the number-one show on television.

PROSPECT: No one ever went broke underestimating the intelligence of homes using television.

The prospect's comments were not an objection to the proposed advertising and did not call for the sales rep to defend the artistic merits of the program. If anything, the prospect has indicated agreement and is ready for a close.

A second trap of creating unnecessary objections is failing to close on cue. There is only a limited window of opportunity to close when a prospect indicates he or she is ready to consummate an agreement. Failing to ask for the order at the opportune moment may mean permanent exile to the land of visceral objections. Consider the following:

SALES REP: The system will pay for itself in eighteen months.

PROSPECT: When can you have us up and running?

SALES REP: A week, ten days max.

PROSPECT: Where would you conduct the training?

SALES REP: At our facility or yours, whichever is most convenient.

PROSPECT: Did you say there was a discount for full payment in advance?

SALES REP: Yes, three percent.

PROSPECT: Let me sleep on it. I'll get back to you tomorrow.

SALES REP: I'll look forward to your call.

We've spent considerable time on visceral objections, a reflection of their more significant role in the new world of business. Today, it's less likely that you'll make a single call on a prospect in which you roll through an entire sales presentation and walk out the door with a signed order form. Strategic alliances and partnerships are, by definition, relationships, and it's through those relationships that you create value and differential advantage over the lower-priced competitor. Assessing people and relationships is far more complex than evaluating product and service criteria, so the attendant reservations and visceral objections will require patience to unearth and deal with them. Move steadily, but don't rush the process. Until all the visceral objections have been handled, there's no point of trying to move into the content of the proposal. Once they've been handled, prospects are positively predisposed to finding ways to work together.

CONCEPT 3: CLOSE ON EVERY CONTENT-BASED OBJECTION

It may take you some time to unearth and deal with all those visceral objections but there's no point of moving into your formal presentation until all of them have been handled. This means it may take some time—perhaps several meetings—to move through the first few steps of the sales presentation. We hope, though, you eventually wind your way to Steps 7 and 8. At this point, prospects will raise one or more content-based objections. If nothing else, they will raise a price objection. Every buyer or decision maker considers it his or her duty to tell you your price is too high, even if he or she believes your price to be fair and is prepared to pay it. Ultimately, virtually every content-based objection boils down to a price objection. Sure, they might really not care for Feature A and Feature B, but they can live with them if the price is right. Or you have a higher-priced product with Feature C and Feature D, and you sell the benefits and value.

With the plethora of information available through the Internet, you probably already know what your competitors have and what they charge. You know there's someone out there who says they have the same thing for less. Prospects will bring this up, as if saying it's the same makes it the same. You're going to get the price objection, and you're going to have to sell your extra value. So, early on, when you're establishing rapport and learning about the prospect's company, attack the inevitable price objection as you explore points of common ground about your respective cultures and philosophies of doing business.

Mr./Ms. Prospect, when we were talking about why people do business with your company, you mentioned quality, experience, uniqueness of your products, service support, and warranty. You didn't say anything about price. Are you the least expensive alternative for your customers?

There may be people out there who have nothing going for them but the lowest price. We just haven't met them yet. Invariably, prospects will respond that they're not the cheapest, then brag about why they're worth the extra price they get. File that in your memory banks and feed it back when the price objection comes up.

Mr./Ms. Prospect, just like your company, we're not the cheapest alternative. But we have feature/feature/feature which will give you benefit/benefit/benefit. And just like you, we offer our customers the best value for the money.

Along the same lines, it's likely prospects will tell you that what you propose isn't in the budget. Generally, that's nothing more than a negotiation tactic designed to wring a concession out of you. "We love your product, and readily agree it's worth your asking price of forty thousand dollars. But all we have in the budget is thirty-six thousand dollars. That's all there is. There is no more." Bob's favorite counter attack is, "If I were in here today offering you ten-dollar bills for eight bucks, I'll bet you could find the money." He then goes on to complete the analogy by explaining how his eight-dollar services provide them a ten-dollar return on investment.

As with visceral objections, whenever you encounter a content-based objection, encourage prospects to elaborate on the objection. Listen, ask clarifying questions, and paraphrase their statements to confirm understanding. Empathize with them through a disarming statement. Then, if you can, your first choice is to refute the objection by bringing in new facts or putting existing facts in a different light. Let's look at some examples.

First, let's consider situations in which you can refute the objection. The easiest of these is when prospects have inaccurate facts or information. Be careful here. Bring in the correct facts, but use a disarming phrase so you don't appear to be telling prospects they're wrong.

PROSPECT: I'm going with ABC.

SALES REP: Could you tell me why you're thinking about doing that?

PROSPECT: They're giving me a five-dollar allowance. You're offering only three dollars.

SALES REP: Oh, well, I can see how that would concern you. But for the amount we were discussing, we have a five-dollar allowance, too. Here, look at this . . .

PROSPECT: Hmm . . .

SALES REP: You need this by Tuesday, right?

We discussed earlier how visceral objections arise because of a negative attitude about you or your company. However, if the negative attitude has arisen due to inaccurate facts or information that can be refuted, deal with it the same way as a content-based objection.

PROSPECT: We're not going to sell your products in our store.

SALES REP: Why is that?

PROSPECT: I read about it in the paper. You're using child labor in sweatshops.

SALES REP: I'm glad you brought that up. I've heard about places like that. It's nice to see that retailers are outraged. We're outraged, too. That's why all our facilities are certified by an international children's advocacy group. Let me show you this article in their magazine.

PROSPECT: Son of a gun. I thought you were the ones.

SALES REP: It's nice to know your suppliers share your concern for children, isn't it?

Sometimes you can refute the objection by putting facts in a different light. This is precisely what you do when helping prospects understand that a higher initial investment will translate to lower long-term costs.

SALES REP: We can give you a complete air-conditioning system for four thousand dollars.

PROSPECT: I've got another bid for thirty-two hundred.

SALES REP: Well, there's no reason to invest more than you have to. But our model has a higher energy-efficiency rating than the other brand. That means you'll save about twenty dollars a month in power bills. In less than four years, it'll pay for itself, won't it?

PROSPECT: I guess so.

SALES REP: What's the best day to install it?

You'll employ a similar approach when you need to consider a residual value at the end of a period of ownership.

SALES REP: Fully equipped, this boat is nine hundred thousand dollars.

PROSPECT: The place across the bay has the same size for one hundred grand less.

SALES REP: I can appreciate your concern. This is a significant investment. But our higher quality workmanship means that in five to ten years, when you expect to sell it, this boat will be worth at least one hundred fifty thousand dollars more.

PROSPECT: Hmm . . .

SALES REP: In light of that, wouldn't you agree that the overriding consideration is the total cost of ownership over its lifetime rather than the initial investment?

PROSPECT: That's a point.

SALES REP: Do you have a marina where you'll be keeping it?

These are, of course, very elementary examples, but you get the idea. Unfortunately, as you know so well, sometimes prospects will raise a negative point that *cannot* be refuted. It stands as a legitimate reason not to buy. We noted the most common example, a higher price. In that situation quickly concede the negatives and sell the benefits, helping prospects to see that the positives outweigh those negatives. The following are other examples:

PROSPECT: Your service doesn't include QVC and C-Span 2. I get those on cable.

SALES REP: You're right, but for the same price we include HBO, Showtime, and NFL Sunday Ticket. On the whole, that's a pretty good package, don't you think?

PROSPECT: I guess I can watch Home Shopping Network and CNN.

SALES REP: In how many rooms do you have a television?

Consider this situation, applying a similar approach to a visceral objection.

PROSPECT: I don't know. Your competition has been working with firms in this industry for twenty years.

SALES REP: You're right. We're new to your industry. But as you've seen, we've been very successful with emerging high-tech companies, haven't we?

PROSPECT: You have at that.

SALES REP: Those companies are lean and mean with highly motivated employees, aren't they?

PROSPECT: They are.

SALES REP: Is that the kind of culture you're seeking to establish here?

PROSPECT: Absolutely.

SALES REP: So our experience in high tech might be very helpful to you, wouldn't you think?

PROSPECT: It's food for thought at least.

SALES REP: How many first-line sales managers do you have?

You will often face a hybrid content-based objection that you can refute partially but not entirely. In that case, refute what you can first, concede the remainder, and then bring up compensating benefits that will more than offset the residual negative. Let's say, for example, that you're a personnel provider specializing in secretarial services.

PROSPECT: One of your employees will cost me forty thousand dollars a year. I pay my secretaries twenty-eight thousand. That's a twelve-thousand-dollar difference.

SALES REP: You're right. There's a twelve-thousand-dollar difference. But what does it cost you for benefits and unemployment insurance?

PROSPECT: About eight thou.

SALES REP: So the difference is only about four thousand a year, isn't it?

PROSPECT: Four bills is four bills.

SALES REP: Certainly. But how long does it take you to train a new employee and get him or her up to speed?

PROSPECT: Oh, I'd say six months.

SALES REP: Is the training easy and fairly cheap?

PROSPECT: Are you kidding?

SALES REP: We fully train all our employees, so they're ready to hit the floor running on day one. You're getting more productivity for that four thousand a year, aren't you?

PROSPECT: Might at that.

SALES REP: How soon will you be needing a new staff person?

By now, you should have a pretty good understanding of visceral and content-based objections. In a meeting with prospects, you should be able to unearth and address issues and relationships that constitute visceral objections and utilize the appropriate tactic to handle content-based objections. But let's take this a step further. Why wait until you're face to face when, with proper preapproach preparation, you could have anticipated and formulated a response for at least 90 percent of the objections you'll encounter in the meeting. It's time for Action Plan Assignment #10.

**Action Plan Assignment #10:
Objections and Planned Responses**

Create a one-page form to prepare in advance for objections you might encounter in any meeting with prospects or customers. On the left side of the page list the objection, and on the right side list how you will deal with or respond to that objection. Have separate sections for content-based and visceral objections.

Making up the form noted in Action Plan Assignment #10 is the easy part. You should complete it in five minutes tops. The challenge, of course, is to have the discipline to prepare the form for each and every call. Some objections are a given and lend themselves to a standard response. But others are unique to a particular situation and may require an investment in time, especially for visceral objections.

Think about it, though. Doesn't it make sense, before a meeting, to seek out and uncover all the relationships, territories, fears, and personal agendas that stand in your way? Those impediments are real and pretending they don't exist won't make them go away. Seek them out in advance and recognize their subtle cues when they appear.

Always take special care to prepare for the price objection. Expect to acknowledge that, no, you're not the cheapest, but then be ready to cite all the components of value that will justify the price. As you likely noted, that's merely an adaptation of the basic feature-benefit statement.

CONCEPT 4:
AFTER DEALING WITH THE OBJECTION, GET BACK IN STEP

Objections have not gone out of style in the new world of business, they've just become different, along with every aspect of selling today. Traditionally, sales professionals viewed objections as barriers to the close, obstacles to be tackled or skirted on the way to the end zone. This may be an appropriate analogy of objections in a simple one-meeting transaction such as the refrigerator. It's inadequate in a scenario describing a long-term partnership relationship.

In dealing with objections, never lose sight of the fact that your objective is to work the process through to its conclusion, formulate an agreement, and get paid. To do that, remain aware of where you are in the ten steps and guide the conversation back onto the path toward agreement.

The old approach to selling positioned objections as happening toward the end of a selling situation, after the formal presentation, the final barrier between the salesperson and the close. Get past the objection and you were home free. That's inadequate for addressing objections in a relationship-based strategic alliance where you might encounter the most significant objections *before* Step 1 of the sales presentation. Whatever objections you face, whenever they arise, just remember where you are at all times and get back in step. Early on, if you unearth and deal with a visceral objection about your competence and experience, you might move into Step 1 and begin inquiring about what they're doing now. Later, after refuting a price objection, you would go to Step 7 with a summary/paraphrase/tie-down ahead of a feature-benefit statement. Always have in mind where you're at in the ten steps, and concentrate on guiding the conversation to get you back in step.

CONCLUSION

In this chapter, we've explored the four key concepts for dealing with objections, barriers, and other impediments. Listen, ask questions, and listen some more. Rather that hiding from objections and hoping they won't appear, encourage prospects early on to discuss all the reasons why they might be disinclined to make an affirmative buying decision, all the reasons why they might be disinclined to do business with you or your company. Of course, similar to a good attorney, you pretty much know what they're going to say and you've formulated your response.

Unearth and handle all relationship-based visceral objections. You got started on this by convincing prospects to meet with you in the first place. Uncover all the emotions, feelings, fears, territories, and established relationships that stand in your way. Eliminate any reservations about working with you and your company before even thinking about moving into the content of your proposal. Once the visceral objections have been neutralized and prospects are receptive to a relationship, it's more of a question of *how* you might partner rather than *whether* they would consider working with you.

As you present, close on every content-based objection. Refute if you can by bringing in new facts or presenting facts in a different light. Otherwise, concede the objection and follow up with feature-benefit statements which illustrate that the positive benefits and value exceed the negatives and costs.

Don't let objections distract you from your ultimate objective, finalizing an agreement on terms and conditions. As soon as it's feasible, get back into the appropriate point of the ten-step sales presentation. Think of those objections and other impediments as signs of an open and frank dialogue between you and the prospect. Talking about and addressing them move you closer together, not further apart. You're nearing the close.

Chapter 7

Closing Is Not the Final Chapter:
Achieving Agreement in Principle

"Closing" is the last chapter in many traditional books on selling, and it's the capstone of many traditional sales training programs, but "closing" is not our final chapter and, in fact, it's our shortest chapter. In this chapter, we'll explore the four key concepts of closing which, in a relationship-intense environment, may not be the endgame in itself but merely the agreement in principle that transitions into the endgame, which *is* our final chapter. We'll review some of the traditional closing techniques, but note how their application must be appropriate and timely. We'll describe how the professional salesperson must first close on relationship to develop a partnership and strategic alliance. After taking a look at underlying buying motives and how to address them, we'll note considerations for persuading the prospect to make a commitment.

CONCEPT 1: MASTER THE BASIC
CLOSING SKILLS AND TECHNIQUES

As a disclaimer, let us state up front that closing is a *process*, not a piecemeal application of techniques. It's essential for the professional salesperson to be familiar with and understand the proper application of basic closing skills and techniques.

Item 1: After Asking a Closing Question, Shut Up

This is the most important item. The reason for asking a question is to get the prospect to speak next. Don't ask a question in the first place if all you're going to do is keep talking. Worst of all, the prospect's silence likely means he or she is giving serious consideration to making an affirmative statement. If the prospect speaks next, you may well have closed, but if you speak next you are, at best, back into the presentation. More than likely, you just talked yourself right out of the sale.

A few years ago, Bob was trying to sell a car he had purchased new just six months before. This vehicle was of the highest quality and would provide its new owner with years of carefree driving. Bob felt, however, that it would be happier in someone else's garage, so he placed an ad in the classifieds. A discerning customer came out to look it over. He took it for a five-mile test drive during which there was no road failure and no critical components fell off. Afterward, standing beside the vehicle, the person asked, "What was the price again?" Bob gave him the asking price, to which the citizen replied, "That's a lot of money for this car." Bob answered, "It's a lot of car." The close! Take special note that this close was not in the form of a question, but in a final statement at the end of a "presentation." Bob had said all he had to say. It was time for the customer to act. They stood there silently for thirty seconds, a minute, two minutes, three. Bob said nothing, silently praying that his beloved vehicle would be adopted into its new and loving home. Finally, the customer spoke. "I'll give you X." The two went back and forth on terms and conditions until it was a done deal. The customer left and Bob had a check in hand

Buck had a similar experience calling on a health care facility. After reviewing all relevant points, he made his closing statement: "Mr. Keith, we've addressed all the considerations we agreed were critical to the project, and we've addressed the time line for its implementation. All we need to get started is your authorization." Then Buck quit talking. It seemed as though two weeks went by, but it was actually closer to forty-five seconds. The prospect spoke next and initiated the paperwork. So what would have happened had Buck been the next one to speak? Probably no sale. The closing statement or closing question opens a window of opportunity. If you speak next, you slam that window shut. Good luck getting it open again.

Item 2: Never Ask a Question That Can Be Answered Yes or No

Instead, use the choice technique, having the prospect select among alternatives, or make an assumptive statement, perhaps in the form of a secondary related question. Don't ask: "Shall I put you down for two hundred?" Do ask: "Will two hundred be enough, or shall I put you down for two hundred fifty?"

On the surface, a secondary related question appears to be one that can be answered yes or no. But the question "Will you be needing this by the first of next week?" is, in essence, a choice technique. Either the prospect will need it by the first of next week, in which case we'll do this (assumptive statement), or the prospect won't, in which case we'll do that (assumptive statement).

Likewise, technically, a summary statement/paraphrase with a tie-down could be answered yes or no, but if it ever gets a no, the sales-person did something terribly wrong leading into it. "Having a health care program would help retain some of those employees, wouldn't it?" is a statement confirming agreement, always expected to get a "Yes." Same thing with, "So, in the long run, it'll cost you less, won't it?"

Be alert for subtle cues that suggest the prospect would be amenable to a closing question. A request for information usually indicates interest, so don't respond with a statement. Instead, answer the request for information with a closing question. When the prospect asks, "Do you deliver on weekends?" don't say, "Yes, we deliver on both Saturday and Sunday." Instead, ask, "Would Saturday or Sunday be more convenient?" Or when the prospect asks, "Do you have volume discounts?" don't merely respond, "Yes, we have a ten percent discount for twelve units and a twenty percent discount for twenty-four or more." Instead, ask, "How many will you be needing?"

Item 3: Employ the Summary Close to Bring Objections to the Surface

Usually, a content-based objection involving price objection is holding the prospect back. Summarize features and attendant benefits previously covered ("We've got this feature with that benefit. It'll help you get this consequence, won't it?" Stop talking to get confirmation. "We've also got . . ."). Wind up with something along the lines of "There are a lot of reasons to go with this. Can you think of any reasons *not* to go with it?" If nothing is cited, close on the spot. If a reason is cited, employ the techniques from Chapter 6 to either refute the objection or yield and cite compensating benefits, then close.

Item 4: If You Encounter High Resistance, Use the Escalator Technique

If you expect your product or service to encounter inordinately high levels of resistance, use the escalator technique, procuring agreement on the benefits before bringing up and identifying the features. As an example, retail stores hate the hassle of resetting sections, so you would open the conversation first by getting them to agree that they want to maximize their return on investment, then to help them see that a good way of doing that is to properly allocate space according to sales. No one wants insurance, so first get them to agree that they need to look out for their families and spare them hardship in case of the unanticipated. People don't exactly jump up and say "Me! Me! Me!" when you bring up the latest multilevel marketing ploy, so start with attaining agreement they'd like to pay cash for a new car a year from now, working at home just two hours a week.

Item 5: Present Profits with High Numbers; Present Costs with Low Numbers

"This will earn you two hundred ninety-two dollars a year. You can save a starving child for eighty cents a day." Sounds great! However, the following statements sound a lot less impressive: "This will earn you eighty cents a day. You can save a starving child for two hundred ninety-two dollars a year."

Item 6: The Closing Funnel: An Application of the Choice Technique

Start with a wide variety of options, and keep narrowing them down until you determine how, not if, you'll structure the deal.

Item 7: If the Final Answer Is No, Get It Quickly and Move On

If, ultimately, the prospect's decision will be negative, get that "No" as soon as possible and move on. Bob learned a variation of this years ago, when he was working with new-product development in consumer nondurables. Ninety percent of proposed new products never make it through the new-product development process. They fail, perhaps as early as concept testing, which is cheap and easy, or after an unsuccessful test marketing, which is complex and very expensive. After that, 80 to 90 percent of new-product launches ultimately fail in the marketplace within a year or two, thus failing to generate profit dollar one. Since 98 to 99 percent of new-product concepts are doomed to failure and will lose the company money, what you need to do is identify the losers as soon in the process as possible and dispatch them forthwith. It never worked out that way. Time and again, management let a dog that would never hunt keep on going through the process one more step after one more step, squandering time and resources. The thinking seemed to be, "Since we've invested so much time and money in this turkey, we can't stop now." This is the same mentality that condemns a stock market investor who works out plans for buying stocks but never develops strategies for selling them. And, of course, it's the consummate time waster for a professional salesperson. Face it, many or most of your contacts will not lead to a successful relationship. If failure is inevitable, realize that nothing can be done to recoup the time and resources you've invested. Cut your losses and go elsewhere.

There are many books out there with hundreds of other closing techniques ranging from the "my dear old mother" close to the Ben Franklin Balance Sheet. One we find particularly offensive is dropping your pen, having the prospect pick it up for you, then handing the prospect an order form to be signed with *your* pen. It is a variation of the drop-the-soap technique, and viewed similarly. Another real winner—Buck actually had a vendor lay this one on him—is the sarcastic close: "Are you telling me you're not interested in making more money?"

We agree that you still have to ask for the order or, at the least, ask to move to the next step in the process. You may even *selectively* employ the basic closing techniques we described. Just don't start closing on content until you've closed on the relationship component. You will not close on details of the honeymoon until first confirming agreement on the marriage.

CONCEPT 2: CLOSING ON RELATIONSHIP

In some selling situations, it is erroneously believed that relationship plays an insignificant role. Sure, you have to act like a decent person and all, but mostly you concentrate on closing on points of content.

In a retail store—selling the refrigerator at an appliance store or a new set of wheels at an automobile dealership—it may be assumed that the objective of the meeting is to move prospects through all ten steps of the sales presentation, finalize the agreement, do the paperwork, and send them out the door signed, sealed, and delivered. If they escape your clutches and get out the door, they're gone forever. If they do buy, it'll likely be something else from someone else, probably someone who knew how to close. Should you be depending on be-backs and callbacks for your future income (1) you haven't been in sales long and (2) you're in for a rude awakening.

You may believe it's a similar scenario if you're making your regular fifteen-minute call every month on buyers. You figure out what they need today, show them your stuff, do your song and dance, go back and forth on the price, sign the order form, and get out the door. Next! About the same thing if you're in route sales, whether that's selling office supplies B2B or vacuum cleaners business to customer (B2C). The old close and go. Remember your ABC's—Always Be Closing. Don't wait until the end of your presentation to lay on a close. Instead, ask a series of "little decision" closes—Red, white, or blue? Will you be needing it by Tuesday?— leading up to the Big Kahuna, the specific request for the order: "Will you be using your Appliance City card today?"

In those situations just described, there is little negotiation beyond details of product components, features, and price. As a result, a salesperson may be inclined to wrap up the details as quickly as possible and move on. Not so fast. You may be missing an opportunity to invest in the relationship.

Although we agree that relationship has a *less* significant role in a one-call close-and-go transaction, let us clarify that a bit by noting that the relationship dimension can enhance closing in *any* selling situation if you assess the relationship component and make a conscious attempt to enhance it, appropriately, before launching even the first trial close. The result is you will close more. You might think this does not apply to you at the extreme low end of the relationship scale, as an order taker selling nuts and bolts at Hardware Emporium or fast food at Hamburger City. It does. At Hardware Emporium, you can invest fifteen seconds to give an analytic product information or talk to an amiable about the weather. Nothing will be different that day—he or she will still buy the seventy-nine-cent mounting bracket—but a week or a month later, when the person needs a $200 chain saw, he or she might be more predisposed to visit your store. Even if you're on salary, ultimately that will pay off for you. Over time, management has a way of discovering who brings in business and who doesn't, and rewards them accordingly. Keep that in mind as you slave away at Hamburger City. Do a little something to enhance the relationship, if only a smile and saying thanks as you hand them their burger, fries, and pop. You just never know when what goes around will come around.

At the next lowest level of the relationship scale, you may find yourself in fifteen-minute appointments with a buyer or selling office supplies door to door, situations which, as we've described, seem to call for you to get to the point and close from the get-go. But even in these ostensibly inflexible selling situations, we challenge you to explore the possibility of introducing a more significant relationship component. If you can't, if there's no way to develop a partnership involvement of any kind, you are doomed to compete against the low-price competitor online. Unless you just love sales so much that making a living is an insignificant consideration, competing on price, as we've seen, is not an option. If your present position offers you no such opportunity, maybe it's time to tap into your network in search of a diffferent sales job.

In the new world of business, "the close" *is* closing on relationship. It's qualitative, an agreement in principle. We agree to agree. All points of content are to be determined and negotiated from this point forward, which *is* the final chapter. Within this context, "closing" constitutes nothing more than confirming agreement to address and work out issues of content. This represents a radical departure from the "Always Be Closing" paradigm. It may be totally inappropriate to as much as even *think* of laying on a close in a first, second, or perhaps even subsequent meetings. In those preliminary meetings, the objective may be solely to get to know each other, learn about problems and opportunities, and discover common ground in your respective business cultures. Allow prospects to close themselves on you and your company in these exploratory meetings. Casually walk through the ten steps to get information about what they're doing now and where they want to go. The more you get them talking about themselves, the more they're closing on you.

During this preliminary process, keep in mind that although you will avoid an overt close on points of content ("500 or 600?" or "Will you need it by Friday?"), you *will* steadily build agreement with summary/paraphrase/tie-down questions ("So, you need compatibility with the tiskets but also need applications for the taskets, is that right?" or "From what you're saying, you like A, but it sure would be nice if you could also do B, wouldn't it?"), which, of course, is Step 7 of the sales presentation. You may selectively go to Step 8 with feature/benefit/tie-down statements, but you will not attempt a formal close on points of content until you have closed on relationship.

Closing on relationship is subtle. It's not a content-based close, where you make a statement to which the prospect responds. In fact, the prospect may not say anything at all, but will communicate with nonverbal cues, especially eye contact. If you're listening aggressively, with your eyes as well as your ears, you just "know" you've sold yourself. Wasn't that just the way it was when you "knew" you were going to get the job offer or "knew" your significant other had fallen for you? In a relationship-intense partnership environment, this constitutes "the close." It is the moment at which the relationship has been validated, and you move on to addressing terms and conditions. The close is relationship based, the next-to-the-last chapter. Negotiation of specific elements of the arrangement is content-based, the last chapter, in which, at the very end of the endgame, the agreement is finalized.

Though the closing on relationship is subtle, it must be formalized. When you recognize that the moment is right, ask a carefully crafted closing question that gently nudges the process into Step 10, negotiating agreement. One of Buck's tactics is the expert close, in which he introduces prospects to colleagues who will be servicing their account or technical people who will develop specifications for a customized proposal. Bob likes to open discussions designed to get on the table all issues to be addressed as part of a comprehensive agreement. As we'll describe in Chapter 8, getting all issues on the table is the initial step of the negotiation process, so this tactic gently shifts the focus from *whether* we work together to *how* we will work together. Give prospects the opportunity to "meet the family," so to speak, and get them to invest time exploring how we can finalize a mutually beneficial arrangement.

CONCEPT 3:
WHAT MOTIVATES PROSPECTS TO BUY

In the new world of business, with its focus on partnerships and relationships, we need to take a different perspective on what motivates prospects to make an affirmative buying decision. We need to go far beyond traditional benefits and value, far beyond the basic closing skills and techniques reviewed earlier in the chapter, to close effectively in this environment.

Advertising and marketing professionals who are masters at understanding motivation and buyer behavior can provide some lessons. Though advertisers and marketers communicate their messages through the mass media, rather than person to person, their ultimate objective is similar to that of a professional salesperson. They want to enhance the likelihood that their target market will purchase their products or services.

Throughout the 1940s and 1950s, most enterprises operated under what was known as a production orientation: manufacture whatever it was they were best at making and then try to find customers to buy it. Since the 1960s, that philosophy has generally been replaced by the marketing orientation: identify the target market's motivations and needs and create products and services tailored to address those motivations and needs. To the professional salesperson, their messages sound very similar to a basic feature-benefit statement: "Wash-O has new blue crystals. Your clothes will look and smell cleaner than ever. Everyone in your family will love you and hug you." Marketers and advertisers, by the way, are well aware that what really motivates the consumer to buy is not so much the benefit per se (clothes that look and smell clean), but the consequence of the benefit (the love and hugs). What really sells are intangible upper-level needs.

You are probably familiar with Maslow's hierarchy of needs. He hypothesized that at the lowest level were basic physiological needs: food, water, sex. These primary needs had to be satisfied before a person could move on to needs at the next level, safety needs: living free of fear of threats emanating from other persons or the environment. This seems to make sense. If you're starving to death, you might be inclined to risk jail or getting shot stealing an apple from the farmer's tree. But if the basic necessities of life are taken care of, you're inclined to start looking for a decent apartment in a safe neighborhood.

Maslow proposed that once safety was secured, a person could move up to social needs: interacting with others and having friends; then to needs of esteem: being recognized and respected; and finally to personal fulfillment: reaching the pinnacle of your life's potential. A couple of notes on all this. First of all, not everyone makes it to personal fulfillment. Some, through no fault of their own, are cut down before their time. Others never get past the point of being fully satisfied with microwave dinners, cable television, a six-pack a night, and a new truck every three years. No problem. Everyone can still be motivated by visions of esteem and personal fulfillment.

Lower-level physiological needs can usually be addressed by tangible commodities, what marketers call a core product. These products are generally undifferentiated and sold on price. People will pay more for product enhancements, but not a whole lot more if those enhancements still address only physiological needs, issues of content. What makes people willing to pay *a whole lot more* is if those enhancements address upper-level needs, issues of relationships. Furthermore, the enhancements in no way need to have anything to do with the product itself. Why will someone pay sixty dollars for a pair of jeans that are of lesser quality than the twenty-dollar private-label brand? Because the sixty-dollar pair is positioned to affiliate the consumer with an aspirational reference group, providing a sense of esteem and personal fulfillment. You can look at this cynically and say that no one has ever gone broke underestimating the intelligence of people who buy jeans, but the fact is that just as love and hugs sell detergent, affiliation sells jeans. Leading marketers of soft drinks do not sell brown pop in a bottle; they sell an image of youth and fun, painting their competitors as old-fashioned and nerdy.

Marketers and advertisers also know that although people are motivated to buy through upper-level needs and feelings (the relationship issues), they often later justify their actions on the basis of lower-level needs, facts, and logic (the content issues). Thus, except for the 25 percent of the population classified as analytics, they do not provide product facts, specifications, and comparisons to help consumers make an informed buying decision. They sell on feelings and emotion, providing those facts, specifications, and comparisons to help consumers justify their decision later. In truth, informative advertising is designed to help consumers rationalize that their emotional behavior was logically consistent.

Before going any further, let us make it absolutely and abundantly clear that in no way do we suggest you misrepresent anything or manipulate anyone. People may tend to make decisions influenced by emotion and relationships, but they will ultimately validate the facts, logic, and content. Should the substance be anything less than they expected and you don't make things right real fast, the relationship component may be irrevocably damaged. So much for repeat business, a long-term relationship, and referrals, and sayonarra to your prospects for a successful career in sales. We *are* saying, though, that you view closing and motivation from a new perspective. Almost from the first page of this book, we've emphasized the importance of enhanced relationships as the foundation for a strategic alliance and partnership. We just got through a segment about closing on relationship. Take this line of reasoning one more step, to address closing. Motivate prospects to make an affirmative decision to reach agreement in principle, and to move into negotiating terms and conditions. Move beyond content-based benefits and value. Motivate them where motivation *is:* upper-level, relationship-based satisfiers. Don't sell them clean-smelling clothes; sell the love and hugs.

We've already dispelled the erroneous assumption that prospects know what they want and will buy on price. If that were true, you'd already be out of work. Still, as we've described, you'll always get a price objection, and one of the basics of Selling Skills 101 is to sell the benefits, sell the value, and justify the price. It always seems to come down to "the bottom line" and the belief that the best road toward the close is to focus on the dollars. Get the numbers right and prospects will initial the agreement. Sounds logical. Problem is, prospects don't really buy on logic. And strange as it may seem, money is way down on the list of motivators. That's not to say that money isn't important. It is; in fact, it's essential. But it may be most important as a way of keeping score in the arena of bragging rights, a relationship issue. If the highest rung you reached on the relationship ladder was for the prospect to be able to brag about how he or she beat you down on price, you pretty much failed at relationship development, didn't you?

Following are relationship-based motivators you should tune into to "close" the prospect into an agreement in principle.

Motivator #1: Take an Active Part in Making Their Dreams a Reality

Few people can tell you precisely what personal fulfillment means for them, but if you can get them talking they'll at least be able to describe some of the markers along the way. If they say "To be worth ten million dollars," follow up with, "So you can do what?" It's what they can cause to happen with the money, not the money itself, that constitutes the dream. Most business professionals have dreams that address upper-level needs of self-esteem and personal fulfillment. If they perceive you as someone who can help make those dreams a reality, they'll be inclined to do business with you.

Motivator #2: Help Prospects Attain Status and Recognition

You can address many of these opportunities outside the formal business environment. Of course, you know better than to position such gestures in the context of "You owe me one." Nevertheless, the fact that you help your prospects satisfy upper-level needs of status and recognition will make them predisposed to doing business with you in preference to a lower-priced competitor.

Motivator #3: Be a Source of Qualified Referrals

Yes, we realize we're back to describing ways to help them make more of that dirty, nasty money that's only a way of keeping score. But do it anyhow. Even people way up there on the hierarchy of needs have sport utility vehicles that have to be filled up with gas and kids that need braces.

Motivator #4: Provide Help and Explanations in Developing Proposals and Plans of Action

There's an old saying in sales about putting yourself in the customer's shoes. Think about the dilemma a prospect faces—you likely experienced this yourself—when confronting an important decision about choosing among alternatives. It's tantamount to a hiring decision in which you have half a dozen candidates with impressive resumes and who performed well in the interviewing process. The manager agonizes over which person to hire and how to go about training, orienting, and assigning. Most of us have been through the process of searching for a job. Wouldn't it have been nice if, after all the candidates had been interviewed, you, one of the candidates, could have consulted with the manager to help determine who to hire and what to do about getting that person on board and up and running? Of course, the manager would never let you do that. You knew you were the best candidate, so it would have been in his or her best interest to get you involved in the hiring decision, where he or she would ultimately hire you. You would have been a lot more productive a lot sooner if you worked with the manager on the details of your integration into the organization.

So what is the difference between hiring an employee and choosing among salespeople, particularly if the selected salesperson will have an implicit relationship with the prospect's company? The answer is there's almost no difference, except that as a salesperson you have the opportunity to get involved with prospects to help them make buying decisions which are in their best interest and to get involved in all the details of implementation, which will further optimize that buying decision.

Don't just submit a proposal and then sit at your desk, waiting for the phone to ring with the good news. Get involved in helping prospects make good decisions selecting among proposals and putting them into action. Your proactive role as consultant and helper, giving them help and explanations, positions you as a partner.

Motivator #5: Be a Source of Advice and Knowledge

One of the great motivators to action is relief from pain and trouble. If prospects have a problem that can be addressed by you, your products, and your services, they'll be inclined to do business with you and close on the details post haste. In the new world of business, the availability of information makes it possible for you to be fully informed about everything affecting your prospect's company and industry. When the news isn't good, be like the cavalry, riding in to their rescue.

Buck had nearly finalized details of a proposal and believed chances were good that it would be accepted. Then, going through an industry e-mail first thing in the morning, he learned that the prospect's company had just downsized by 10 percent. Conventional wisdom would suggest that you leave the prospect alone since this might not be a good time to talk about spending money, but Buck saw it differently. He immediately called the prospect to ask about how the downsizing had affected him and his department. The manager explained he was going to have a problem trying to get more done with fewer resources. Buck's response was, "I can help you do that." The deal was done.

In the preceding example, it was obvious to the prospect that he had a problem. Often, though, there are threats and problems that prospects are not even aware of, at least not yet. That's where the incredible explosion in availability of information can help you motivate them to act. As their primary information resource, you can keep them apprised of all relevant developments on the horizon, with proactive solutions you can provide.

Motivator #6: Relieve Prospects of Hassles

Here we have the essence of a partnership relationship, in which prospects perceive you not as a supplier but as a colleague. Just as an employee would say to a manager, "I'll handle that for you," the professional salesperson takes a proactive role in assuming responsibilities. Don't wait to be asked, but step up and take charge, managing a task as a business gesture, not expecting payback per se but ever mindful that such actions will cause prospects to be inclined to do business with you and will willingly pay more for the privilege.

Motivator #7: Help Prospects Avoid Risk

We've noted how it's a given in sales that there's always someone out there who says they have the same thing for less. And we've described how you must sell the value of you yourself, personally, rather than fight it out on price against the competition. Take that perspective one step farther by pointing out the other edge of the sword.

Don't just sell your value on the upside, also help your prospects avoid risk on the downside.

Some people, particularly amiables and analytics, are more averse to risk than others, but everyone, to some extent, can be motivated by reducing the possibility or impact of downside risk. If you have insurance beyond that required by law or the holder of your mortgage, you're one such example.

Here's a little game you can play to illustrate. Walk up to someone at random and say, "Take a coin out of your pocket. Flip it and call it in the air. If you call it right, I'll give you ten dollars. If you call it wrong, you give me five dollars." Chances are a vast majority of subjects will take you up on the offer. There's an equal probability of winning ten dollars or losing five dollars, or, as the statisticians would say, an expected value of winning $2.50.

Next, go up to someone and modify the proposal slightly. "If you call it right, I'll give you a million dollars. If you call it wrong, you give me half a million dollars." Now, there's an equal probability of winning a million dollars or losing $500,000, or an expected value of winning $250,000, but unless you're playing with someone who just won the lottery, don't expect too many people to take up your offer. The mere possibility of losing $500,000 is unthinkable, so people won't play the game.

Dealing with prospects is similar to having an insurance policy. Sure, they expect to pay a little more, but they reduce the downside risk so it's well worth it. Sometimes, though, prospects will play you off against the low-priced competitor, conveying to you that a downside risk does not exist. They either naively believe that to be the case or they're just throwing it out there to get a concession. Bring up the issue of downside risk.

No one gives things away for nothing. If the price is cheaper, something is missing. The competitor can say it's the same, the specifications may be the same, but since when does that make it the same? Occasionally, prospects weigh choices that can save them pennies but could cost them millions. A decision that could save them $10,000 might result in a recall that would cost $5 million. Is it worth the risk? And, naturally, point out the impact in terms of upper-level needs. "Sure, if you save ten thousand dollars, you'll get an 'attaboy' from your boss. But if you lose five million dollars, what will happen to your career, your family, your dreams?"

Motivator #8: Provide Service and Follow-Up After the Sale

This is a corollary to the prior two motivators, helping prospects avoid hassles, work, and downside risk. If you're there after the sale, they will be more confident that value received will exceed investment, so they will be more inclined to work with you and make the decision now. And as you already know, service and follow-up will help you generate repeat business and referrals.

CONCEPT 4: PROVIDE A COMPELLING REASON FOR PROSPECTS TO ACT NOW

It's a law of human nature that no one wants what they can have and everyone wants what they can't have. Evolution has programmed us this way, and it's what ensures a continuous improvement of mankind, at least technologically. It's also a law of human nature that no one will finalize any kind of deal, including selection of a mate, as long as there remains any reasonable possibility that there's something better down the road. This is illustrated each spring in rituals conducted at high schools throughout the land, where debutantes delay until the last minute accepting a date to the prom with a nerd like Bob in the hope of getting an invitation from a star athlete and student leader like Buck.

Prospects are no different from debutantes. No one is going to let you close them today if they know you and your offer will be there tomorrow since a better deal might just show up between now and then. They have nothing to lose by waiting a little longer before making a final decision. And no one is going to be all that interested in you, your products, and your services until it looks as though they might no longer be available or, even worse, someone else, perhaps their competition, gets them.

It all goes back to our analogy of viewing yourself as a prospective employee in the hiring process. As you probably learned in the first series of interviews for your first job, no one was going to make you an offer on a given day if they knew you'd still be available tomorrow. It was only when you conveyed great interest in the company and the job, tempered with the need to give an answer to your second choice if that was what you had to do, that your potential employer, faced with the reality of not getting invited to the prom at all, made you an offer. If none of this has ever happened to you, if you always got a quick offer on a job interview and always got accepted for a date, perhaps you were a star athlete and number one in your class at an Ivy League school. Along the same lines, if you consistently close prospects on the spot, without giving them a compelling reason to buy now, something is wrong. Perhaps you're selling ten-dollar bills for eight bucks.

A fundamental component of preparation for the sales encounter is to present prospects with some reason for making a timely decision. Within our context of closing, that means reaching agreement-in-principle and getting to work on specifications, terms, and conditions. Just be careful how you do this. Don't lie, and don't paint yourself into a corner.

If you've ever bought a home through a competent realtor, he or she almost certainly implored you to make an offer once you'd found a property you really liked. Recently, a salesperson was sued and convicted in such a situation by lying about other supposedly interested parties and the amounts of their prospective offers. That's not only unethical, it's stupid. You can convey a compelling reason to buy now in vague generalities that are consistent with facts. Others have looked at this house (qualified buyers or, at the least, the neighbors), it's possible an offer will come in as soon as tonight (the probability of that event is not zero), and I believe we should submit an offer of at least X (which is the appraised value).

In dealing with prospects, potential employers, or debutantes, there's no reason to lie. There's also no reason to put facts immaterial to your proposal on the table. Convey that if you can't put things together in the immediate future, you might not be able to do it at all or won't be able to give them the same deal. This is where you must be very careful about the perils of painting yourself into a corner. If you say, "This offer is good only until four o'clock today," you're boxed in. Should they call at six, you must tell them the offer has expired or you've totally lost your credibility. Worse, you've emboldened them to ignore any future deadlines and to question how firm you are on a "final offer." Instead, say: "I can guarantee this offer until four o'clock today. After that, it's anybody's guess."

Similarly, you might say:

- "I can reserve this now, but it might be gone as soon as tomorrow."
- "You have your choice of dates now, but I may get an e-mail this afternoon that will book me for a month."
- "I need a ten percent deposit to hold this for you."

Even more effective are impending events beyond your control.

- "There's a price increase next week."
- "Zero percent financing ends January second."
- "If we don't process this today, it will go on next month's production run."
- "The truck leaves Dallas at three. Do you want us to load your order on a pallet for you?"

All these tactics employ deadlines to convey to prospects a need to act or face the possibility of losing out. In the traditional transaction, this was the consummate "close," the capstone to all the little decisions that had narrowed down the options as you moved the prospect down the closing funnel. And if you're an order taker, selling a generally standardized product or service with little potential for customization and with only minor considerations for a follow-up or relationship after the sale, this is the last chapter for you. Smile, thank the prospect for doing business with you, and move on.

On the other hand, if your product or service will be individually tailored to the unique needs of your prospect in a relationship-intense partnership and strategic alliance, the close was a qualitative and subtle nudge to achieve agreement in principle, affording you the opportunity to attempt to quantify details. Contrary to the traditional perspective, the close did not finalize the deal, but has embarked you on the process of seeing whether you and the prospect can put a package together. At this point, you've agreed to try to agree.

CONCLUSION

In this chapter, we've described tactics designed to confirm agreement-in-principle, the affirmation that you and the prospect are going to work things out under some yet-to-be-determined terms and conditions. You're going to do business together! However, now is not the time to relax and get ready for the celebration you've planned once all the details have been hammered out. The devil is in all those details which will determine how favorable and how profitable that agreement will be. You're moving into the endgame, but in truth, the real game has just begun.

Chapter 8

Negotiating the Partnership:
Reaching Agreement on Points,
Terms, and Conditions

In the previous chapter, we looked at closing from a different perspective. Yes, in a traditional selling situation, with little or no latitude on points of agreement, terms, and conditions, the sales rep will run straight through all ten steps of the sales presentation, close, and go. But in a relationship-intense strategic partnership more typical of the new world of business, closing represents agreement in principle. You've closed on relationship and agreed to agree. That is, both sides are prepared to work out the specific details of a partnership if—and it's a big if—agreement can be reached on all the points, terms, and conditions. To go back to our analogy of a candidate for employment, the prospective company is amenable to hiring you and is prepared to make you a job offer. The question is, Will the offer be such that you can afford to take it? Sure, the company wants you as an employee, but if the most pay you'll get is $100 a week with no benefits, it's unlikely you'll be able to work things out. The flip side of the coin is if you're a recent college graduate looking for $10,000 a month, the employer may not exactly jump at the chance to hire you unless, of course, you can bring an incremental $20,000 a month in profits to the company, in which case the employer might be ready and anxious.

In this chapter, we'll explore the four key concepts for reaching agreement all the points, terms, and conditions of your partnership. First, we'll address the essence of power and leverage to enhance your bargaining position and help you construct a profitable agreement. We'll look at some negotiating tactics and countermeasures to employ and be on the lookout for. Then we'll describe a strategic approach to negotiation, a game plan for the process. Finally, we'll introduce some innovative approaches that can enhance your partnership and make it a better deal for both parties.

CONCEPT 1: THE ESSENCE OF POWER
AND LEVERAGE

A major theme of this book has been the importance of focusing on prospects and their needs. Make meaningful gestures toward others, without expecting something in return, and ultimately you'll be paid back anyhow, a function of the law of large numbers. We stand on everything we've said, to which we will now add: Having sold the relationship, moving on to attempt to finalize points, terms, and conditions, never forget that your number-one priority is looking out for number one.

There are far more similarities than differences between personal relationships and professional relationships because both include all the subtleties and dimensions of human nature and interpersonal communication. Back in Chapter 3, in the 2 × 2 communication-style matrix, we looked at two of the most important behavioral components, sensitivity and assertiveness. Let's now go a bit more deeply into assertiveness, since it's basic to a major resource for effective negotiation: power and leverage.

Power and leverage are always in play in any interpersonal interaction. It's a game you have to play. You can't elect not to participate. If you're perceived as strong, you'll come out better. If you're perceived as weak, people will either take advantage of you or decide you're not worthy of their attention at all. To successfully negotiate a strategic partnership, you must understand the essence of power and leverage, and enhance your position.

A fundamental tactic for enhancing your power is by setting the tone of the dialogue, taking control of the communication environment. In Chapter 3, we described how people can make "one-up" dominant statements, high on assertiveness, which can lead to confrontation. We counseled you not to respond in kind but to employ a neutral statement to establish an adult-adult dialogue. Viewing that from a perspective of power, this would not make you appear unassertive or submissive. On the contrary, you enhanced your power by refusing to allow the other person to control your behavior.

Along those same lines, we trust that you have learned the futility of attempting to assert yourself over others through demands and commands. It is a lot more effective to let them know what you have to offer, and that they are free to go elsewhere if they wish. Of course, in this case you, too, are free to go elsewhere, and you imply that plenty of others are interested in engaging you. Your power over others is enhanced by offering freedom and getting them to choose to deal with you.

These simple examples make an important point about power in negotiation. Power is an intangible that just "is." You just have a sense that certain people have power and confidence. By contrast, those people who attempt to overtly demonstrate power and confidence by what they say and do often lack what they're attempting to convey. Let's take a look, then, at a few points that can help power to "be."

Point 1: Knowledge Is Power

There is nothing more basic to the process of negotiation: the more you know, the better the outcome will be for you. Early in this book, we described how the information revolution helps you learn everything about your prospect and your competition, which was important for prospecting and proposal development. It's critical as you negotiate terms and conditions.

As we've said, you will always get a price objection and generally prospects will try to play you off against the competition. Have knowledge of what the competition has to offer, and what they provide in value above and beyond price and specifications. Learn all about their reputation and experiences enjoyed or suffered by their customers. Get a sense of whether your prospects would really seriously consider going with your competitor. Knowledge can help you get a sense of whether that competitor is viewed as a viable alternative by your prospects. That knowledge gives you power.

We've urged you to be a back-door sales rep, to help get ideas of prospect problems and needs that could be addressed with your products and services. All that work helped you develop a well-targeted presentation and proposal. Now, as you negotiate the details, there's another payoff.

Technology can get you information anytime, but personal sources of information from prospects themselves may be hard to get within the framework of the formal negotiation process. It's logical that as you're working on terms and conditions, prospects are unlikely to reveal information that would be helpful to you or detrimental to them. On the other hand, such information is far more likely to be available at a time well before the formal process, or from people at operational levels. Be alert for indiscreet remarks such as, "The boss' brother used those guys a couple of years ago and wound up suing them" or "We're down to a one-month supply, and you're the only ones who meet the technical specs." Such nuggets of information today can significantly affect your power in negotiations six hours or six months later. Of course, you won't make a big deal about it and brag about what you know, but just simply say: "I'm sorry, but I can't help you on the price. You can go with the competition if you wish, but I really believe we're a better value in the long run." Stop talking, and don't gloat.

The ten steps of the sales presentation are designed to glean a plethora of information from your prospects, all of which will come into play in the negotiation. Especially helpful is Step 4, uncovering an unmet need or dissatisfaction, particularly if you're making a proposal to an account currently served by the competition. Should you be able to address those unmet needs or dissatisfactions, you have power. For starters, there's good reason for the prospect to divorce the competitor and marry you. Even more important, you won't have to beat competitor's price.

There's another issue that must be addressed concerning the exchange of information in negotiation. There is an element of deceit in communication, perhaps not to mislead directly, but at least to allow the other party to reach a conclusion you wish him or her to. Let's be very careful with this, particularly since it's within the context of mutual benefit and trust. We are not advocating that you lie except under the most egregious circumstances. One such example, a favorite in ethics classes, is the case of a boat smuggling Jews out of Nazi Germany. A Nazi patrol boat comes alongside and asks, "Do you have any Jews on board?" The captain replies in the negative, lying, and is allowed to proceed. Most students would agree there was no breach in ethics and that the lying was justified. A similar example, closer to home, was back in the days when Buck was taking Bob's sales class at the university. One morning an angry gentleman burst into the room and shouted, "Where's that weasel Buck Hall? I heard tell he kissed my daughter behind our trailer." Buck was actually cowering in a small supply cabinet, but Bob, with no ethical qualms, explained that Buck had dropped the course and not been seen for weeks.

Except in such extraordinary circumstances, we would agree that lying is not ethical. From a pragmatic point of view, however, lying is plainly and simply a bad idea because you can get caught, resulting in a loss of credibility and respect. Beyond that, lying can get you in serious legal trouble if you knowingly misrepresent or fail to disclose germane material facts with resultant damages to the other party. That's called fraud, and it can cost you big time or a long time. Having said that, much of the time you can either refuse to answer or, how shall we say it, respond with a creative interpretation of the facts. We had an example of this in Chapter 7, where the real estate agent raised the possibility of a competing offer as a compelling reason to buy now. It's the same thing when you tell a prospect you can't guarantee a promotion will still be available Monday. Of course you can't guarantee it, because you can't guarantee the earth won't be struck by an asteroid or attacked by aliens over the weekend, obliterating all life-forms on the planet. Just don't say it *won't* be available if it might just *be* available.

Outside the context of fraud, generally you do not have to lay all your cards on the table. You do not have to tell the prospect you must close the sale today or be living on the streets tomorrow. On the other hand, since knowledge is power, the person on the other side of the table has every right to discover, if he or she can, the fact that you're desperate, and treat you accordingly, without mercy. You have no obligation to disclose that you are authorized to make a price concession if you are confident the prospect will accept your proposal as it stands. Likewise, the prospect is free to convey that he or she has numerous alternatives even when you're the only one who met the specs. "The truth" is furtive. "I have only fifty thousand dollars in the budget" becomes "the truth" by saying it, as does, "Well, maybe I could get another five thousand dollars from another budget."

Negotiation is a game of power and information, played out in an ever-changing context of time. As in chess, you make moves in the pursuit of an objective, with an element of deceit consistent with a relationship based on trust. Yes, that sounds like a contradiction, but even in your closest personal relationships, you still negotiate within that context. You may have no viable alternatives, but you'll say to your significant other, "Go ahead and date other people if you'd like. Several others have shown an interest in me lately, and I might just go out with some of them." Unless you're a fool you would never, even if it were the truth, say, "No one else wants me. If you go out with other people, I'll just sit home and cry."

Keep all this in mind as you begin the process of exchanging information, seeking to finalize points, terms, and conditions. Certainly, you want to help your prospects satisfy their needs and give them the best you have to offer, personally and professionally. But first and foremost, you're looking out for number one and you want to get paid. It's enlightened self-interest. Your prospects are playing it that way, and you must also play it that way. If you can't play the game, you may close some sales, but they likely won't be profitable sales and you won't have commanded optimum respect from your prospect. Bet your significant other doesn't treat you very well, either.

Point 2: The Power of Commitment

You must absolutely, positively, unequivocally believe in yourself, your company, and its products, services, and support. You cannot fake this, and it is essential in negotiating the partnership. It's the commitment that not only gets the sale but gets the price.

From the first meeting with your prospect until the final agreement is signed, sealed, and delivered, you will, time and again, have to look your prospect and others in the eye and convey, "We're the best. Not the lowest price, but the best value. We'll be there for you all the way. I won't let you down. You can depend on me." In the negotiation, it's part of the game for the prospect to tell you the competition has better products at better prices. You must believe—without reservations—that's not true. You must believe your products and services are worth the price or you'll never get the price. Way back in Chapter 1, we suggested that you evaluate your company and the company you keep. Here's where the belief in your company, or lack thereof, comes into play.

On a personal level, you must believe in the value you bring to the table or you have nothing to offer over the low-priced online competitor. This means a commitment to do what you said you'd do, when you said you'd do it. In turn, that leads to commitment on the part of your prospect and other buying influences in the prospect's company.

He or she is willing to take a stand and advocate doing business with you and argue against going with the low-priced alternative. Many of these conversations will take place during intense private sessions among principals in the buying organization. At that time, just who is going to stand up for you and how strongly?

Bob learned this lesson firsthand soon after launching his own firm specializing in sales and management training. He made a call on a firm whose sales manager was a person he'd dealt with regularly over a ten-year period with his former employer. Their relationship had always been good because Bob had always done what he promised, on time. After a couple of meetings, Bob developed and submitted a proposal for a comprehensive and innovative training program that, if accepted, would have been the first significant project for his new company. About a week later, Bob got a phone call confirming agreement, initiating a series of follow-up programs and referrals that were the foundation for his business in the next several years. But it was several months later, as the activities were being conducted, that Bob was having a conversation with another manager who told him the rest of the story. It turned out that soon after Bob submitted his proposal, a representative from his former company had called on the prospect, urged the prospect not to do business with Bob, and promised that the former company would develop and conduct the same program for no charge, an offer apparently too good to refuse. The managers all got together to discuss the situation, and initially it appeared that the obvious choice was to go with the low-priced—free— bid. Then, the sales manager stood up and said, "We've always been able to depend on Bob. The rest of the people in his former company have never been there for us." The commitment of the sales manager had turned the tide. Keep that in mind when you make the commitment to do what you said you'd do. Sooner or later, maybe in ten years or more, the commitment to your promises may help gain the commitment of a key influence in a buying organization. The chickens always come home to roost.

Another side of commitment, dealing with your reasonable and rational perspective of looking out for number one and getting paid, is that you have the right to expect customers to do what *they* said they would do and live up to commitments *they* made to *you*. Buck recently granted a prospect a 12 percent discount on a project if payment were made by the end of the year, but as of December 31, no check. So, on that last day of the year he phoned the prospect's company and explained, very politely, that they needed to cut a check that afternoon or the invoice would be voided and a new one issued, sans the discount. Their accounts payable department explained that the check would be issued along with the regular batch, in mid-January, but Buck held firm. The discount was contingent on a check being cut that day. It was done. Did it make any difference to Buck's company if they received the check on January 15 instead of December 31? Probably not. But it would have sent the wrong message to the clients, implying they need not live up to their commitments. Better to establish, early on, that clients are expected to live up to their commitments, too.

Both Bob and Buck routinely negotiate agreements with clients in which a portion of the costs for program development is paid up front. They clearly spell out to clients that work will not begin, or work on a project will be suspended, if payments are not received as agreed. Bob has a policy of collecting in advance 50 percent of the fee for conducting programs, as confirmation of scheduled program dates, with the remainder of the fee due upon conducting the program. Should a client wish to change a program date, another 50 percent is due as confirmation of the new date, with nothing more due upon completion. This permits a client to make one change, with no additional cost, in case unforeseen circumstances so dictate, though it occasionally leaves Bob with nothing to do for a few days. However, should the client wish to make subsequent changes, it's another 50 percent for confirmation of the new date. On several occasions, clients have requested a second change of program dates, pleading events beyond their control, but Bob always holds firm. It's an extra 50 percent to change a second or subsequent time. Every time, the client has managed to find a way to schedule the program and avoid the extra charge.

Most salespeople will have experiences similar to those of Bob and Buck. It all points to the need for an explicit written understanding of what each party is expected to do and when. Prospects have every right to expect you to fulfill your commitments, and you have every right to hold them to theirs. It's an essential component of mutual respect.

Point 3: The Power of Attitude

Our last point—the power of commitment—touched on the fact that your attitude can profoundly affect the outcome of a proposal. Let's go into that in greater depth.

Back in Chapter 3, we touched on the power of attitude and described how relationships are always being defined, either growing or dying. The status of relationships most certainly affects a negotiation, so it's essential to ensure that all relationships are growing and flourishing. This is often called the power of courtship. As in a marriage, if the courtship ends at the altar, disaster is on the horizon. The courtship must never end, though it's important to couch that attitude within the context of want, not need. Certainly communicate that you want the business, but never convey need, that you're unwilling to walk. You will never command respect in a personal or professional relationship if the other side perceives that you will not turn on your heels. All they have to do is wait you out, ticking off one concession at a time until they finally throw a bone to the whipped dog. This is basic human nature, and another example of the necessity of developing negotiation skills in business and life. We sympathize with you in wishing life was different than it is, but that won't change reality.

As we will describe in Concept 3, after all other points have been determined the negotiation likely will come down to that nasty old money. At that time, you should have a very specific range of agreement in mind. At the high end is your objective, what you're shooting for as the optimum outcome. At the low end is your walkaway number, the point at which you perceive that no agreement is the best alternative. These numbers need to be quantified in advance to properly plan a negotiation strategy. Similarly, the other side should have a low number at which they'd ideally like to buy and a high number beyond which they will not go. If there's no overlap in the ranges, no agreement will be possible without going back to the table to explore alternatives. If there *is* an overlap, agreement should be attained. Just *where* that agreement is attained will depend on the negotiation skills and the attitudes of the respective sides. This is the most basic, least sophisticated form of negotiation, piecemeal bargaining over price after all other variables have been determined. As we'll see later in the chapter, this is not an ideal situation and is subject to impasse, especially if the respective positions are far apart. We'll describe strategies to either avoid piecemeal price haggling entirely or, at the least, to minimize the gap between positions. But first, let's take a look at a typical piecemeal price negotiation.

Let's say, for example, that someone is selling a house. He or she would like to get $500,000, but would settle for as little as $450,000. You're interested in buying the house and would like to get it for a bargain basement $420,000, but would be willing to go as high as $480,000. Clearly, a deal should be struck, somewhere in the range between $450,000 and $480,000. But where? That remains to be seen.

Don't convey to the owner that you love the house and can't live without it. To do so would ensure that you do the deal at the high end of the range or even above. If the owner perceived your attitude, or just noticed you frothing at the mouth, you might even wind up paying $520,000. Instead, you would try to appear fairly nonchalant, communicating that you were a serious qualified buyer, but, utilizing some of the tactics we'll describe in the next section, that you can offer only $400,000. Since knowledge is power, you would have uncovered the fact that the owner had already bought a new home in another city and had been stuck with two mortgage payments for the past three months. Let's say the owner counters with $475,000, halfway between his or her objective and bottom line, a price now within the range of agreement. Certainly you would not agree on the spot, realizing that the $25,000 concession would indicate that further concessions of $10,000 or $15,000 or more were still to be had. Perhaps you counter with $420,000, matching the 5 percent move, leaving you at the bargain basement objective. Now the fun begins, in which your power of attitude will affect the ultimate outcome.

If the seller makes another significant concession, say $15,000, to a price of $460,000, you can readily respond with a concession of your own, albeit smaller. You might go up $10,000, to an offer of $430,000, leaving the two parties only $30,000 apart. Though you can't be sure of the seller's bottom line, you can calculate the halfway point between the positions as $445,000, very favorable to you. It's the seller's turn. You sit back and wait for the next concession and respond in kind. The seller drops to $450,000, you go to $438,000.

The scenario as described so far is ideal for you, but perhaps overly optimistic. Reading between the lines—and we'll return to this example in greater depth later in the chapter—the negotiation posture of the seller indicates weakness, a willingness to keep making concessions, partially matched, until a point is reached at which the difference between the positions is insignificant: "I'll agree to your price if you buy the pizza." Certainly it's in your interest, perceiving this weakness, to let the game play out since it's favorable to you. This is the game played by adept buyers against salespeople, anxious to make a sale, who are unskilled negotiators. One side perceives that the other has a greater need to make a deal, and of course, takes advantage.

Let's back this up, then, to a situation in which the need to sell equals the need to buy. The seller drops to $475,000. You counter with $420,000 and wait for another concession but surprise, the seller says no; that's as low as he or she will go. The seller has just lobbed the ball back into your court. Yes, you can raise your offer again, but two concessions in a row without getting one in return makes you look very, very weak indeed. The seller appears to be holding firm, but just how firm is he or she? Are you willing to put this to the test, to risk not getting the house? If not, go ahead and throw in the towel and offer the $475,000 or at least $470,000. Rationalize that it's only money. But if you're willing to assume risk for potential reward, turn on your heels. Do not raise your voice and say, "Four hundred twenty thousand dollars. Take it or leave it." Even if that were your top dollar, such a statement would only aggravate the seller. Instead, say, "I'm sorry, but four hundred twenty thousand dollars is the best I can do. I won't buy anything else before six tonight. Please call me if you change your mind." Or, if you prefer, "I'm sorry, but four hundred seventy-five thousand dollars is more than I can go. Please let me know if you can do better." Prepare to go, and under no circumstances make another concession. The seller will make the next concession, or it's a no go. Chances are very good that he or she will say "Wait!" or at the least phone by 5:45. Will you take the chance?

If you have the power of commitment, and truly believe in your company, products, services, and yourself, you should have the power of attitude. You want the prospect's business, but you don't need it. You are selling value that's worth the price. Sell that value! And sell the price! Be willing to say: "I'm sorry. I just don't think we'll be able to get together on this." If you just can't and won't walk out that door without a deal, you'll never know what might have been. You'll always be underpaid, and pay too much.

Point 4: The Power of Legitimacy

The power of your position in negotiation is enhanced by having authoritative standards and justifications underpinning your proposal. In its most basic form, the power of legitimacy is the power of the printed page. A sheet specifying your prices is more authoritative and powerful than merely stating them. Banks are great at this. "Here it is on our letterhead. A thirty-year mortgage is X percent interest with Y points." Since it's written down, most customers never challenge the terms.

When you go into a negotiation, always have in writing your prices, terms, and conditions. If applicable, include the attendant rationale on which they are based. Have as little authority as possible to alter your pricing.

Many salespeople are under the erroneous assumption that they could close more deals if they had more authority, whereas the reverse is true. You are in a stronger bargaining position, more likely to get your price, if you can look your prospect straight in the eye and say, "I'm sorry. I just can't do that." Then, call upon your powers of commitment and attitude, and sell the value.

You enhance the power of legitimacy by engaging the power of expertise, including technical people or other support personnel to explain salient points of your proposal. Their interaction with peers and colleagues within the prospect's company can enhance commitment within the buying organization. In addition, take advantage of the information revolution to procure articles and data from scientific and trade sources that support points in your proposal. It's one thing to tell prospects your products are built to last, it's something else to pull out the results of a test conducted by a leading university.

Use the power of legitimacy to question any statements or presumptions made by the prospect. Ask yourself, "Says who?" If you fail to challenge assumptive statements such as, "It will take us ninety days to process payment," "We'll have to get an independent verification of this by X," or "Our cost to arrange that is Y," think to yourself, "Says who?" Allowing such seemingly innocuous statements to pass unquestioned allows the other side to set terms and conditions in what amounts to a unilateral concession on your part. Recently, one of our colleagues was placing an order on which he needed delivery within five days. He was told that would incur an additional shipping charge of twenty-four dollars, to which he replied, "Says who?" As a first step, it was determined the upcharge should be sixteen dollars, not twenty-four, and as a second step that standard shipping would get it there in plenty of time.

Point 5: The Power of Competition

We've talked about some of these points elsewhere, but let's briefly tie up the loose ends. Sure, there's someone out there who says they have better products and services for less, and buyers will play the competition against you in an attempt to wring out concessions. In some cases, though, you go into the negotiation with the power of knowledge that prospects are playing you against the competition, knowing that in actuality, the competition is not a viable alternative for them. By contrast, inadequate knowledge of the competition may weaken your negotiating position, with a detrimental effect on the outcome. A professional association was recently negotiating with hotels in New Orleans for facilities to conduct a major meeting event. Initially, the hotel was very inflexible about services and prices, knowing it was the only establishment in the city that could handle the event. Then, the clients let the word leak out that they were considering moving the event to Chicago or Atlanta and were soliciting competitive bids. In fact, it was too late to change the meeting site but, of course, they did not feel ethically compelled to so inform the New Orleans hotel, which became considerably more flexible when faced with what it erroneously perceived to be the power of competition.

Point 6: The Power of Time

Negotiation is a process involving the interplay of knowledge, tactics, and power, all within the context of time. Time plays a crucial role in this process, in several distinct ways.

One of the roles of time is derived out of the power of persistence, investing your time and getting prospects to invest their time in efforts to find creative solutions and reach agreement. From your point-of-view, this is your power of commitment and an unwillingness to give up, consistent with the principle of bailing out as soon as possible if the ultimate result will be unfavorable. The other side of this equation involves getting your prospects to invest their time and energy. If they have invested many hours over weeks and months, evaluating your proposal and negotiating points, terms, and conditions, they will become increasingly inclined to work the process through to agreement lest all their efforts be for naught. You will enhance this through skills we will discuss in Concept 3, in which both sides have gained something through the initial stages of negotiation and are thus inclined to move the process to conclusion and agreement rather than lose benefits already in hand.

A second role of time is deadlines, yours and the other side's. There are self-imposed deadlines and real deadlines. "I've got to get this done by Friday" is a self-imposed deadline if it means only that you'd prefer not to work over the weekend. It's a real deadline if you're being shipped off to Saudi Arabia on Saturday. A rule of thumb in negotiations is that real movement starts to take place near, or even a bit past, deadlines. Your power in the process is significantly enhanced if you can discover the other side's deadlines without having them find out yours. If someone is trying to sell his or her motorcycle before being shipped out to Saudi Arabia on Saturday, his or her bargaining position and expectations will be far lower Friday night than they were Monday morning. Unless, of course, the seller knows you need to have a bike and be on the road in the next two hours to make it to Sturgis.

The third role of time, closely related to deadlines, is that reality changes over time. If you're in a position to outwait the other side, and know it, you're in a position to outnegotiate them. What was untouchable a week ago may be wide open to discussion today. Yesterday's unacceptable offer is received with open arms. Twelve-step veterans know that everything is one day at a time. I'll love you forever— today. I'll never do that—today. When Bob moved to Florida, he put his home in Athens on the market for a net $55,000, with a bottom line of $51,000 (what he had invested in it). Very soon after listing the property, he was offered $46,500, which he turned down. Six months later, he took $41,000 and was glad to get it.

The changing of reality over time works to your advantage with the power of persistence. The account that was unreachable a year ago might be had today, especially if the competition neglected to continue the courtship after the sale. Salespeople living in the past—not twenty years in the past like Willy Loman, but in the reality of only a few months ago—may be missing opportunities today. The events of

September 11, 2001, are generally acknowledged as having had a profound effect on the business and political landscape, apparent to the most casual observer. Not so obvious have been the incremental changes, inexorable, day to day, in the weeks, months, and years since then. These changes don't slap us in the face as a monumental event, but they add up quickly over time. The world and reality are very different today than a year ago, and they will be significantly different a year from now. The information revolution of the new world of business makes it possible for individuals to learn about and act upon emerging opportunities before the general public is even aware of them. A year from now, most people will look back at all the changes and say, "Of course that had to happen. Why didn't I see it coming?" People who know reality changes over time, and is changing at an exponentially increasing rate, will be the first to discover those emerging changes and act on the opportunities that surface alongside them.

CONCEPT 2: TOOLS OF THE TRADE— TACTICS AND COUNTERMEASURES

To this point, we've described considerations for establishing a strong posture in negotiation, optimizing power with the use of information and appropriate communication, all within the context of time. Now we'll look at some of the tools of the trade, negotiation tactics, and their attendant countermeasures. We need to preface this segment similarly to its counterpart in the last chapter, specifically by noting that negotiation, as closing, is a process, not an isolated application of tactics. You will utilize these tactics as appropriate, but all as part of an overall strategic approach to negotiation, the subject of Concept 3. There is a major difference between closing and negotiation, however, which is that whereas closing is a tactic employed almost exclusively by the salesperson, negotiation is a game that two can play. Thus, it's absolutely essential to spot tactics employed by the other side, since a perceived tactic is an ineffective tactic.

Experienced buyers are all adept negotiators, as are most professional businesspeople spending their company's or their own money. They will all employ tactics designed to get the products or services, on which you achieved agreement in principle, at the lowest possible price. No, they will not feel badly that you don't make any money on the deal. Yes, they will still sleep well at night knowing that you must subsist on peanut butter sandwiches and your kids get their clothes secondhand. They will employ a wide variety of tactics to get you to lower your prices and make other concessions, and once they wring a concession out of you, like a shark smelling blood, there will be a feeding frenzy with you as the carcass. To get that nasty, grimy money out of their pockets and into yours, know the tools of the trade.

Tactic 1: It's Not in the Budget

As we noted in Chapter 6, this is a popular variation of the price objection. We actually look forward to this tactic because it usually means agreement has been achieved on everything *but* the price, so now we're getting down to the nitty-gritty. The objective of this tactic—and *all* negotiation tactics—is of course, to get you to make a concession so as to accommodate the "budget," which is probably a figment of the imagination anyhow. If you offer better value than the competition, and that value exceeds price, they'll find a way.

Tactic 2: Emotional Pleas

Why would people resort to cheap emotional pleas in negotiation? Because they work. Your parents taught you this one early. "How can you even think of going camping for the weekend? Your Uncle Harry and his companion will be visiting, and you know how much they look forward to seeing you. Why are you so selfish? Can't you be thoughtful and do something nice to others at least once in awhile?" Guilt is a great emotional tactic, highly likely to yield a concession when followed by silence. "You gotta help me on this. I'm putting in ninety hours a week just to buy food for my family. You're making lots of money with this. Can't you just please give a little guy a break?" Equally effective is imploring you to fairness. "I'm interested, yes, and I think you should make a profit. But you've got to be fair about this. C'mon, what can you do for me?"

Sometimes, an emotion of mild aggravation and disgust works well. "Fred, you've just got to do better than this . . ." or, to tick it up a notch, "Fred, you've just got to do substantially better than this . . ." Always, of course, follow the emotional plea with silence, letting "You love me, don't you?" or "Why can't you be fair?" or its business counterpart sink in. The first one to speak loses, which of course is you, making a concession.

Loud emotional outbursts, profanity, or ranting and raving are usually not as effective as guilt trips or pleas to fairness. The only acceptable response to all such shameless tactics is to acknowledge them with a disarming statement, mentally grade them on a scale from one to ten, and shift the discussion to content.

Tactic 3: Silence

A quick follow-up on the last item, tying up a point we've stressed on several prior occasions. One mark of a competent salesperson, or a competent negotiator, is his or her ability to handle silence. We've noted the importance of shutting up after asking a question, particularly a closing question. Now, be aware of it as a negotiation tactic. So, when the other party says, "Fred, you've got to do substantially better than this . . ." allow about twenty seconds of silence, then say, "Sheila, it's a good proposal. It's worth the money," and shut up for the duration. The other party speaks next, even if it's ten minutes after the cows come home.

Tactic 4: Extreme Initial Positions

Opening with a "relatively extreme" position can be an effective negotiation tactic, assuming it is handled properly. The risk is that if the other side is confident about their expectations, your initial position may incline them to dismiss you out of hand rather than taking your opening position as a starting point for serious negotiations. To minimize that risk, have some justification for the offer—the power of legitimacy—and present it in positive relationship terms. If done properly, the extreme initial position immediately reduces the other side's expectation level. They may not do it consciously, but they will do the math to calculate the midpoint between the proposals, where you'd be if you split the difference.

Let's go back to the example of the house, for which the owner wants $500,000. If you had any reason to believe the owner was anxious to sell, instead of an initial offer of $400,000, why not come in about 30 percent lower, say $350,000, particularly if you know—which of course, you should—that's significantly more than the seller paid for it twelve years ago. Using the "It's not in the budget" tactic, agree the house is worth the asking price but you can't afford it. Applying the powers of competition and legitimacy, point out comparable foreclosures available at your price. Then, make a personal appeal, note you have preapproved financing and are prepared to close within seventy-two hours, and shut up. Chances are very good that by the time the seller speaks next, the bottom-line number will have dropped from its initial $450,000 to the split-the-difference price of $425,000. Starting the concession game from there should yield you a somewhat better outcome.

If you're on the other side of the table, don't mishandle that extreme initial position if there's a chance you could ultimately reach an acceptable agreement. Perhaps respond with, "I'd love for you to have the house, and I'll try to help us put a deal together. But three hundred fifty thousand dollars just isn't a reasonable place to begin talking [note the appeal to fairness]. Please look at your numbers again and see what you can do." In other words, sorry, I won't respond with the concession game yet. It's still your turn. Another countertactic, which you might employ first and would certainly employ if the next offer was $355,000, would be to respond with an extremely small, almost insignificant concession. "Tell you what. I can't do three hundred fifty-five thousand dollars, but here's what I can do. I'll go four hundred ninety-nine thousand, five hundred dollars, but I'm taking the washer, dryer, and hot-water heater." In other words, two people can play this stupid game. Do you want to make a serious offer or not? Then, naturally, shut up.

Tactic 5: Communicate Through Diminishing Increments

This was also illustrated in the house example, where an initial $25,000 concession by the seller suggested that at least one more five-figure concession might be in the wings. Had a second concession been an equal amount of $25,000, it would have communicated that there might have been *much,* much further to go. The buyer, you will recall, went from $400,000 to $420,000 to $430,000 to $438,000, communicating through increments that the final agreement would be somewhere in the $440s, not higher than $450,000.

We'll fine-tune our points on concessions in Concept 3, but stay with the basic house example at this point. Essentially, the game is going along well if your concession is met by one of equal size by the other side, as long as you're progressing to a split-the-difference midpoint that is favorable to you. This sort of tit-for-tat scenario is particularly effective against people with a compromiser negotiating style willing to initiate the process from the starting point of your extreme initial position. Just don't make it too easy for him or her. Convey that you're almost killing yourself to modify your offer. "Wow, I don't know how I'll be able to do it, but I'll increase my offer by twenty thousand dollars." If you've just made such a magnanimous gesture, certainly it's only fair that the seller will respond in kind, as you steadily march toward the split-the-difference mark. Employ a guilt trip if you think it would be effective. "I've raised my offer by twenty thousand dollars. I'm trying to be fair. Don't you think you should be fair to me and lower your asking price by twenty thousand dollars? I'm just trying to be reasonable. Please try to be reasonable with me."

Tactic 6: The Nibble, the Salami, and Other Funny Money

Experienced buyers know that a good deal can be made a very good deal just by asking for one more thing that will wrap up the agreement. The most basic tactic is the nibble, asking that something be thrown in. "Okay, I'm ready to buy the suit. Will you throw in the tie?" or "I think we can get together on this. Can you give us the extended warranty for years two through five?" After negotiating as good a price as you're going to get on a car, ask: "Can you give me free oil changes for the next two years and no charge for labor on my thirty-thousand-mile service?" See what happens. You'll probably get something you wouldn't have gotten without a nibble.

Similar to the nibble but a bit more sophisticated is the salami, designed to get an apparently minor unilateral concession. Here's the anecdote behind the name of the tactic. You're out on a picnic, just you and your significant other, and for lunch you're having, what else, a salami. Someone walks up to you on the blanket, grabs the salami, and runs off. What are you going to do? Well, since someone just took off with your lunch, you'll probably set off after him or her, retrieve the salami, and reprimand him or her severely. By contrast, what if he or she walked up, cut off just a thin slice of the salami, and ran off? Since it was only a small slice, and you still have the remainder of the salami, you'd probably let him or her go rather than permit the event to negatively affect the ambiance of your date. Hence the tactic of asking for just a little something at various points in the negotiation process. A thin slice here, a thin slice there, and, hey, that son of a gun got my whole salami.

This is the point of so-called funny money where, to paraphrase a famed senator from the Midwest, a penny here and a penny there, pretty soon you're talking about big money. A penny a pound is significant when you're talking 100,000 pounds. "Just throw in the shipping" might not show up in the sales department budget, but could cost the company half its profit on the deal.

Sure, one thin slice off the salami, in the form of a nibble, might be a reasonable concession for achieving agreement today. But just remember that one thin slice times 100,000 is a lot of salami.

Tactic 7: Disinformation

Be very wary and skeptical of information that just happens to land in your lap, especially if receiving the information seems too good to be true. It probably is. We noted this tactic in the example of a client dealing with hotels in New Orleans by leaking information about considering moving their event. In case you hadn't noticed, humans use this tactic routinely. "Please don't say a word to Bill, but if he doesn't call me by Wednesday I'm going to make other plans with someone else." For this tactic to be effective, you must be confident the third party will relay the news, and it's guaranteed he or she *will* relay it if you specifically ask him or her *not* to.

Another common application of this tactic is buyers who let you think you're being very clever snooping around their office. There will be a seemingly important document on your competitor's letterhead on the buyer's desk. After being sure you've spotted it, he or she will arrange to be called away for a few moments, permitting you the opportunity to lean forward, peer over the desk, and read, upside down, that the competition has beaten your price by 15 percent. You, of course, cannot admit your apparent indiscretion and so cannot convey your "knowledge" directly. But when the buyer says, "Alice, I hope you understand we're considering a number of alternatives, and price will be a very important point," your expectations have already dropped by at least 10 percent, maybe the whole 15 percent. When a month later you discover that the competitor's document was a phony—yes, early on you too learned how to print out documents with anyone's logo—you're in no position to complain since you had no business reading it in the first place.

A last point is to be on the lookout for vague promises such as future business at very favorable prices in return for today's business at an inordinantly low price. Such vague promises are not worth the price of the paper they're printed on, which they're not, even if the other party believes he or she is sincere in making them. "We'll take care of you down the road" is translated as "You've been had today. And if you were so easily had today, why should you expect us to show you any respect down the road?" Get it in writing!

Tactic 8: Limited Authority

We looked at this one back in prospecting and qualifying, noting how critical it was to speak to decision makers who have the authority to finalize an agreement. That done, buyers may still throw in the need to run everything by a person or a committee to get final approval, and that person or committee will want a nibble or a thin slice of salami, perhaps with a cracker and condiments, to ice the deal. Head this one off at the pass. When you make the offer of a final concession that brings both sides together, ask directly: "If I do this, will you initial this agreement today?" If that's affirmative, you have a deal. If there's a higher authority ploy, you've withheld the offer of your final concession contingent on agreement. Hold to the understanding that the final concession will constitute the last nibble.

CONCEPT 3: A STRATEGIC APPROACH
TO NEGOTIATION

So far, we have described ways to enhance your power position in the negotiation process and tactics that are commonly employed. You will utilize these tactics at appropriate moments and hopefully recognize when someone is laying them on you. None of this, however, will be particularly useful outside the context of an overall negotiation strategy. A strategic approach starts with something you've heard a time or two before: get prospects to talk. As you do, look beyond their stated positions and get a sense of what they really want, need, and care about. Then, show them how they can get all those things as you maximize the flow of money out of their pockets and into yours. If that concept seems familiar, it should. It's just another play on the feature-benefit/price-value theme, the difference being that in negotiation it's quantatative instead of just qualitative.

Double-check to be sure of a couple of perspectives you must have going in. First of all, understand that if you must make a deal, you won't like the deal you get. Yes, you've put in a lot of time and work to get this far, and you've "closed" in the sense that you've reached agreement in principle and have moved on to terms, points, and conditions. So near and yet so far. Sure, it's great to close a sale and get the order. But in the relationship-intense new world of business, where there is considerable latitude on specifications, prices, and terms, it's more important to close a *profitable* sale. Better to lose half the sales, even at this point, rather than make a series of concessions that leave you with only a third the profit. Be prepared to walk.

With these key perspectives in mind, lets look at a strategic approach to negotiation. As in chess, our applications of power and utilization of tactics will all take place under the umbrella of this overall game plan.

Strategy 1: Get Everything on the Table
Before *You Start to Negotiate*

There are a number of schools of negotiation that advocate addressing one issue at a time. The idea is to reach agreement on the easy issues first, by which time, through the power of investment of time, both sides are more inclined to be accommodative on the tougher points. We've come this far, let's not lose what we've gained, let's work things through to a final agreement. This approach to negotiation may be valid and useful in numerous environments, but business just doesn't happen to be one of them.

That piecemeal approach to bargaining fails to take into consideration a major characteristic of business negotiations, namely that at the end of the day agreement hinges on price. Since every other variable in the equation affects the price, you can't finalize price until you've reached agreement on everything else. Thus, before starting to go back and forth, get everything on the table. Brainstorm, and keep probing for variables. Ask yourself: What other points, what other considerations can we make part of this agreement that will make it a better deal for both parties?

Everything is negotiable; anything can be talked about. Go ahead and put it on the table, though that, of course, does not imply tacit agreement to any point or concession. When you get the "It's not in the budget" tactic, or even the more emphatic "There is zero budget for that," consider it neither a deal breaker nor a reason for making a concession. Simply say: "Fine, we'll have to talk about payment terms. What else do we need to address?" In sales, there's a lot to be said about just showing up. In negotiation, there's a lot to be said about just staying on the playing field.

Taking the time to get all the issues on the table also permits you to get a sense of the other side's hot buttons. Beyond the content-based features and benefits, try to get a sense of individual relationship issues and personal agendas that are being played out, and how you could address these to generate a more favorable agreement. Your unique ability to satisfy upper-level needs could prove the difference between a profitable sale and no deal at all. Can you make your prospects feel important, with a more favorable and visible profile in their organization? Can you help them launch a project that could have positive implications for their career track? Will they gain personal recognition by increasing productivity?

There was a pitching coach of a not-terribly-successful ball club in a major midwestern city who had a habit of walking out to the mound and saying something such as, "Whatever you do, don't throw him high and inside. If it's high and inside, he'll knock it out of the park. Remember: Just don't throw him high and inside." The pitching coach would go back to the dugout, and all the pitcher could think was, "High and inside. Don't throw it high and inside." So, where do you suppose the pitch went? Of course, high and inside. And where do you suppose the ball went? Right again.

The point to that little anecdote applies to this first strategy of negotiation. As you're getting everything on the table, you're going to hear a lot of things you don't want to hear in the form of objections and demands. Fine. But instead of thinking "Don't throw it high and inside," do think "Just keep it low and outside." In other words, stay focused on the positives—the target you're aiming for—instead of the negatives—the least you'll settle for.

Keep the other side talking, and encourage them to elaborate. Get a sense of the relativity of variables, points that are of great value to one side but of little consequence to the other. Generally, this comes down to a simple exercise in price-versus-value. Say, for example, that you have a concession that costs you $1,000 but is worth $3,000 to the other side. It is absolutely in the interest of both parties that the concession be made, perhaps with a comparable concession from the other side. At the least, make the concession in exchange for a price increase of $2,000, leaving each party $1,000 better off than before. By contrast, if a concession that costs you $3,000 is worth only $1,000 to the other side, the concession should not be made at all.

You can note in the prior example that there is a wide range of possible agreements. If the concession is made, both parties gain if the price is increased between $1,001 and $2,999, though, of course, one party gains a whole lot more at the respective extremes. Negotiation skills and tactics will determine whether one side or the other consistently benefits inordinantly more as variables and price adjustments are determined. But a key point is that it is absolutely in the best interest of both parties that agreement be reached if there is a favorable relativity of variables. Failure to agree hurts everyone. If transportation will cost them $8,000 and you can do it for $5,000, both parties lose if you initial an agreement in which they handle the transportation. The dance is to identify shared concerns without giving away how little a concession costs you or how much it benefits you. In a truly collaborative negotiation, both sides would simply lay their numbers out on the table. That might well happen in the context of a strategic alliance and partnership, or it might not.

Strategy 2: Trade Concession So That Both Sides Benefit

Let's now take our points on concessions to the next level. You'll recall our very simple case of the house, in which the parties alternated price concessions, moving toward a midpoint. As we noted, if the process of alternating concessions is moving you toward a satisfactory outcome, all well and good. We classify this example, however, as a "very simple case" because implicit is the fact that there is only one variable to be negotiated, the price. The assumption in the example is that all other points, terms, and conditions have already been determined according to the relativity of variables. For example, the above-ground swimming pool is worth more to the buyer than it would be to the seller, who would have to empty it, disassemble it, cart it off, and set it up somewhere else. The pool stays. By contrast, if the buyer were a contractor it would be cheaper and easier for him or her to fix the leaky roof. The buyer handles it, and so on for every variable until you get down to the final one, price.

The problem with this approach is that you have left the one key variable, price, to the end. At that point, the respective sides will have to fight it out over the price, piecemeal, a lose-lose scenario subject to gridlock. If the buyer offers $420,000 and the seller is asking $480,000, any concession is a "lose." Should the buyer up the offer to $430,000, nothing is received in return for the gesture, except the hope that the seller will absorb an equal loss and drop to $470,000. We've said that it's fine to play this game if the outcome is heading where you want it to, but the reality is that each succeeding concession will be more and more difficult to attain. Very possibly, the buyer will hit $435,000, the seller $455,000, and neither will be willing to budge further. Impasse. Game over. No deal.

We suggest, therefore, that you not merely agree on all the other parameters and then fight it out piecemeal on price. Don't *make* concessions, *trade* concessions. By all means encourage the other side to make unilateral concessions, particularly early in the process. In the house example, pleas for fairness, the power of competition, and a final "Let's get down to business. What can you do for me?" followed by silence, might get the price from $500,000 to $475,000, with the buyer getting nothing in return. On your part, of course, there's an iron-clad rule. Never make any concession without getting *something,* hopefully of equal or greater value, in return. So, yes, to whatever extent possible, encourage the other side to make initial unilateral concessions. When you perceive you have as many of them as you can get, then, go back and forth *trading* concessions according to the relativity of variables, allowing each side to come out ahead on the exchange.

Back to the house example. We wish to avoid an endgame of potential gridlock in which, according to our example, we were fighting it out piecemeal on price with the buyer unwilling to go higher than

$435,000 and seller unwilling to drop below $455,000. At this point, you can say, "That's my final offer. Take it or leave it," and turn on your heels. To take such a position, you must believe you have the power to compel the seller to acquiesce to your demands. If, indeed, your perception of strength is correct, the seller may cave in, or at least accept $438,000, but he or she won't be happy with the idea of one big final concession and the whole thing might just fall apart. Better, then, to play out the power game in increments as you trade concessions rather than wait to the end and fight piecemeal over price.

As an example of what we mean, let's consider the above-ground pool. We saw that according to the relativity of variables, it made sense that the pool remain. But at what value? Let's say the pool, as it sits, is worth $5,000 as value added to the property but would yield the seller only $500 if removed. We trust you would not be so foolish as to say, "Oh, I just love that pool," because that would peg its value at $5,000. Even if you were inwardly panting with fantasies of private poolside adventures at midnight, you would convey that the pool was of no interest to you and that the owners were free to take it with them. If, on the other hand, they wished to leave it, you would be willing to accept it at a value of $600. Go back and forth a little, and settle on letting it remain at a value of $1,000. Now, let's take a look at what just happened. The seller came out ahead, salvaging an extra $500 for the pool, but you in effect, procured a price concession of $4,000 on the sales price when the value-added of the pool was reduced from $5,000 to $1,000. Similarly, if you, as a contractor, can fix the leaky roof at a cost of $2,000, but it would cost the seller $4,000 to hire you or someone else to do the job, you should volunteer to fix the roof in return for the price reduction of the full $4,000. Playing the game this way, the person with the favorable power position will consistently attain agreement at the extreme of the range for every exchange dictated by the relativity of variables. The big difference is that the other party still comes out marginally better on each trade *and* (and this is the big point) at the end of this process, when you're down to the final variable, price, the difference in the positions has been radically reduced, perhaps even eliminated.

As another example, more typical of a B2B negotiation involving numerous variables, let's go back to the situation in which transportation will cost the prospect $8,000 and you can do it for $5,000. We noted that under those circumstances it only makes sense that you handle the transportation.

Yes, but do it right. Don't merely agree that you should take care of the transportation, move on to the next variable and similarly agree to its dispensation according to the relativity of variables, and finally fight it out piecemeal over price. At that time, even if you're in a superior power position, you run the risk of hitting an impasse if the difference between the respective positions is large. A better approach would be to trade concessions on the variables one at a time, generally with the parties agreeing on a point in exchange for an adjustment in the price. Thus, you would propose to handle the transportation in exchange for a price adjustment of $8,000, which would represent a break-even for the prospect but would be a net gain of $3,000 for you. You might go back and forth ultimately agreeing to adjust the price by $7,500. Both sides win. The prospect comes out $500 ahead but you, apparently in the superior power position, come out $2,500 ahead, the same effect as getting a $2,500 concession at an endgame piecemealing over price. Proceeding in a similar manner through all points of agreement, you end with a much smaller difference in position when you iron out the final variable of price because, a slice of salami at a time, you have already guaranteed yourself an agreement on terms favorable to you.

Strategy 3: Balance Firmness on Content with Enhancement of the Relationship

Through this chapter so far, you may have the impression that we're advocating you take a firm posture in negotiating points, terms, and conditions, with an eye toward attaining a final agreement in your favor. We are. Having said that, we caution you to do so in a proper manner. In other words, don't lose sight of the fact that your primary objective is to establish a long-term relationship that will yield repeat business and be a source of referrals. In other words, be a decent person, always. Get input from the other side, let them talk, and work to establish collaboration within this context of competition. Sympathize with their hardship in paying you what you know you're worth, and reassure them that you'll be there after the transaction.

As you near final agreement on price, it may not be to your advantage to take an inflexible "take it or leave it" stance. Let them have something, if only a face-saving gesture. We know of one sales professional who gave a prospect tickets to an important football game for the upcoming weekend, saying he wouldn't be needing them since he wanted to get down to details of implementing their project and would work Saturday and Sunday. This gesture cost very little, but it was a nice thing to do. Even when you have the other side right where you want them, don't take full advantage of your position.

Do keep in mind throughout the negotiation process that enhancement of the relationship means commanding respect as a competent professional who plays the game with fair-minded toughness. It's nice to have people like you, but being liked is not necessary while on the playing field of a high-stakes game of hardball. Should you feel it necessary always to be liked, you will not achieve optimal outcome and you will probably lose some degree of respect. There is plenty of time to be liked after you get off the negotiation playing field when, in a break of the action, the prospect smiles and says, "We got more than we expected." When the word gets around, which it will, that you consistently exceed customer expectations, no one will have a problem with your firm stance in negotiations. In fact, they'll respect you for it.

CONCEPT 4: INNOVATIVE APPROACHES FOR THE NEW WORLD OF BUSINESS

Now that you're prepared to knuckle down and hammer out a negotiation of all the final points, terms, and conditions, let's note some approaches that may make the entire process a whole lot easier. These tactics may have had limited applications in the past, but can open many doors of opportunity in the new world of business.

Tactic 1: Reciprocity

This basic tactic has been around forever, but is nevertheless often overlooked. Its premise is simple. If I do business with you whenever I need the product or service you sell, you should do business with me whenever you need the product or service I sell. I use you for all my dry cleaning, so you buy your insurance from me. We use your hotel for our convention, so you feature our products in your bar and restaurant. Take a look at every place you drop your hard-earned cash and see whether there's an opportunity to formalize a reciprocal arrangement. Who knows? It might even lead to a strategic partnership in which you refer business to each other. Or more.

Tactic 2: Help Them Find the Money

As we've stated, there will always be a price objection and there's never enough money in the budget. Those are tactics all buyers use every time but, in fact, often they really *do* have a problem finding the money. Help them locate the resources and it's a whole lot more likely that you'll be able to close your proposal as it stands.

Many prospects market their products or services through distributors or up-channel partners, many of whom are competing with other distributors or up-channel partners. If your proposal will help your prospects more effectively market their products or services, those distributors or up-channel partners will benefit as well, so why not have them finance some of the investment? Some of these distributors and up-channel partners are anxious to procure a higher proportion of your prospects' business, and want to increase their shares of market in their respective industries. They may have co-op advertising and marketing funds you can tap into, or promotional dollars that can be directed toward your proposal. Just don't rely on your prospects or anyone else to do the selling for you. Initiate the contact yourself, and make your prospects' up-channel partners your prospective strategic partners.

Buck regularly does this in developing sales training programs for his clients. Instead of teaching generic selling skills, he involves numerous manufacturers and provides them with program segments to present information and features of competitive advantage. Role-plays are customized to teach sales reps how to sell those specific products and their attendant benefits. Manufacturers contribute a significant proportion of the prospects' training investment, and directly benefit. Furthermore, these activities have enhanced the relationships between manufacturers and distributors, creating a stronger strategic partnership. Money well spent.

Bob has found money available from packaging and container manufacturers. He's done training for salespeople who market products available in a wide variety of glass and metal packages, different plastic and cardboard multipacks, employing a variety of in-outlet marketing and promotional devices, utilizing numerous types of point-of-sale materials. Manufacturers of these supplies and component parts contribute to program costs and feature their products at the training site. Bob also includes the partner products in role-play exercises. Here, too, training is more realistic, partnerships are enhanced, and they find the money.

Tactic 3: Barter

You were probably practicing barter even before you knew the meaning of money, such as when you traded your pet frog to the kid next door in exchange for some of her mom's cookies. Even today, if you own the lawn mower and your neighbor is adept at cutting with his or her hedge trimmers, it might work out nicely for you to mow his or her lawn as he or she is doing your hedges. Especially with the smaller specialized companies common to the new world of business, barter just makes sense. According to the National Association of Trade Exchanges Web site <www.nate.org>, 20 to 25 percent of world trade is transacted through barter, with 65 percent of NYSE-listed firms engaging in barter at the corporate level.

Barter offers numerous benefits, most significant of which is a dramatic increase in your purchasing power. For example, you might trade $1,000 worth of goods, the variable cost of which was $400. In exchange, you might receive $1,000 worth of legal services. The bottom line is you received a full $1,000 retail value for an investment of your $400 variable cost. It's very unlikely you could have negotiated a price discount this deep, even paying cash up front. Since it's a similar situation for the firm that provided you the legal services, both parties have won. An even more significant implication is that such an arrangement is a great starting point for a strategic alliance and networking partnership.

Barter frees up cash that you can direct at vendors who do not accept trade but do offer substantial discounts for cash. It opens up credit lines you can offer to prospects who need them. Barter can help you clear out excess inventory and optimize utilization of resources. If you have skilled employees on your payroll, in areas as diverse as Web development to market research analysis, why not make the most of that resource by making it available to others in exchange for products and services you need in turn. We know of companies who do advertising for hotels and airlines in exchange for lodging and transportation. We know accountants who do people's taxes in exchange for yard maintenance and auto repair.

You can set up one-on-one relationships with businesses you know and trust if each of you wants what the other has to offer. As an alternative, you can expand opportunities for trade by joining a trade association that acts as a broker and third-party record keeper. These associations offer services such as employee bonus plans, lending of credit to clients, and bill paying with trade credit dollars. For more information, and to locate a trade association near you, check out the National Trade Association <www.ntatrade.com> or the International Reciprocal Trade Association <www.irta.com>.

CONCLUSION

This was the final chapter, where we addressed the endgame: reaching agreement on points, terms, and conditions. Negotiation is a very serious game in which you must consciously convey an attitude of strength and confidence. Yes, you and your prospects are developing a relationship predicated on mutual respect and trust. Even so, those same prospects, especially if they're experienced buyers, will react to indications of weakness about the same way a shark responds to blood.

If you believe in yourself and your company, you'll be able to operate from a position of strength, selectively apply negotiation skills and tactics, and reach an agreement which is a good deal for the prospect and a profitable sale for you.

Epilogue

Traditional books on selling, and many traditional sales training programs, have viewed the sales cycle as a finite process. Begin with prospecting and qualifying. Get the appointment, make the pitch, and submit your proposal. Hammer out the terms and conditions. Get paid. Next!

We have presented the sales profession in a different light for the new world of business, in which negotiating agreement is the beginning of the process, not the end. It is from that point forward, formalizing the relationship, that will lay the foundation for the strategic alliance that will lead toward repeat business and referrals. You have not closed a sale, you have opened an account.

From this point forward, if you deliver all you promised and more, you're solid for repeat business and referrals. But if you're selling a big-ticket product or service and you fail to deliver, your customers may be inconvenienced, lose their jobs, or be out of business. And they won't forget you.

Stay in touch after the sale and if there's anything in the product or service delivery that is not 100 percent, bring it to the customers' attention before they even find out about it, even if they probably never would have found out about it in the first place. Don't even *think* about sweeping something under the rug. As Buck has always said, "It's not a problem if you fix it." No excuses and no blaming others. Take ownership of the problem and just fix it!

There's only one thing you want to hear at the end of the process for customers, when your products or services have been delivered in full. They should say to you, "We got more than we expected." This will translate to repeat business and referrals, and it means you have successfully fought the battle against the low-priced competitor. Now the sales cycle begins anew, continuing to grow and carrying you to higher and higher levels of success. We'll see you at the top of the mountain.

Index

Page numbers followed by the letter "f" indicate figures.